'I DON'T BELIEVE IN MURDER'

STANDING UP FOR PEACE IN WORLD WAR I CANTERBURY

Margaret Lovell-Smith

CANTERBURY UNIVERSITY PRESS

First published in 2023 by
CANTERBURY UNIVERSITY PRESS
University of Canterbury
Private Bag 4800, Christchurch
NEW ZEALAND

ISBN 978-1-98-850336-3

A catalogue record for this book is available from the
National Library of New Zealand.

Editor: Gillian Tewsley
Indexer: Robin Briggs
Book design and layout: Smartwork Creative, www.smartworkcreative.co.nz

Front cover image: Protest against the imprisonment of youths for non-compliance
with the Defence Act, Victoria Square, 9 March 1912 (detail) (The Director, Zealandia
Milling Co Ltd. Photograph 421, Canterbury Museum)

Printed by Caxton, New Zealand

Published with assistance from
Canterbury History Foundation, Chris Barfoot, Christchurch City Council's Intangible
Heritage Fund, New Zealand History Research Trust Fund, Peace and Disarmament
Education Trust, and Quaker Peace and Service Aotearoa New Zealand

'I DON'T BELIEVE IN MURDER'

CONTENTS

ACKNOWLEDGEMENTS

There are many people who helped make this book a reality. I sincerely thank the following individuals and funding bodies – without their support and assistance, the project could not have been completed.

I would like to give special thanks to Dr Kate Dewes who, as a director of the Disarmament and Security Centre (DSC), initiated the Voices Against War project, and who provided support and editing advice throughout the writing of the book. The book is a development and extension of the Voices Against War website (http://voicesagainstwar. nz/), and I'd like to acknowledge the partnership between the DSC and the University of Canterbury's School of Humanities and Creative Arts, which took responsibility for the preparation and maintenance of the website. Associate Professor Dr Jane Buckingham edited the content for the website, and Jennifer Middendorf and the team at the UC Arts Digital Lab designed and developed it. I thank them all for their contribution.

Dan Bartlett, who worked for the Voices Against War project as a University of Canterbury 2015 summer scholar, provided the impetus to get the book underway, and a successful application to the New Zealand History Research Trust Fund in 2017 encouraged us to persevere. In 2019 Dan Bartlett received the Community Historian award from the Canterbury History Foundation, which supported his further research. Although our original plan to co-write the book didn't eventuate due to Dan's later work commitments, his research and drafts were incorporated into several chapters, and Dan helped later with editing the text and accessing images.

Dan Richardson, the 2018 summer scholar, wrote two articles for the website; and Martin Crick carried out research into the contribution made by English Quakers to the New Zealand peace movement. I thank all those who commented on part or all of the draft manuscript including Martin Crick, Clare Simpson and Jared Davidson, who also assisted with locating information at Archives New Zealand. I particularly thank Professor Jim McAloon for reading and commenting on a later draft of the whole book. Responsibility for the text, however, rests with me.

I feel very fortunate to have met with many relatives of conscientious objectors (COs), including four who had a direct link as children: Ron Nuttall (now deceased), son of Thomas Nuttall; David and Geoffrey Stedman, sons of Silas Stedman; and Sally Page, daughter of Robin Page. The scrapbook about Robin Page's wartime experiences, compiled by Robin's aunts and which included numerous original letters, proved to be an invaluable source of information. Eleanor Bodger provided access to copies of CO Frank Money's diaries and letters, which included first-hand accounts of his experiences in prison. Letters and photos from the Worrall family made available by Edith Lucas née Worrall, including William Worrall's letters from prison, were greatly appreciated.

Other relatives of anti-militarists and objectors who provided photographs and information included Noel Curr, Brent Efford, Elwyn Goldsbury, Philippa Gordon, Noel Hendery, Jan and Peter Kradalfer, Bronwyn Pollock, Paul Ridder, Wendy Robinson, Patricia Smith, John Williams, Peter Williams, Hugh Worrall, Jill Worrall and the late Joy Turner. Others who gave helpful information include Brian Smith, who provided digital records of the Baptist Church magazine, and Tony McCahon and Margaret Naismith, who helped with enquiries into the Richmond Mission. Megan Hutching's research into the early days of the Women's International League was very much appreciated.

Many of the images in the book came from the Canterbury Museum, and I am extremely grateful to the Museum staff, especially Sarah Murray, Head of Collections and Research, for their support. As a museum volunteer I was able to combine my research interest with a data-entry project on the Charles Mackie Papers and Pamphlets, and I thank the museum staff who supervised this process: Joanna Szczepanski, Dan Stirland and Frances Husband.

My thanks go to all those who helped with images and research enquiries: archivists at Christ's College and Christchurch Boys' High School, and staff at the Alexander Turnbull Library, Archives New Zealand Te Rua Mahara o te Kāwanatanga in Christchurch and Wellington, Auckland City Library, Auckland War Memorial Museum Tāmaki Paenga Hira, Ara Institute of Canterbury, the Christchurch City Libraries, the Kaiapoi Museum, the Macmillan Brown Library at the University of Canterbury, the Methodist Church of New Zealand Archives and the Presbyterian Research Centre.

I thank Catherine Montgomery and Katrina McCallum of Canterbury University Press for agreeing to publish the book and for their ongoing support throughout the process, and editor Gillian Tewsley for her thorough scrutiny of the text.

Finally, I am extremely grateful for the financial support received from the Canterbury History Foundation, Chris Barfoot, the Christchurch City Council's Intangible Heritage Fund, the Peace and Disarmament Education Trust, and Quaker Peace and Service Aotearoa New Zealand, whose generous contributions enabled the book to be published and made available at an affordable price.

Margaret Lovell-Smith, September 2022

ABBREVIATIONS

AML	Anti-Militarist League
CMA	Christchurch Ministers' Association
CMT	compulsory military training
CO	conscientious objector
CPS	Christian Pacifist Society
CTLC	Canterbury Trades and Labour Council
CWI	Canterbury Women's Institute
ICW	International Council of Women
ICWP	International Committee of Women for Permanent Peace
ILP	Independent Labour Party
LRC	Labour Representation Committee
NCW	National Council of Women
NMWM	No More War Movement
NPC	National Peace Council
NZSP	New Zealand Socialist Party
OC	Officer Commanding
PLL	Political Labour League
PPU	Peace Pledge Union
PRU	Passive Resisters' Union
RAB	Religious Objectors' Advisory Board
SDP	Social Democratic Party
UDC	Union of Democratic Control
UFL	United Federation of Labour
ULP	United Labour Party
WCTU	Women's Christian Temperance Union
WEA	Workers' Educational Association
WIL	Women's International League
WILPF	Women's International League for Peace and Freedom
YMCA	Young Men's Christian Association

INTRODUCTION

'I don't believe in murder,' said Harry Cooke in 1911 – the first of Canterbury's young men to be imprisoned for refusing to take part in compulsory military training (CMT) in the lead-up to World War I. Similar statements were made by many other anti-conscriptionists and conscientious objectors (COs) who took a stand against conscription and military service. 'War is legalised murder,' 20-year-old Robin Page declared at his court-martial in 1918. The result of his stand was 16 months in prison.

Books that give insight into how soldiers were thinking and feeling during the war have become common with the publication of soldiers' diaries, letters and biographies. With one or two notable exceptions, however, the personal stories of those New Zealanders who chose the path of resisting militarism and war have barely been heard, and rarely has their bravery been recognised. 'I verily believe that it would take a braver man to stand down than become a soldier,' wrote Canterbury's tennis star Anthony Wilding to his mother Julia in September 1914 after he had decided to fight for the empire;[1] he was killed less than a year later, in May 1915, at the Second Battle of Ypres. Robin Page's mother Sarah wrote, 'It takes more courage to be a C.O. than a soldier. No glamour nor band.'[2]

The Voices Against War research and education project was initiated by the Christchurch Disarmament and Security Centre (DSC) in 2015 in order to record the thoughts, beliefs and motivations of the individuals who made a stand for peace before and during World War I. The DSC was ideally placed to undertake such a project, as it was in Christchurch that the peace movement took hold most strongly and provided leadership for the rest of the country. The name 'Voices Against War' reflected our intention to include, in every story on the website, some words spoken or written by the subject of each article.[3]

The project aimed to identify, research and publicise the stories of women, men and their families throughout Canterbury who, before, during and after World War I, opposed conscription and militarism, supported the COs, and advocated the settlement of international disputes by arbitration. The project was begun in the midst of the centennial war commemorations and would, it was hoped, provide an antidote to what often seemed to border on a glorification of war, with constant talk of heroism, sacrifice and freedom, rather than words such as killing, carnage and grief that might better describe the reality of war. Geoffrey Troughton and Philip Fountain have written that the effect of the commemorations overall was to 'reinforce the centrality of warfare in shaping global geopolitics and national identities'. The commemorations also further normalised and entrenched 'the institution of war', they said.[4] Certainly the many displays, events and publications surrounding the centennial commemorations conveyed the general impression to the public that the country as a whole had been united in the war effort.

Much of the commemoration leveraged emotion, empathy and even jingoism at the expense of critical remembrance and analysis, and the CO experience received scant attention. The Museum of New Zealand Te Papa Tongarewa's immensely popular commemorative exhibition, *Gallipoli: The scale of our war*, for example, made little mention of either conscription or conscientious objection, and Canterbury Museum's exhibition *Canterbury and World War One: Lives lost, lives changed* contained only a single, small display devoted to conscientious objection.[5]

The Anzac myth dominated the commemorations: the idea that our national identity distinct from Britain was forged in the trenches alongside our Australian comrades. Little was said of the fact that the Anzacs fought in support of Britain's imperial and economic interests (as well as our own economic interests), and there was little recognition of the uncomfortable fact that the first military alliance with Australia was during the New Zealand Wars of the nineteenth century, when the New Zealand colonial government fought Māori over sovereignty and land.

This book is an extension and development of the Voices Against War website. It encompasses three separate but interconnected topics: the history of the peace movement in Canterbury from 1911 to 1919 and its ongoing legacy; the story of pre-war resistance to CMT; and the imprisonment of objectors and seditionists during the war. With its focus on the peace movement, and the beliefs and experiences of the resisters and COs in just one region, it breaks new ground. But it is not the first book to be written about the wartime COs. Two notable examples are by Harry Holland and Archibald Baxter.

Holland's *Armageddon or Calvary*, published soon after the war, set out to publicise the shocking results of the New Zealand Government's conscription policy.[6] As editor of the anti-militarist Federation of Labour newspaper *Maoriland Worker*, Holland was well informed about the COs, and had himself been imprisoned in 1913 for sedition. A major focus of his book was the revelatory account of the 14 COs sent to Europe to turn them into fighters. The memoir written later by one of the 14, Archibald Baxter, published in 1939 as *We Will Not Cease*, gives a moving insight into Baxter's beliefs and his appalling experiences as a CO. A later retelling of the story of 'The 14' by David Grant in *Field Punishment No. 1* (2008) added further details and context to Baxter's story.[7] The extremity of the suffering and horror described by Baxter, however, may have contributed to the lack of other memoirs by COs, who were very aware that time spent in a New Zealand prison was in no way comparable to the suffering either of the objectors sent to Europe or of the soldiers serving in the trenches. As Baxter was from Otago, his story has not been included in this book, though an account of one Canterbury man, David Gray, who was mistakenly sent abroad as one of 'The 14', is told in chapter 6.

The parameters of the study

The young men who, in the pre-war period, were prepared to go to prison for their beliefs became the first Pākehā political prisoners in our country's history. This was not the first instance of passive resistance in Aotearoa New Zealand, however, and there had been other political prisoners before them.

In June 1877, with growing concern at the loss of Ngāi Tahu reserves and despair at the contemptuous attitude of the Crown, Ngāi Tahu leader, tohunga and prophet Te Maihāroa led a heke (migration) of around 150 people from Temuka in South Canterbury, 181 kilometres up the Waitaki Valley, where they established a new kaik (village) – a peaceful settlement called Te Ao Mārama (now Ōmārama). They were evicted from their settlement in late 1879, and could only watch as the local militia destroyed their houses and crops.[8]

In the North Island, meanwhile, a pacifist community established by the spiritual leaders Te Whiti o Rongomai and Tohu Kākahi at Parihaka became a centre for peaceful protest against confiscation of land. When government militia invaded Parihaka in 1881 they were greeted by quietly seated Māori: their leaders were arrested and imprisoned, the village destroyed and its inhabitants dispersed.[9]

The young Pākehā resisters in the pre-war period did not experience the full force of military violence, but their incarceration for minor offences was still a brutal shock. Identifying who they were was more difficult than expected; how we arrived at the figure of 'about 50' young Cantabrians is discussed in chapter 3. The young men, or boys – some as young as sixteen – were imprisoned not directly for their beliefs, but because they refused to pay fines imposed for offences against the Defence Act. They were initially jailed in the country's prisons alongside criminals, until, in response to public concern, the government decided to detain them instead in military detention barracks. Were they prisoners or detainees? The deprivation of liberty was basically the same and, therefore, I would argue, they were all 'prisoners of conscience'.

The 65 Canterbury men who became prisoners of conscience during the war were readily identified using the Ministry of Culture and Heritage's invaluable lists of imprisoned conscientious objectors and convictions for sedition. In the process, I have accepted Tim Shoebridge's criteria for inclusion in the list of COs and, like him, I have not included military defaulters or military prisoners.

A conscripted man who was imprisoned after he refused to be medically examined, or to accept the issue of kit at camp, was clearly an objector to military service by any definition. A man who opted out of the process by hiding in the West Coast bush was – by the Defence Department's definition – a defaulter, or, if he had been attested for military service, a deserter, rather than an objector. If apprehended by the authorities he would be sentenced to a period in prison. … The department categorised such men as 'military prisoners' but not as objectors.[10]

Shoebridge listed 286 men imprisoned as COs during the war and 101 arrested for sedition (not all of whom were imprisoned). There must be many examples, however, of cases where there is little distinction between an 'objector' and a 'defaulter'. Chapter 5 includes the case of Peter Scott Ramsay, who was known to be a socialist and a CO. But when he went into hiding in rugged mountainous country near Lake Wakatipu to avoid arrest he became a military defaulter.[11]

Historians on both sides of the Tasman are now exploring new ways of understanding the nature of dissent. In papers presented at a 'Dissent and the First World War' conference in Wellington in 2017, they demonstrated that dissent could be open or hidden, consciously or unconsciously expressed. Their research further undermined the myth that New Zealanders were united behind the war effort.[12]

The question of numbers

Historian Jared Davidson has argued that there were many more objectors to military service than appear on Shoebridge's spreadsheet. By including groups such as those religious objectors who were considered 'genuine' and who accepted non-combatant service on the Weraroa State Farm at Levin; some who had been punished at the Wanganui Detention Barracks; and Māori military defaulters, Davidson puts the total number imprisoned at 670. Then there were the objectors not included in the prison count, including additional men transported overseas; the 196 who were serving in a non-combatant role; those who deserted from training camps and remained at large; and those religious objectors who were successful in their appeal against military service. Altogether, Davidson estimates there were somewhere between 1500 and 2000 people, with an upper figure of 3000 objectors during the war.[13]

Then there were those who evaded the state altogether. The government statistician estimated that 3500–5000 men never registered and therefore couldn't be balloted. Some went into hiding; others left the country. Historian Paul Baker estimated that between 2800 and 6400 men deliberately evaded service and were never found.[14] Davidson concludes the total number of dissenters is closer to 10,000 – and this doesn't include any women; or objectors who had no need to identify themselves because they weren't called up, or were not eligible for military service.

This book focuses on the objectors who can be identified; it does not attempt to quantify the number of Canterbury objectors who 'went bush' for the duration of the war. It does, however, mention some individuals whose stories have become known.

There was a considerable amount of public support for those who resisted conscription, whether openly or secretly. Both before the war and in the final years of the war, crowds of about 2000 Christchurch women and men were prepared to come out and show their opposition to conscription.

This study is confined to objectors from Canterbury. We have included in the total of 65 Canterbury 'prisoners of conscience' individuals such as Frank Money, who had spent most of his life in Christchurch and had only recently moved to a farm in the North Island, possibly to try and evade the ballot, but we have omitted others such as Jim Thorn, who spent his early life and formative years in Christchurch but had lived overseas and had moved to the North Island in 1914. He is, however, mentioned in the text.

Reassessing the enthusiasm for war

Individual writers from as early as the 1920s have recorded a variety of responses to New Zealand's involvement in the war. Stephen Smith, for example, recalled that at the outbreak of war, many people had 'a very real premonition of the tortures of mind to be endured and the terrible losses to be sustained during the struggle that had been forced upon us'.[15] Paul Baker, in his thorough study of conscription and the war, described the wildly enthusiastic response of many young men and boys, but he noted that 'the response of most adults was more sober than is usually assumed … Most adults who congregated in the streets did so less for celebration than for reassurance in the face of frightening uncertainty.'[16]

Other historians have discussed the lack of homogeneity in New Zealand society at the time. Jock Phillips examined the cultural diversity of groups with differing attitudes to war and Megan Hutching has written about the small minority of women's groups who agitated against war.[17] Citing statistical analysis done by Nicholas Boyack, historian Graham Hucker concluded that only a small proportion of the 193,254 males of military age living in New Zealand in the pre-war period actually rushed to enlist.[18] Similarly, the rush to enlist is just one of the myths about the war that are demolished by Stevan Eldred-Grigg in his 2010 book *The Great Wrong War: New Zealand society in WWI*. Citing a diversity of views from newspapers, literature, letters and diaries, his refreshing critique notes that several newspapers and citizens expressed fear and anxiety rather than enthusiasm at the outbreak of war.[19]

Different regions greeted news of the outbreak of war in different ways. A more accurate approach to gauging the level of enthusiasm for the war is that taken by historians in other Commonwealth countries, who have a 'focus on local and regional studies, and the experience of individuals rather than persisting with general accounts that purport to be the national view'.[20] In Britain, Cyril Pearce has stressed the importance of studying local experience and perspectives 'anchored firmly outside London', rather than attempting 'a national picture based on national sources'; such attempts 'perpetuate the nonsense that England, or even worse, Britain, can be viewed as the homogenous whole which it very clearly was not'.[21]

Fortuitously for this project, historian Gwen Parsons had already carried out a regional study of attitudes to the war through an analysis of Christchurch newspapers. She found 'significantly more ambivalence among the civilian population than has generally been suggested'.[22] The debate was very much along class lines: the Christchurch ruling elite supported the war, while the labour organisations and working class in general did not. Censorship, said Parsons, 'ensured that patriotic material dominated the public domain during the war, almost to the exclusion of any anti-war or anti-conscription material'.[23] While more recent general histories or online articles often acknowledged opposition to war or conscription, she noted, they gave limited attention to the body of academic literature which discusses it. In an earlier article, Parsons discussed the arguments put forward by those on both sides of the debate – those for and against support for the war.[24] The pro-war discourse used anti-German arguments, the importance of defending British liberty, and concepts of duty and sacrifice to argue that the war was both justified and legitimate; whereas those who opposed the war presented socialist and Christian pacifist arguments, while also appealing to the same traditions of British liberalism as those who were pro-war.

A note on sources new and old

The most important sources for the history of the peace movement were the archives of the National Peace Council (NPC), the 'Charles Mackie Papers', in the Canterbury Museum. Mackie generated an enormous amount of correspondence as secretary of the NPC, especially in the pre-war period. The papers also include reports, printed publications, cartoons, flyers, tickets and other ephemera, some of which were posted on the Voices Against War website as graphic items and have been included in the book as illustrations.

Digital sources that are now readily available have been invaluable. The National Library of New Zealand's 'Papers Past' project[25] provided easy access to newspaper reports of meetings of peace groups and women's groups, letters to the editor, and reports of objectors' military board hearings and court-martials. Reports that quoted the objector, giving insight into his beliefs and motivation, provided the 'voice' of many of the individual COs. Because COs were officially part of the military, the digital personnel records of servicemen in World War I available on the Archives New Zealand website were another useful source of information.

Charles Mackie (1869–1943) was the hard-working secretary of the National Peace Council from 1912 to 1943. (Canterbury Museum)

Numerous other published and unpublished sources are listed in the bibliography. Two of special significance are Elsie Locke's ground-breaking and comprehensive *Peace People: A history of peace activities in New Zealand* (1992), and Elizabeth Plumridge's 1979 thesis 'Labour in Christchurch: Community and consciousness 1914–1919', which interprets complexities of the labour movement while also highlighting the women's and anti-militarist movements.[26]

The outpouring of books that accompanied the centennial commemorations of World War I included several about what has traditionally been known as the 'Home Front'. The most comprehensive of these, *The Home Front: New Zealand society and the war effort, 1914–1919*, by Steven Loveridge and James Watson, showed that the anti-war movement was now accepted as one part of the mosaic of groups and beliefs in World War I New Zealand,[27] with coverage of the anti-war movement and objectors to military service, illustrated by photographs and cartoons.

Jared Davidson's 2019 book *Dead Letters: Censorship and subversion in New Zealand 1914–1920* has further opened up the topic of 'dissent' during World War I. With censored letters in the government archives as the starting point for each chapter, much is revealed about those whose letters were censored and seized during the war.[28] One of the targets of the military censor was Charles Mackie, and the success of the peace movement in Christchurch owes much to his commitment. But it was also due to foundational work done by the women's and labour movements who, over the previous 20 years, had created a receptive climate of opinion among a network of individuals – as described in the first chapter.

CHAPTER 1

THE PROGRESSIVE NETWORK OF RADICAL CHRISTCHURCH 1880s–1910

While historians have recognised the presence of radicalism in Canterbury 'from the earliest stage of formal settlement',[1] contemporary writers often dismissed Christchurch as a stronghold of strange religions, cranks and faddists. Depending on your political viewpoint, many of the same 'cranks and faddists' could be hailed as the most progressive thinkers.

The 'long depression' of the 1880s, with its accompanying unemployment and poverty, had led to the formation of a number of radical political groups, and with the election of a Liberal government in 1890 there were high hopes that some longed-for reforms might be achieved. By the 1890s there was a ferment of ideas in Christchurch with numerous groups and individuals discussing new ways of organising society. Most of the radical thinkers belonged to more than one group and the interaction that developed between them was to play an important part in the later peace movement. Workers' rights and the development of trade unions were the priority of labour groups. Women's groups, while their focus was on women's rights and women's and children's welfare, shared with the labour groups a concern for world peace, and the need for international arbitration to settle disputes between nations.

The growing confidence and visibility of progressive women in Christchurch owed much to the numbers of women receiving a university education. Canterbury College, a constituent college of the University of New Zealand (and the forerunner of the University of Canterbury), had admitted women to non-degree classes from the time it opened in the 1870s, and the first women had graduated from there in 1880. In 1881 Helen Connon became the first woman in the British Empire to graduate with an MA degree. At the age of 25 she was appointed 'lady principal' of the recently established Christchurch Girls' High School, where other recent graduates were employed as teachers.

Canterbury College gained a reputation for welcoming women students, including those from other parts of the country. By 1889, 47 women had graduated from the college, and in 1891 and again in 1898 women arts graduates from the college outnumbered men.[2]

It took an American 'missionary', however, to introduce an organised women's movement to the city. Mary Clement Leavitt, a visiting speaker and organiser from the Women's Christian Temperance Union (WCTU) spent two weeks lecturing in Christchurch in 1885, preaching a message that was revolutionary but that didn't upset traditional notions about how Christian women should behave.

To belong to the WCTU women had to pledge total abstinence from liquor, and the WCTU worked towards prohibition in the liquor trade. But the WCTU was about more than just alcohol: its motto was 'For God, Home and Humanity', and the policy advocated by the world leader was that women should become active throughout society. The Christchurch branch was formed at a meeting on 15 May 1885 with a membership of 44, which had risen to 85 by December 1889.[3]

The WCTU was the first women's organisation in New Zealand with an organised national structure; and because the constitution of the world WCTU included among its several objectives 'the establishment of Courts of National and International Arbitration, which shall banish war from the world', it had a department of peace and arbitration from the time of its founding.[4]

This department of work received a boost in 1889 when William Jones, a visiting lecturer and former secretary of the English Peace Society (founded in 1816), spoke about international arbitration and advocated the formation of local peace societies. Addressing a meeting of the WCTU, Jones told his audience that, from his personal observation, women and children suffered the most during wartime, and he urged them to take an interest in how to bring about more healthy and rational ways of settling disputes between nations. The Christchurch Peace Society was formed a few days later, with Anne Murgatroyd as secretary and a membership fee of threepence. It was a modest fee, because the aims of the society were modest: members were to use their influence individually. Jones' suggestion that such a society could issue circulars and arrange lectures was apparently not taken up.[5] The following year the Christchurch WCTU followed the example of Wellington

Women's Christian Temperance Union members at their National Convention, probably at Kaiapoi in 1899. Kate Sheppard is standing fourth from right. (WCTU)

and Dunedin in formally making the peace society a department of the WCTU – though it seems to have been largely inactive.

But while they may not have taken up the peace issue at this time, WCTU members in the early 1890s were gaining confidence and advocacy skills as they worked on many other issues, including the campaign for women's right to vote.

Christchurch women become politically active

The women who became most involved in the peace movement in Christchurch during World War I all had connections with the successful women's franchise campaign, led from Christchurch by Kate Sheppard as national superintendent of the WCTU's Franchise and Legislation Department.

Alongside the WCTU a more avowedly feminist and non-Christian organisation, the Canterbury Women's Institute (CWI), was formed in Christchurch in late 1892, and several of the most politically active women from the WCTU joined this group as well. The CWI had a wide-ranging programme of reform that included the abolition of the upper house (the legislative council), the removal of all legal and civil 'disabilities' from women (such as not being able to hold public office), equal marriage and divorce laws, the economic independence of women, old age pensions, and equal pay for equal work. Among its activities in 1893 was collecting signatures for the last of the women's suffrage petitions. (Women's suffrage was passed into law in September 1893.)[6]

The CWI went on to convene the first meeting of the National Council of Women (NCW) in April 1896 at the Canterbury Provincial Council Chambers in Christchurch. This was to be the Women's Parliament. Women had won the vote but were still excluded from government; a women's council was an opportunity for them to meet together, hear papers on serious social issues, and debate and put forward their own vision for society, just as the male politicians did in Wellington. The meeting was attended by delegates from women's organisations throughout the country. The NCW also welcomed as speakers many of Christchurch's most innovative male thinkers, including Alexander Bickerton, the foundation chemistry professor at Canterbury College, who was a popular lecturer; Edward Tregear, a socialist and secretary of labour for 20 years; and James O'Bryen Hoare, a radical former clergyman. Elizabeth Taylor, an active member of the WCTU who gave a paper on 'Marriage and divorce', was accompanied to the meeting by her husband Tommy Taylor, a prominent prohibitionist and city councillor who was elected to Parliament that same year. Wilhelmina Sherriff Bain, a Southland teacher who had agitated for more pay for women teachers and had recently moved to Christchurch, convened the meeting as president of the CWI and was elected treasurer; and Annie Hookham, a former teacher who was active in the CWI, gave a paper on 'Constructive socialism'. Kate Sheppard became the first president of the NCW, and Ada Wells became secretary. The women delegates to the first NCW meeting represented societies that had worked for women's suffrage. They respected and admired Sheppard as their natural leader: intelligent, well organised, diplomatic and hard-working, she was an obvious choice.

The first NCW meeting did not discuss international questions. But just a few months later, with Wilhelmina Sherriff Bain as chair, the CWI agreed that 'national and international disputes should be settled by arbitration', and that 'war among civilised peoples is a contradiction in terms'.[7]

In August, when Jessie Mackay issued a challenge to all the women's political societies in the country to support a national protest urging England to 'effectively' intervene in Armenia, where the Ottoman authorities had massacred thousands of Armenians, the CWI opposed the move. Sheppard, as vice-president of the CWI, argued, 'If the Institute now urged war it could never again uphold arbitration principles.'[8] She elaborated on this in an editorial in the WCTU's *White Ribbon* magazine: by all means condemn the British Government for its apathy, she wrote; but she asked the unions to pause before they declared themselves in favour of war. 'The W.C.T.U. is a Peace Society. Nothing but the clearest conviction should cause our Unions to depart from their avowed principles … What Armenia needs is present assistance and self-governing power for the future. England can give her these more quickly by the purse and diplomacy than she could by the sword …'[9]

A progressive network

A number of idealistic organisations were developing in Christchurch that often combined elements of Christianity and socialism, and their members formed a network of like-minded people. WCTU members Kate Sheppard and her sister Isabel May were on the committee of the Christian Ethical Society, established in 1890 with the object of 'the advancement of truth and love', and which held regular meetings for about three years. Members strove to 'follow the spirit of Christ in dealing with men', in recognition of the fact that 'the good of all is the best for each'.[10] Topics discussed included 'Socialism and its developments', 'Simplicity of life', 'Vegetarianism' and 'The emancipation of women'. Members included Alexander Bickerton, Annie Hookham and several clergy. James O'Bryen Hoare was another member: he had been dismissed from the ministry in 1895, and this had freed him to found 'Our Father's Church' with the object of testifying to 'the idea of merging all the churches in one brotherhood, all acknowledging the fatherhood of God'.[11] Fellow radical Harry Atkinson believed that Hoare, with his attitude and spirit, was 'a driving force behind the emergent socialist sub-culture in Christchurch'.[12]

Hoare was instrumental in starting another group, the Fabian Society, in 1896 – a short-lived group who believed in achieving socialist ideals through education; its members included Harry and Rose Atkinson, Annie Hookham, William Ensom, and the Christian socialist Eveline Cunnington, who was well known for her social reform work; she was a member of the ladies' committee of the Canterbury Female Refuge, a prison visitor and an advocate for prison reform.[13]

The Progressive Liberal Association began in 1893 as a prohibitionist offshoot of the Liberal Party: its platform was one of 'radical liberalism rather than out-right socialism'. Among its members were Tommy Taylor and Rose and Harry Atkinson, as well as several people known to the Atkinsons through other groups: William Ensom, James McCombs, Elizabeth Henderson and her older sisters Christina and Stella, and Louisa Blake.[14]

There were familial connections, too: Eveline Cunnington was a cousin of Sarah Saunders Page and her brother Samuel, who until 1914 was editor of the *Lyttelton Times*. Their father Alfred Saunders, had been a friend of Kate Sheppard's and a supporter of women's franchise in Parliament.

The Christchurch Socialist Church: Brotherhood and equality

Harry Atkinson came from a leading Taranaki family. While living in Wellington in the early 1890s he had become familiar with the ideas of the Fabian Society, and during three years in England he became involved in the Manchester Labour Church, whose founder, John Trevor, believed that the movement for the emancipation of labour was the 'great religious movement of our times'.[15] Harry returned to New Zealand in 1893 with his English wife Rose, and found work as a fitter at the Addington Railway Workshops. In 1896 he established the Christchurch Socialist Church, based on his experience in England. Other left-wing groups were appearing throughout New Zealand at the same time, but Atkinson's organisation was the only one to openly espouse socialist ideals.[16] Membership was small, and included many of the people the Atkinsons already knew through the Progressive Liberal Association, such as Eveline Cunnington, James McCombs (who shared

Rose and Harry Atkinson in 1901. (Alexander Turnbull Library)

Taylor's political and prohibitionist views), and Elizabeth Henderson, known for her work as secretary of the Children's Aid Society. Other members included Stella and Christina Henderson (both of whom were Canterbury College graduates), Louisa Blake, and Annie Hookham and her father Henry.

Atkinson later said that, for him, socialism was 'not a set of dogmas but a living principle, a striving after human betterment under all circumstances ... the spirit of socialism envisages a higher plane of living for all individuals than merely the gaining of a living'.[17] The Christchurch Socialist Church similarly defined its objectives as: 'promoting a fellowship amongst those working for the organisation of Society on the basis of Brotherhood and Equality. It affirms the Principle that only as we learn to live purer and better lives can we benefit by any measures of Social Reform.'[18] Belonging to the church meant seeking a whole new way of living; its members met weekly to discuss topics such as 'Why we want equality', 'What is the socialist's business' and 'Human nature and socialism'.

In 1896 Atkinson met Jack McCullough, a tinsmith employed at the Addington Workshops, who had been impressed by Atkinson speaking about the socialist church in Christchurch's Cathedral Square:

> Someone squatted outside the rails and spoke into the pit under the locomotive at which I was working and the voice said, 'Do you know what it is like to want to hug a man?' I don't know what I answered. I remember I was rather embarrassed. The voice continued, as I peered out through the spokes of the wheel: 'That's what I felt like, listening in the square on Sunday.'[19]

Atkinson and McCullough became firm friends and spent Sunday afternoons together 'expounding socialism' in the square. The Christchurch Socialist Church imported and disseminated socialist literature from overseas – the *Labour Prophet* and the *Clarion*, among many others. From 1897 Atkinson published a monthly journal, *The Socialist*, which promoted the idea of an independent New Zealand labour party.[20] In 1897 he hosted the British labour leader Ben Tillet on a visit to

Christchurch; while Tillet was here, 6000 people gathered in Hagley Park for a demonstration in support of British engineers' call for an eight-hour day.

It was Rose and Harry Atkinson's membership of a wide range of organisations that provided a crucial link between the labour movement and the idealistic groups discussing social reform, including the women's movement where Rose was active in both the CWI and the WCTU.[21] Harry was later proclaimed the 'Father of New Zealand Socialism' for

A view of the Addington Railway Workshops, where Harry Atkinson worked as a fitter and where he formed a lifelong friendship with Jack McCullough. (Christchurch City Libraries)

Jack McCullough, leading tinsmith at the Addington Railway Workshops, is seated eighth from left in the second row in this photo of smiths at the railway workshops. (Christchurch City Libraries)

his role as mentor of a socialist subculture that developed around the Socialist Church. It was marked by strong friendships among individuals who went on to be leaders in the labour movement, including Jack McCullough, Jim Thorn and James and Elizabeth McCombs (born Henderson – they married in 1903). By 1914 Christchurch had the 'strongest local labour organisation', while Atkinson's later commitment to the peace movement has been seen as a forerunner to New Zealand's anti-nuclear and peace movements.[22] Edith Searle Grossmann, a novelist, journalist and feminist, reported that most of these radical Christchurch groups from the late 1890s consisted of the same people under a different name: 'On Sunday they are Our Father's Church, on Tuesday the Progressive Liberals, on Wednesday the Metaphysical Club, on Thursday the Children's Aid, and on Friday the Women's Institute.'[23]

'Lay down your arms' and the czar's initiative

At the second NCW meeting in Christchurch in 1897, Wilhelmina Sherriff Bain read a paper on 'Peace and arbitration', and her resolution that the council believed war to be a 'savage, costly and futile method of settling disputes hostile to that realisation of brotherhood which is essential to the progress of humanity' was passed with just three dissenters. The resolution called on the women of Australasia to cooperate in promoting permanent peace, gradual disarmament and the agreement to abide by arbitrative principles.[24] The *Lyttelton Times* commended the council for promoting 'the most practical lines that have yet been projected for dealing with the terrible curse of war'.[25]

While Bain was the main instigator of papers on peace and arbitration at NCW meetings, it was Sheppard who, through her editorship of the *White Ribbon*, was arguably more influential on the topic. Unsigned editorials, presumably by Sheppard, expressing support for the stand taken by Bain and the NCW, and reports of peace initiatives overseas were published regularly alongside reports of WCTU conventions, meetings of the NCW and local women's organisations. In this way information was disseminated and connections were maintained with women throughout New Zealand. An editorial titled 'Lay down your arms', published in September 1898, referred back to the reaction to

Delegates to the second meeting of the National Council of Women, held in Christchurch in 1897. Ada Wells and Kate Sheppard are seated in the second row, second and fourth from left respectively. Sheppard's sister Isabel May is seated centre front. (Macmillan Brown Library)

their 1897 resolution, when NCW members had been told 'by critics both in and out of the council' their ideas were absurd and utopian and they should stick to subjects that were suitable for their intelligence.[26] With good-humoured irony, Sheppard countered this by arguing that it was outdated among civilised nations to believe that 'preparation for war is the best guarantee of peace': 'Owing, possibly, to our limited intelligence we have never been quite able to see the force of this argument … Reason, equity, humanity, and, ignoble though it sounds, the pocket, are the arguments one would expect to hear among highly civilised peoples.'[27]

The heading for the editorial, 'Lay down your arms', was the title of a popular novel, *Lay Down Your Arms: A realistic romance of modern war*, which had caused a stir in Europe on its publication in German in 1889. Written by the pacifist Baroness Bertha von Suttner, it was first published in English in 1892 and was reviewed by some South Island newspapers in 1893. The book was phenomenally successful, dealing as it did with women's place in society as well as war and peace, and it went through a dozen editions in a very few years. The book had inspired the formation of peace societies in Europe and apparently influenced the Russian czar Nicholas II, who invited other European nations to take part in an international conference on peace and disarmament.

The 1898 NCW meeting sent a letter to the czar, thanking him for his manifesto. Sheppard said his circular had 'sent a thrill throughout the whole world. And little wonder.' Preparing for war as a guarantee of peace was both evil and absurd, she argued, as well as being ruinously expensive:

> All Europe is practically composed of army camps. Armed for what? 'The preservation of peace', say the military experts. What an absurdity! What an evil! Russia is impoverished by the heavy drain on her finances. Germany is held in the iron grip of a military despotism. France has become a byword among the nations through her sacrifice of justice to the moloch of an armed tyranny. England, which, perhaps, suffers least by this folly of a military peace, lavishes many millions on her army and navy, and cannot afford to pension her worn-out citizens. And these evils, we have been told, must be suffered for the preservation of peace.[28]

In another editorial she expressed a hope for mutual disarmament among nations: 'The maintenance of huge armies by the nations is as dangerous a practice as the carrying of revolver and bowie knives by individuals.'[29]

At its next meeting in Auckland, the NCW passed a resolution deploring the continued increase in armaments throughout the world and warning against Australasian involvement in any British war: 'the people are crushed by the ever-increasing expenditure and … alienated from each other by the rivalries of their respective rulers. The Council deprecates any project likely to involve Australasia in the participation of warfare, and strenuously protests against any Imperial consideration of the colonies as a recruiting ground for Imperial militarism.'[30]

The New Zealand WCTU also expressed pleasure at the czar's proposal for a Peace Congress, and in May 1899 when the first international peace conference was meeting at The Hague – an outcome of the czar's initiative – the 'Ladies' Gossip' column in the *Canterbury Times*, probably written by 'lady editor' Jessie Mackay, wrote a long review of von Suttner's book, noting in particular that it had been written by a woman:

> There is much significance for us in the fact that the hand which gave the chief impetus to the great Peace movement in Europe was that of a woman … women may be forgiven if they feel some pride in the fact that the work of a sister has not only influenced the world generally in favour of peace, but also has greatly moved the Czar of Russia, who read her book with absorbing interest, just before he issued his famous Peace Rescript.[31]

The fact that the peace conference had met was seen by the writer as 'proof of a widespread desire to be set free from the demon of war'.[32]

Imperial militarism and the South African War

With the outbreak of the South African War in October 1899 the optimism and hopes engendered by the peace conference were dashed. Instead, imperial militarism was very much in the public mind. As historian Michael King said, New Zealand liked to see itself as 'one of the most loyal – if not *the* most loyal – of Britain's children', and there was popular support for New Zealand's involvement.[33]

The Christchurch Socialist Church did not support the South African War, drawing criticism from the press and from some of its own members. The church devoted two meetings to the war and organised a public lecture titled 'For the honour of the flag';[34] and it passed a resolution in which it regretted that the House of Representatives had 'played false to the highest interests of humanity in offering to send a cavalry force to South Africa to aid in what is purely a work of capitalist aggression in the Transvaal, and a base and degrading misuse of British power against a weaker State'.[35] Several speakers at the meeting held in the Art

Gallery highlighted the hypocrisy of Britain in contrast with the admirable qualities displayed by the Dutch settlers; they claimed that 'many internal reforms were required before Great Britain could consistently undertake to educate by means of aggressive warfare, a self-reliant and brave people, who had gone far afield to secure a home where they could dwell in peace and safety'.[36] An editorial in the *Lyttelton Times* criticised the Socialist Church's reasoning, and this led to a spate of letters from those who defended the socialists, including Rose Atkinson. The situation of women factory workers, the unemployed, the slum dwellers and those living in crowded workhouses was far worse than any Boer outrage, she argued. 'These people are the people we ought to fight for with all our strength … and the Socialist feels this.'[37]

In addition to criticism from the press, Atkinson and McCullough faced opposition from their colleagues at the Addington Railway Workshops, where support for the war was strong. Railway workers even organised a parade to celebrate the end of the siege of Mafeking, a small town that was surrounded by Boer forces for seven months; the procession was reported to be the second largest ever seen in Christchurch.[38]

Individuals in the local radical network who spoke publicly against the war also drew criticism. Tommy Taylor lost his parliamentary seat in the 1899 election partly because of his opposition to New Zealand sending a contingent to the Transvaal to assist Britain. He was one of five MPs to oppose the move, having told the House that 'this may be a capitalistic war … The Boers were given this area. If gold had not been discovered there, if the power behind wealth had not become centralised in the Transvaal their independence would never have been questioned.' He also criticised England for being 'prepared to flaunt her flag and talk sentiment while for generation after generation she leaves a large

Tommy Taylor. (Alexander Turnbull Library)

portion of her population in abject poverty'.[39] A newspaper commentator responded with: 'a partisan of the Boers is usually marked off by oddities of belief on other matters. Fad goes with Fad.' The writer named the Socialist Church in Christchurch and T. E. Taylor to prove their point – in a dismissal of Christchurch radicals that was to become increasingly common in the years ahead.[40]

The National Council of Women responds to the war

Sheppard's disappointment was evident in her December 1899 *White Ribbon* editorial 'And there shall be peace', in which she deplored the fact that 'the two great nations of the Anglo-Saxon race should be engaged in war':

> After hoping so much from the recent Peace Conference, the disappointment is keen that no other way of settling the present dispute could be found save the savage and murderous warfare that today is in full force. We can only hope now that its very virulence will bring it to a speedy conclusion. Let us do all we can to discourage the vain, arrogant, and blatant war spirit, to urge the substitution of arbitration for Mausers and Lyddite, to remember that Boer and Filipino are our brother men, and be willing and anxious that right rather than might should prevail.[41]

The war was still on Sheppard's mind the following year when the NCW met in Dunedin in May. Her presidential address included comment on the war which, she said, 'had brought sadness into many homes … we cannot but cry in an agony of disappointment, "How long, oh, how long will the war spirit exist between nations?" And the answer is given, Just so long as greed and selfishness exist in the hearts of men … I am firmly convinced that no people can be truly great who delight in war.'[42]

A paper from Bain at that same meeting condemned spending on the arms race and military training, but also spoke strongly against the spirit of militarism that had seen New Zealand send troops to the South African war. Patriotism was false, she said, that could not respect the patriotism of other people. The resolution passed unanimously by the council on this occasion deplored the militarism that was extending its ravages over the world, and said that difficulties between nations were always capable of peaceable settlement, 'if mediatory methods be employed in time'. The council 'strenuously' advocated the establishment of a permanent court of arbitration, 'which shall adjudge the claims of the strongest and weakest States on the basis of equal justice to all'.[43]

Bain's paper and the discussion that followed prompted a strong response in the Dunedin newspapers and caused a division within the NCW between the minority who, like Bain, were both feminist and pacifist, and those who were not. Sheppard, ever the diplomat, felt obliged to clarify the council's position the following day. A letter was sent to the *Otago Daily Times*, signed by the three officers, Sheppard, Ada Wells and the treasurer Jessie Williamson (from Whanganui), explaining that, while the council supported the broad principles of peace and arbitration as expressed in the resolution, the council's executive was at fault for not having ascertained that Bain's paper was going to deal with the present crisis and not just with general principles. 'The opinions of three members must not be taken as an expression of the policy of the council,' the letter read.[44] Bain and Louisa Blake (from Christchurch) were clearly two of the three members referred to who had spoken against New Zealand's involvement in the war. Blake, a delegate from the CWI, supported Bain: in a letter to the *Otago Daily Times* she wrote that she too spoke on behalf of humanity. Great Britain should have submitted to arbitration, and 'just because the Boers did not give way quite to

Wilhelmina Sherriff Bain led the call for international peace and arbitration at the National Council of Women meetings. (*New Zealand Illustrated Magazine*, January 1903, p. 261)

our lines … that was no reason why we should crush them out as we were going to do'.[45] Blake had earlier defended the Boer point of view and deplored the glorification of war in a letter to the *Lyttelton Times*: 'If one-hundredth part of the energy that is now spent in our newspapers and at meetings, in songs, and so forth, in rousing the war spirit were expended in furthering the cause of peace, peace would speedily become, queen of the earth.'[46]

In arguing that war was a question 'pre-eminently for women' and that arbitration and peace education were largely the responsibility of women, Bain was referring to women's experience as childbearers and nurturers of their families.[47] The belief that women had a special responsibility to work for peace and against war because of their maternal role was one that feminists could agree with; but not all were also pacifists.

Another letter from Bain to the *Otago Daily Times* responded to the controversy she had caused and encapsulated her personal convictions. Conflict was an evolutionary process, she wrote. Human warfare had done service in the past but the battlefield was no longer necessary. 'I confess that I am imbued with a sense of the sacredness of human life as compared with property … I plead the cause of brotherhood. Beautiful as is the sentiment of patriotism, the solidarity of mankind is a still grander ideal.'[48]

Sheppard once again referred to the tragedy of the South African War in her presidential address to the 1901 meeting of the NCW, held in Whanganui. While she argued for principles of peace and arbitration and sounded a warning against the

Louisa Blake, who was active in the Children's Aid Society, the Progressive Liberal Association and the Canterbury Women's Institute. (*New Zealand Illustrated Magazine*, November 1901, p. 85)

Ada Wells speaks to the 1901 meeting of the National Council of Women, held in Whanganui. (Auckland War Memorial Museum Tāmaki Paenga Hira)

spirit of militarism and the glorification of war, she nonetheless con-ceded that the world was not perhaps sufficiently civilised to 'lay aside our arms':

> That war is the most cruel, the most unfair, the most costly, and least permanent method of settling a dispute cannot be sufficiently emphasised. It may be that the world is not yet sufficiently civilised, not sufficiently permeated with the spirit of Christianity for us to dare to altogether lay aside our arms and rely solely on just and humane methods of adjusting our differences. But even if it be still necessary to rely on force for the safety of our homes, and the preservation of our liberties, there should be no vain, no bombastic ideas of glory to be found in the killing or maiming of our fellow creatures … Surely then, it is for us to discourage this rampant war spirit, and to urge with all earnestness and at every opportunity the principles of Peace and Arbitration.[49]

She welcomed the end of the South African War the following year, but lamented the way both sides in the war had been fighting for the same ideals. The real enemies of peace that needed to be fought, she wrote, were identified by Petrarch as 'avarice, ambition, envy, anger and pride'.[50]

By 1903 the NCW, which had started with such energy and enthusiasm seven years earlier, was running into difficulties. Sheppard left for England that year, intending to stay there permanently; and although she returned to Christchurch the following year, poor health caused her to play a less active part in the women's movement from then on. The meeting held at New Plymouth in 1903 was not a full NCW convention: it was attended by just six women, including Christina Henderson and Bain from Christchurch. A paper on 'Peace and arbitration' was read by Bain and a resolution passed, almost word for word the same as that passed in 1901.[51]

Bain's feminist and pacifist commitment took her to the international stage when she travelled to Berlin in June 1904 to represent the New Zealand NCW at the Quinquennial Meeting of the International Council of Women (ICW). There she found that peace was a widely held aspiration among the delegates.[52] The ICW had shown a strong commitment to world peace: it had a standing Committee on Peace and Arbitration, and in 1902 had issued a statement, intended as a discussion paper, expressing support for the Court of International Arbitration, which had sat for the first time on 18 May 1901 – an outcome of the 1899 Hague Peace Conference.[53] From Berlin, Bain travelled to Boston to attend the Thirteenth Universal Peace Congress in October 1904, a meeting attended by both men and women. Here she found that many 'powerful and eloquent speakers' were urging arbitration, just as the New Zealand NCW had done since 1897, as 'the only human [sic] method of settling differences between individuals, communities and people; and gradual, simultaneous, and proportional disarmament was repeatedly advocated'.[54] One of nine invited speakers at a meeting that considered 'the duties and responsibilities of women in regard to peace', Bain reported that New Zealand was still divided by the issue of its involvement in the South African War, but that New Zealanders spoke optimistically about the 'growing realization of the futility of warfare. The love of peace for its own sake is becoming more and more freely expressed among us.' She also spoke about the New Zealand NCW's stand for peace, and she mentioned the system of industrial tribunals introduced by the Liberals in New Zealand in 1894 (the Industrial and Conciliation Arbitration Act), which settled disagreements between employers and employees and was credited with having resulted in 11 years without strikes.[55]

The 'Clarion' settlers and the New Zealand Socialist Party

Meanwhile New Zealand's small but burgeoning socialist movement had been boosted by the arrival of almost two hundred British socialists, who sailed out to the colony in 1900. The group were subscribers to the *Clarion*, a popular British socialist newspaper, and had given themselves the moniker 'Clarionettes'. Among them was the Yorkshire tailor and future Cantabrian socialist – dubbed the 'conscience of Christchurch socialism' – Frederick Riley Cooke, his wife Ida, and their four sons.[56] The group hoped to establish a cooperative settlement in New Zealand, with social as well as political ideals: 'In our village we should have plenty of social life. Most of us would be fond of books and music. Some who wish to join later are expert musicians ... We could lay out a lawn for tennis and croquet; we should have a cricket and football field, and realise in every way a fuller life than is possible in our present conditions.'[57]

Although the settlement was ultimately abandoned due to a lack of suitable land, other Clarionettes continued to arrive in New Zealand until at least 1903. Many of the settlers went on to become prominent in New Zealand's socialist movement. Fred Cooke, for example, was present at the founding of both the Wellington branch of the New Zealand Socialist Party (NZSP) in 1901 and the Christchurch branch in 1902, and he contested the Christchurch East electorate seat for the Socialist Party in 1905, 1908 and 1911. The party advocated equal pay for women at a time when few trade unions held a similar view; and it aimed to educate people towards 'the organisation of New Zealand as a Co-operative commonwealth in which the land and all the instruments of production, distribution, and exchange shall be owned and managed by people collectively'.[58]

The establishment of the Socialist Church and the Socialist Party ran in tandem with the development of a strong trade union movement, which was underway long before the 1890s. The arrival of new immigrants in Canterbury in the 1870s who had previously been involved in the British trade unions had brought a 'forward movement' of unionism in the region, and over the next decade there was a proliferation of unions and labour organisations. The Canterbury Trades and Labour Council (CTLC) was established in 1890, comprising unions of typographers, bookbinders, carpenters, bootmakers, tailors and tailoresses, shipwrights, boilermakers, painters, butchers and labourers.[59] Despite

New Zealand Socialist Party Conference 1910. Fred Cooke and his wife Ida were among the attendees – Ida as the proxy delegate for Rongotea. Ida is third from the left in the front row; Fred is sixth from the left. The other two women present, both from the Christchurch Socialist Party, were Mrs L. R. Wilson (first on the left of the front row) and Mrs D. Whyte (fifth from the left). (Alexander Turnbull Library)

a setback to unionism caused by the defeat of the maritime strike in 1890, there was rapid growth in the number of unions and union membership, spurred on by energetic leaders. Jack McCullough, who was vice-president of the CTLC in 1899 and president in 1901, was said to have founded 17 trade unions in just one year; Ted Howard, became organiser of the General Labourers Union in 1908.[60]

In 1904 the conference of the Trades and Labour Councils established the Political Labour League (PLL), an independent labour party to put up political candidates for election. The league's Christchurch leaders included pacifists McCullough, Howard and James Thorn. A willingness to cooperate was still a feature of Christchurch's radical groups, and in April 1903 the Socialist Party, Socialist Church, CWI, WCTU and the Progressive Liberal Association agreed to hold quarterly meetings to discuss topics of general interest. This 'networking' was a major contributing factor to the strength of the peace movement in the city later on.[61]

When the NZSP held its first national conference in Wellington at Easter 1908, the subject of militarism provoked a long discussion that concluded with a statement of solidarity with workers around the world: 'This Conference of Socialists in New Zealand recognises that the workers of the world have no quarrel among themselves, and affirms the principle of universal peace as in the best interests of humanity.'[62]

Reaction to the 'dreadnought' battleship

The principle of universal peace received a direct challenge in March 1909 when the New Zealand Government decided to donate a battleship to Britain. Justifying the decision, Liberal Prime Minister Joseph Ward told the papers that the 'Motherland' felt: 'her supremacy on the seas is now seriously threatened by the amazing naval activity of the German dockyards … [A]ll thoughtful men in Great Britain recognise that the Empire must set itself with the utmost determination, and, if necessary, sacrifice itself to maintain the naval supremacy upon which not only our honour but our national greatness depends.'[63] According to Ward, New Zealand stood 'among the first in the British Dominions for a ready and loyal response where the necessities of the Empire call for it.'[64] Parliament authorised expenditure of up to two million pounds on the battleship (the *HMS New Zealand* ultimately cost 1.7 million), to be paid for with a loan, and a second ship would be provided if necessary.[65]

Trade unionists were foremost among those who disagreed with the gift of the dreadnought battleship. Alfred Hart, a painter and former president of the CTLC, spoke strongly against the gift on behalf of the council, calling it a 'delirious farce'. 'There was no doubt,' he said, that 'the burden of providing the money to pay for this Dreadnought would fall heaviest on the workers.'[66] A meeting of the CTLC condemned the gift. James Thorn, who had joined the Socialist Church (which continued to meet until 1905), was secretary for the CTLC and had been a parliamentary candidate for the PLL in the 1905 election, wrote to the *Lyttelton Times* to criticise the decision, citing the economic improvidence of building a battleship, and the inhumanity of war.[67]

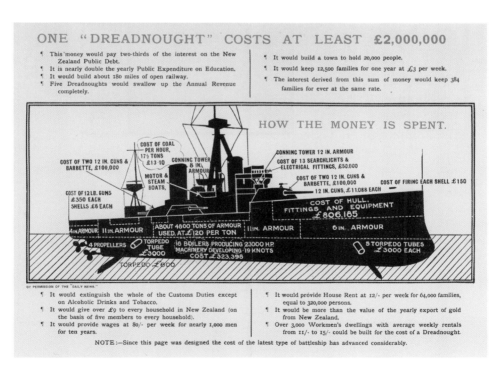

Detail of a large poster produced in England and adapted for use in New Zealand with local information. (Canterbury Museum)

> On the ground of financial necessity, this Cabinet of waste-
> ful squanderers dismisses scores of men from public works and
> shops … and then glibly and heartlessly proclaim their intention
> to put the people in bonds to build an engine of destruction! The
> inhumanity, the brutal inhumanity! … I should like to know
> what the ordinary German has done to have developed in us this
> spirit of disgusting bombast. Can any of the workers here … tell
> me any one sound reason why we should hate the Germans? The
> Germans are men and women, just as we are. They love, laugh,
> sing, get sad, just as we do. Have they done us any injury? Have
> they? If not, what justification is there to lust for their lives?[68]

Thorn, whose father had ordered him to enlist in 1900, had returned
from service in the South African war a pacifist after witnessing the killing of civilians there. He also wrote an open letter to the local clergy in
which he said that militarism was incompatible with the teaching of
Jesus of Nazareth. On his return to New Zealand he secured work at the
Addington Railway Workshops, where he came under the influence of
McCullough.[69]

Taylor, another of Thorn's men-
tors, vigorously opposed the gift of
the dreadnought at a special meeting of MPs. This led to calls for
him to resign from Parliament, and
twice he was threatened with violence by unruly crowds. His main
argument was that the decision was
unconstitutional because it had been
made by Cabinet, not authorised
by Parliament. When Taylor called
a public meeting at His Majesty's
Theatre in Christchurch to protest
against the unconstitutionality of
the cabinet decision, the theatre was
filled to overflowing, with a crowd of

James Thorn, c. 1936. (Alexander Turnbull
Library)

2000 outside. The meeting, chaired by McCullough, proceeded despite heckling from a portion of the audience who sang patriotic songs and disrupted with catcalls, kazoos and an 'insistent whistle', especially when unionists Alfred Hart, Harry Atkinson and Dan Sullivan addressed the meeting.[70] Most, however, were there to support the motion opposing the 'unconstitutional action of the Cabinet', and it was duly passed.[71]

There was opposition to the government's offer of a dreadnought from Christians, too. Charles Mackie, a leading Baptist layman, argued that Christ had taught peace on earth and goodwill towards all people. Arbitration should be adopted for settling international disputes, and Christians should be sending messages of peace and goodwill to fellow Christians throughout the world. 'Instead of War Leagues, form Peace Unions; instead of shouting for more "Dreadnoughts" raise our voices for Peace,' he concluded.[72] Christchurch printer and journalist Louis Christie was another whose opposition was based on his Christian beliefs and 'on the necessity for a better understanding among the nations and the extension of the principle of the brotherhood of man'.[73]

Although the *HMS New Zealand* was decommissioned and sold for scrap in 1923, the country continued paying off the loan well into the 1940s. The government's maritime largesse was the opening salvo in what would become a series of military commitments to the British Empire.

CHAPTER 2

'RAISE OUR VOICES FOR PEACE': THE PRE-WAR PEACE MOVEMENT 1911–12

New Zealand's participation in the South African War provoked an outburst of patriotism and jingoism. There was increased concern for military preparedness and a part-time reserve grew to 8000 men. Schools introduced a weekly regime of voluntary military exercises, and a National Defence League was formed to advocate for compulsory military training (CMT).[1] The enthusiastic welcome given to British war hero Lord Kitchener when he visited New Zealand in 1910 on a mission to reorganise and coordinate the defences of the British Empire reflected the country's eagerness to play its part, while also being well prepared to defend itself. Those in favour of CMT in New Zealand argued that it would help in the defence of the empire; that New Zealand needed a large military force to make it safe from a possible influx of Japanese or Chinese immigrants; and that military training would improve the mental, moral and physical health of young men. It was supported by schools such as the strongly imperialist and militarist Christchurch

Boys' High School and by its parent body, Canterbury College, where college staff encouraged British patriotism and the students responded by forming an Officers' Training Corps in 1909.[2]

The 1909 Defence Act had introduced CMT for teenage boys – the first country in the British Empire to do so. All boys had to join the junior cadets when they turned 12 (later raised to 14), and were required to do 52 hours of training a year, which included shooting practice, marching in formation and taking part in mock battles.

The registration for military training of all young men between the ages of 14 and 20 began in April 1911. Posters appeared at 'post offices, police stations and other conspicuous places, informing all male inhabitants of New Zealand … that they must register themselves within 60 days'.[3] Māori were included in the scheme, but military training was not enforced in rural areas where most Māori lived. Some were part of cadet schemes at their schools, however.[4] Failure to register would result in a fine of five pounds. Registration continued until the middle of July,

A *Weekly Press* photo of public school cadets in Victoria Square, Christchurch, May 1907. (Canterbury Museum)

by which time the government had a roll of over 30,000 men and boys available for the Territorial Force. But around 25 per cent of those eligible to join the senior cadets and the Territorial Forces – 13,000 young men – had failed to register. This was a difficult situation for the government: it did not have the resources to cope with more than 30,000 men and boys in the territorials at this stage, but at the same time it wanted to demonstrate that it was enforcing the Act. As a result, enforcement was always going to be selective rather than wholesale, and the first boys to be prosecuted for failing to register came from pacifist, socialist and/ or working-class backgrounds.[5]

For Christians the arguments against military training were moral. As they saw it, killing people, and training young men to kill, was against the teachings and example of Christ and was therefore wrong. Besides, a compulsory scheme violated people's freedom to make decisions based on their conscience, and undermined the moral authority of parents; and finally, they did not want their sons exposed to immoral behaviour at military training camps.[6]

Baptist Christians took the lead in establishing the first enduring peace group in Christchurch, prompted into action by the Defence Department's attempts to involve churches in the process of registering boys for military training. A letter from the Christchurch Ministers' Association (CMA) asking churches to provide names of eligible boys who could be drafted into an interdenominational corps prompted a strong reaction from Oxford Terrace Baptist Church member D. W. Jones, who objected to the churches being used as recruiting grounds for the army. Enlisting the help of Mackie and another church member, C. von Bibra, a meeting of the Baptist Lay Preachers' Association was held on 23 May 1911, where a resolution was passed condemning the attitude of the CMA and the churches 'that have fostered and abetted the spirit of jingoistic militarism instead of strenuously opposing it from the beginning'.[7] They protested against the introduction of CMT and called on Christians to 'passively resist' the government 'or any other body whose laws and requirements are in opposition to the principles of the Christian faith'.[8] Three days later the Baptist lay preachers held a public meeting at the Salvation Army barracks where they resolved that

CMT was a 'direct violation of the law of liberty of conscience', and 'in direct opposition to the growing ideal of humanitarian advancement and the universal brotherhood of humanity'.[9]

Even at this early stage the anti-militarist meetings attracted both support and opposition. A group of about sixty students from Canterbury College seated themselves in a solid body in the centre of the hall and disrupted the meeting using tactics that included loud singing and turning out the lights. But members of the Socialist Party had also turned up in force, and the resolution was passed by a show of hands. After the meeting the college students reconvened outside the Supreme Court and attempted to carry a motion: 'That this meeting believes in compulsory military training'. Ted Howard and Fred Cooke spoke against the motion, and the meeting ended in 'disorder and uproar'.[10]

Socialists and Christians working together continued to be a feature of the Christchurch peace movement. Many of the anti-militarists were recent migrants who referred to England as 'Home' and saw themselves as part of a proud English tradition of freedom of conscience. This paradox is encapsulated in letters exchanged between Robert Milligan and Mackie in 1912, in which Milligan regretted that Christchurch, 'which is spoken of as being so "English" should have earned the unenviable reputation all over the Dominion for their opposition to the Defence System', to which Mackie replied that it was not surprising that 'English' Christchurch was anti-military, because conscription was un-English.[11]

The publicity created by the May 1911 meeting resulted in Louis Christie approaching Charles Mackie, and together they convened a meeting of sympathisers in the Young Men's Christian Association (YMCA) Buildings on 21 June, where the National Peace and Anti-Militarist League was formed, with Christie as secretary and Mackie as treasurer.

The peace movement is established

About six weeks after the National Peace and Anti-Militarist League was formed it was decided that two organisations were needed: a National Peace Council of New Zealand (NPC), to be based in Christchurch, and a 'working league', which would join those already at work in Auckland, Wellington, Waihi and at Runanga on the West Coast. At a packed meeting in the Caledonian Hall, chaired by Mackie, the resolution to form a league was carried unanimously and a constitution recommended by the NPC was adopted.[12] The Christchurch Anti-Militarist League (AML) and the NPC were both working towards the repeal of the compulsory clauses in the Defence Act; however, while the AML was a local membership organisation with aims of protesting against militarism and promoting principles of peace by distributing educational literature, the NPC had a broader vision of working for the settlement of international disputes by way of arbitration: it aimed to educate public opinion and play a national coordinating role, while also corresponding widely with peace organisations overseas.[13] In practice, many of the same individuals played leading roles in both organisations and worked together at house-to-house leafleting, organising public meetings, hearing papers from members, organising socials and supporting the young men who were resisting military training.

The Christchurch AML had the names and addresses of 216 members or supporters listed in its record book. The NPC, in contrast, did not seek to have a large membership; instead it had around twenty members who were either appointed as delegates by sympathetic organisations or elected by the council members. The delegates came from the AML, the Canterbury Trades and Labour Council (CTLC), several individual trade unions, the Socialist Party, the Society of Friends (Quakers), the Fabian Society, and the Canterbury Women's Institute (CWI).

Some previous histories have said that the AML began in June 1910 — a claim that seems to derive from a misinterpretation of a statement made by Louis Christie in November 1911

IMPORTANT ANTI-MILITARIST MEETING.

In view of the result of the General Elections and the fact that orders have been issued to the effect that the Compulsory Military Training Scheme is to be rigidly enforced early in January, it is imperative that some bold action should be taken by our League. An Important Meeting of Members and Sympathisers will be held on Tuesday next, December 19th at 8 p.m. in the Caledonian Society's Rooms, Worcester Street, to discuss the situation, and to carefully organize for immediate vigorous action, if such becomes necessary. You are urged to attend, and to bring any friends who you know are in sympathy with this movement.

F. McCullough, Secretary.

Frank McCullough calls anti-militarists to an important meeting. (Canterbury Museum) that the league had started in 'June last'.[14] The fact that the two groups are often referred to in newspaper reports in 1911 and 1912 as if they were still one organisation, and that Mackie was still using printed letterhead of the 'National Peace and Anti-Militarist Council' as late as May 1912, all adds to a confusing picture.

It is evident in NPC records that there was some dissatisfaction with Christie; when he was re-elected secretary in April 1912, several of Mackie's supporters resigned. The situation was resolved by Christie resigning, clearing the way for Mackie, who had been appointed national organiser in February 1912, to become secretary of the NPC.

Christie also resigned as secretary of the AML in October 1911 and was replaced by a young resister, Frank McCullough (son of Jack and Margaret McCullough), who was, in turn, replaced by trade unionist Henry Worrall in May 1912. Methodist minister Rev David McNicholl was elected president at the first AGM of the AML in August 1912, but his involvement ended when he moved to Thames in April 1913.[15]

In September 1911 the movement produced its first issue of *The Anti-Militarist*, 'A journal of Protest and True Patriotism', edited and published by Louis Christie. Three issues were produced in 1911 and a fourth in April 1912, with most of the content coming from activists in the Christchurch movement. They reported on events such as the jailing of young resisters, recent meetings and protests, along with some news from abroad.[16] Within a few months, leagues had been established in other towns throughout the country, including Invercargill, Gore, Dunedin, Nelson, Feilding and Hastings. By November 1911 there were reported to be 16 leagues around the country, all loosely connected to the Christchurch organisation – although later reports suggest that

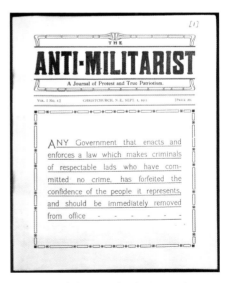

Front page of *The Anti-Militarist*, September 1911. (Canterbury Museum)

most were short-lived. Christchurch was the heart of the resistance movement, and confirmation of its leading role came in November 1911 when 25 delegates from anti-militarist leagues, the Wellington Branch of the Federation of Labour, the Auckland Peace Society, the Society of Friends, the Women's Christian Temperance Union (WCTU) and some individuals met in Wellington. The conference decided to organise a campaign advocating repeal of the compulsory clauses of the Defence Act, to be conducted by the National Peace and Anti-Militarist League from its Christchurch office.[17]

Charles Mackie, c. 1907. (Canterbury Museum)

Organising a successful campaign

Charles Robert Norris Mackie, the diligent and long-serving secretary of the NPC, first became interested in the peace movement in England as a young man, and fought 'strenuously for a peaceful settlement' at the time of the South African War.[18] Born in Christchurch in 1869, Mackie and his family left their sheep station 'Lavington' on the south bank of the Rakaia River in 1884 and went to live in England.[19] After the death of both his parents Mackie returned to Christchurch. He joined the Oxford Terrace Baptist Church, probably drawn there by the ministry of the Rev Joseph Doke, who had spoken out against New Zealand's involvement in the South African War. The proceeds of Mackie's family's land investments apparently supported him throughout his life, and once he had settled in Christchurch he devoted his life to voluntary work. He married a widow, Ethel Manttan (née Nuttall), in 1914, and the couple lived at the Avonside house they called 'Lavington' for the remainder of their lives.[20] By 1902 Mackie was playing an active role in the Baptist Church at local, regional and national level. He was the missionary organiser for the New Zealand Baptist Union for three years, a role he carried out with 'skill and thoroughness'.[21] A year-long trip to India, the United States and the United Kingdom from October 1909 left a lasting impression. There was a 'deep response given to any reference to peace' he said of the three conferences he attended while he was away.[22]

Mackie came into the role of secretary organiser for the NPC with clear ideas about how to organise a successful campaign. Catering for all branches of the community in the movement was important, and he advised having officers who represented various interests so as to avoid the dangers of 'class troubles'. The work of the group should be largely educational, and members needed to have 'plenty of work'. He suggested dividing the city into wards, each with its own committee to organise a propaganda campaign; encouraging one or two members to become sufficiently knowledgeable to be able to do public speaking; distributing literature house-to-house while at the same time gaining signatures of supporters on a protest form were all suggested; and getting women's organisations involved. He proposed that peace group members visit *all* organisations – including trades councils, WCTUs, bible classes and debating societies – to ask that CMT go on their syllabus.[23]

The programme of work carried out by the NPC from 1912 followed Mackie's strategy. Distribution of literature was a major activity: Mackie reported that over the next few years the NPC printed or distributed 656,040 leaflets, pamphlets and circulars.[24] Much of the literature distributed was imported from England but several booklets written by local citizens indicated a strong measure of support from a range of individuals.

Robert Laing, a leading botanist and science master at Christchurch Boys' High School, originally prepared his publication *Shall War and Militarism Prevail?* (1911) as a series of lectures for Eveline Cunnington's Girls' Social Science Club in 1910. Laing particularly wanted to educate people about 'Imperialism as it appears in the documents of history and the ideals of peace as promulgated by pacifists in all parts of the world', including the falsity of the popular paradox: 'If you wish for peace prepare for war'.[25]

Three other locally produced pamphlets were written by Charles Reginald Ford (known as Reginald), who had served as ship's steward and assistant to Captain Robert Falcon Scott on the *Discovery* voyage to Antarctica in 1901–04. When he returned to Christchurch in 1906, Ford became a land agent and architect. Before he left Christchurch in 1913 he wrote three pamphlets opposing conscription and CMT, published articles in the *Maoriland Worker*, and attended the national peace conference in November 1911. Between June 1911 and August 1912 the NPC distributed 20,000 of Ford's pamphlets, *The Defence Act: A criticism* (1911); *The Case Against Compulsory Military Training* (1912) and *The Cost of War* (June 1912).[26]

Morgan Williams was a Kaiapoi farmer, a socialist and anti-militarist who encouraged the NPC to hold meetings in Kaiapoi and Rangiora. His 22-page booklet *The Great White Elephant*, published in 1914, countered the popular belief that preparing for war was the best way to preserve peace.[27] The real object of CMT, said Williams, was to provide the raw material for an expeditionary force, as demanded by Britain, and to strengthen the hands of those who were clamouring for military training in the United Kingdom. Like many of the anti-militarists, Williams had a personal interest in CMT: his younger brother Reg was a leading figure in the protest movement.

In addition to distributing literature the NPC arranged to publish an 'advertisement', written in the form of articles, in *The Reformer* – a monthly paper published by the Canterbury No-licence Council, which worked for the prohibition of alcohol in local areas by way of the 'no-licence' vote held at the time of each general election. The 'advertorials' appeared from December 1912 until at least November 1913.[28]

Opposition and support for the peace movement

At first the NPC found the press to be hostile, abusive, and unwilling to publish anything in favour of their work: 'it was not until the force of the movement was realised by the numbers of letters received that the columns were more freely opened to us'.[29] There was one newspaper, however, that consistently supported the work of the peace movement – the *Maoriland Worker*, which, in 1911, became the official organ of the

Federation of Labour. Like the NPC and AML, the *Maoriland Worker* equated CMT with conscription. It saw military training as a form of state oppression and it believed that a conscript army had the potential to be used by the capitalist class against the working class.[30]

In November 1911 opposition to the NPC took the form of a direct attack. The Agricultural and Pastoral (A&P) Show that took place in Christchurch every November was a good opportunity for the NPC and AML to reach a large number of people. Having gained permission to set up a stall at the 1911 show, the NPC was unprepared for personal intervention by the commandant of the New Zealand Forces, General Alexander Godley, who told the A&P committee that the NPC's literature was inflammatory and illegal. When Harry Atkinson, who was manning the stall, refused to leave, he was escorted from the grounds by a sergeant and a constable. The NPC later brought an unsuccessful suit against the A&P Society for breach of contract. There was another attack the following year when the peace council, not permitted to have a stall at the show, distributed some 30,000 leaflets from a nearby section. A band of 15 men drove up in motorcars, pulled down the peace council's tent and went off with their flag.[31]

Support for the peace movement – and opposition to it – were also evident when Mackie and William Ensom visited towns south of Christchurch, including Ashburton, Timaru, Waimate, Oamaru, Dunedin and Invercargill, in June and July 1912. In the smaller towns they found only a few supporters who came from some labour groups and trades unions, a few clergy, a few socialists or, in Timaru, the congregation of the Unitarian Church. Ignorance of the scope and meaning of the

THE GREAT WHITE ELEPHANT
From Morgan Williams' Pamphlet, "The Great White Elephant."

Cartoon, probably drawn by Heathcote Mann, from Morgan Williams' booklet. (*Maoriland Worker*, 4 March 1914, p. 5)

The Christchurch Incident—Militarism Presents Its Only Argument.

'Militarism presents its only argument' refers to the incident when Harry Atkinson was expelled from the National Peace Council stall at the Agricultural and Pastoral Show for giving out 'inflammatory and illegal' material. (Heathcote Mann, *Maoriland Worker,* 24 November 1911, p. 8)

Defence Act prevailed. After some serious leafleting in Invercargill, 70–100 people attended a public meeting and a league was formed. Meetings in Timaru, Gore and Dunedin were disrupted by opponents, including cadets and territorials. A branch of the Peace Society in Gore had given up because no one attended meetings. A meeting of 50–60 in Waimate gave the speakers a good hearing and carried a resolution against the Act, and the most encouraging meeting was with a vigorous branch of the Housewives Union in Invercargill. Most people they met thought the country needed to be defended and that discipline was good for youths. Mackie and Ensom's conclusion was that the workers, including many small farmers, were against the Act, but much more education was needed by way of meetings and the distribution of literature.[32]

William Ensom and his wife Annie (Sarah Ann) were among the most committed and generous members of the NPC. Annie was a successful businesswoman who, with her mother, had developed the 'Mrs Pope's' variety store. She married Ensom in 1902 when she was 62. From 1907 the Ensoms divided their time between Timaru and Christchurch, where William was manager of the Timaru branch of the NZ Express

Company. When they joined the NPC they already knew many of the members through their membership of groups such as the Progressive Liberal Association, the Fabian Society, the Socialist Church and the CWI.[33]

Contrasting Christian responses

Local churches and clergy on the whole were not prepared to take an active interest in the fledgling peace movement. A typical view was that of the Rev H. Williams, who wrote that he was thankful that military training had been established, and was confident that military discipline would be 'of benefit to the national character'.[34] Mackie deplored this attitude. He speculated that it might be because New Zealand clergy had never lived in Europe: 'They cannot seem to fathom the depths of Militarism probably from the fact that few of them have seen its effects in the older lands.'[35] Mackie himself had lived near St John's Wood Barracks in London and felt he was well informed about the immoral side of military life.

A deputation from the National Peace and Anti-Militarist Council in August 1911, however, persuaded the CMA to unanimously pass a resolution protesting against the compulsory clauses of the Act and pledging to work towards the repeal of those clauses. Charles Murray, a politically active Presbyterian minister in Sydenham, was a leader in the Ministers' Association and remained a strong supporter of the peace movement, though he declined to join the NPC. 'Christ is the way of love and peace, and the only solution to international, national and social complications. Christ's commandment to love one another admits no exceptions,' he told Mackie.[36]

In contrast to other churches the Society of Friends (Quakers) has a

William and Annie Ensom, c. 1914.
(Canterbury Museum)

'peace testimony' at the core of its Christian belief. There were not many members in the New Zealand society at the time, but it was still a part of the London Yearly Meeting, and even before the Defence Act was passed, British Quaker Thomas Hodgkin was despatched to New Zealand to try and ensure that a conscience clause was added to the

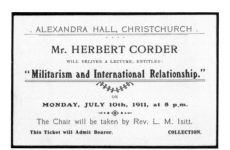

. ALEXANDRA HALL, CHRISTCHURCH .

Mr. HERBERT CORDER

WILL DELIVER A LECTURE, ENTITLED:

"Militarism and International Relationship."

ON

MONDAY, JULY 10th, 1911, at 8 p.m.

The Chair will be taken by Rev. L. M. Isitt.

This Ticket will Admit Bearer.   COLLECTION.

Ticket for the Herbert Corder meeting, 10 July 1911. (Canterbury Museum)

Act. A number of other British Quakers visited New Zealand to advise and encourage members, and inevitably they became involved in the peace movement here. In July 1911 when British Quaker Herbert Corder addressed a large public meeting in Christchurch on 'Militarism and international relationships', numerous people joined the newly formed National Peace and Anti-Militarist League. The following year Alfred Brown and William and Harriette Alexander came to New Zealand and Australia as a Friends' Peace Deputation. Brown spent most of his time

The first Annual Meeting of the New Zealand Society of Friends, held in Christchurch in May 1912. Percy Fletcher is standing sixth from the right in the back row (in front of the man with a beard). (Macmillan Brown Library)

in Australia, while the Alexanders worked for the peace movement, primarily in Auckland and Wellington.[37]

The Annual Meeting of the New Zealand Society of Friends consistently opposed militarism, and wrote to the government deprecating the movement towards CMT. Louis Christie and his family, and John and Ellen Howell were among those who attended the 1912 annual meeting, held in Christchurch. The Howells had arrived in Auckland in 1901 and moved to Christchurch in 1906, where John, who was a pioneer in technical education, transformed a series of night classes into the highly successful Christchurch Technical College. British Quakers also supported the New Zealand peace movement financially, and John Howell was on a small committee set up to allocate the funds received from England for the campaign against CMT. The contributions were considerable: an estimated £1783 was sent to New Zealand pre-war.[38]

Bristol Quaker gets involved

English Quaker Thomas Churchus (T. C.) Gregory, who worked at a printing works in Bristol, became directly involved in the struggle against militarism in the colonies when he received a copy of the 1909 New Zealand Defence Act. Gregory was so appalled by the idea that a British colony was introducing CMT that he printed a leaflet criticising the Act and distributed it to others in his neighbourhood. Gregory's name and address appeared in an article criticising the leaflet, and his cause became widely known in New Zealand. Anti-militarists, including Mackie, were happy to send him further information about their opposition to the Act and, provided

John Howell, the first director of the Christchurch Technical College, was a Quaker and a strong supporter of the peace movement. (Ara Institute of Canterbury)

with such ammunition, Gregory published at least 10 leaflets warning British emigrants of the consequences to them and their families if they emigrated to New Zealand, Australia or South Africa. A booklet entitled 'Warning to emigrants: New Zealand: Plain facts about conscription', published in March 1912, was compiled mainly from writing by New Zealanders. Some of Gregory's leaflets ran to several editions: A 'Warning to emigrants' published in January 1913 was the fourth edition, and had a print run of 25,000.[39] His campaign against militarism in the colonies became a burning passion.

Another English Quaker, Elizabeth Josephine Peckover, was a member of a family who had provided generous donations to the New Zealand NPC. She issued a leaflet, 'Boy heroes for conscience sake in New Zealand', which painted a harsh picture of the consequences of having a Christian conscience in the colony, and showed how the introduction of CMT appeared to an English Quaker:

Boys from 14 years upwards, whom the recent Defence Acts of New Zealand consider to have no conscience because they are under 21, are being prosecuted and imprisoned, some with hard labour and solitary confinement, merely because their belief in the New Testament teaching of the brotherhood of man compels them to refuse compliance with the newly enacted regulations for military drill.[40]

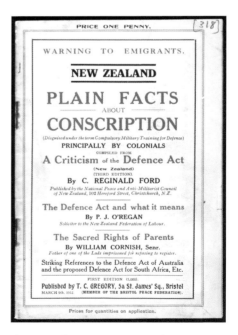

The cover of T. C. Gregory's 'Warning to emigrants' pamphlet, published in Bristol in March 1912. (Canterbury Museum)

Labour movement resistance

Christchurch's successful peace movement owes much to Mackie's commitment and willingness to work for the NPC as if it were a paid job. But his outstanding contribution was the ability to work alongside those with whom he must have had some disagreement. Whether they were Christian pacifist like himself, socialist or humanitarian, Mackie took care that meetings and deputations were representative of the whole cross-section of anti-militarists.

Socialists in Christchurch, while they supported the activities of the NPC and the AML, continued to protest against the Defence Act. A 'large gathering' attended a protest meeting against CMT, organised by the Socialist Party in His Majesty's Theatre in July 1911. The meeting, chaired by Ted Howard, condemned the imprisonment of a Wellington boy, William Cornish, who had refused to register under the scheme. It pledged not to support any candidate who was in favour of CMT and condemned the government for building a dreadnought battleship. On 18 July Hiram Hunter, vice-president of the CTLC, wrote to the *Lyttelton Times* condemning Ward's autocratic decision-making. In a reference to the 1909 imperial conference in London, where Prime Minister Joseph Ward had said the New Zealand people were prepared to increase their contributions for imperial defence, Hunter asked:

> Were the people of New Zealand ever asked about Imperial
> defence schemes, or compulsory military training, or whether
> they are prepared to rear children to be trained as conscripts,
> to make targets in any part of the world if called upon? … Sir
> Joseph Ward has acted as an autocrat …[41]

That same month, 17-year-old Harry Cooke became Christchurch's first young resister to be imprisoned for failing to register for military training. Press reports on his court case highlighted his socialist allegiance, even down to the colour of his tie: sporting a 'flamboyant tie of a shrill red', Harry told the court, 'I don't believe in murder, and I won't be trained to be a murderer.'[42] The reports downplayed any notion of heroism in his stance: they described him as 'very young, very thin, very nervous, and very "do or die"'.[43] He was fined, and informed that non-payment would result in imprisonment. Harry refused to pay, and

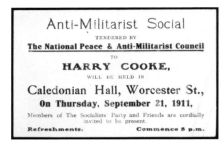

The ticket for a social held for Harry Cooke on 21 September 1911. (Canterbury Museum)

in August was sent to Timaru to serve 21 days in prison. He was fare-welled at the station by a large group of supporters.

In his preparedness to go to prison on a matter of principle, Harry was following the example of his father Fred Cooke, who was serving a second short term in Lyttelton prison for refusing to pay fines incurred after he was convicted for speaking against conscription without permission in Cathedral Square. Characteristically, when he was interviewed on his release he criticised the prison as a place that did not 'give a man any possible chance of reform; it is a place for crime, imbecility, and degeneracy'.[44]

When it was revealed that Harry Cooke and other young political prisoners were being incarcerated alongside criminals, there was a public outcry, and in August 1911 the government announced that in future it would prosecute only 'in special cases'.[45] With a general election approaching the Liberal Government was anxious not to make the Defence Act an election issue; as a result there are just three names on the *Maoriland Worker*'s 'Roll of Honour' of boys imprisoned for their beliefs in 1911: William Cornish of Wellington, Peter Thompson of Nelson, and Harry Cooke of Christchurch.[46]

On Cooke's release from prison in September he was greeted at Christchurch Railway Station by a large enthusiastic crowd, and he was carried to the already overflowing King's Theatre where, reportedly, between two and three thousand young men were unable to get in.[47]

The battle of Choral Hall

While Harry Cooke was serving his sentence in the Timaru jail, 'probably the most riotous and disorderly meeting ever held' in Christchurch took place in the Choral Hall, organised by the NPC and the AML to protest against the Defence Act. The large crowd who gathered for the 'public indignation meeting' was a sign of the strength of local socialist and labour organisations:[48] there were 'hundreds present opposed to the Conscription Act', and the resolutions were carried by 'over 800 to 21'. The organisers had become aware a few days before the meeting that 'college students, volunteers and rowing clubs were organising to create disorder and chaos', and they issued tickets to avoid any disruption, but on the evening of the meeting 'it was plainly apparent there was mischief brewing'.[49] Many supporters of CMT had gained admission by forging tickets, and a large contingent had gathered outside the hall.

> At a signal from the outside, the college hooligans inside tried to rush the side door to let the outsiders in. For a brief period there was a mixing of people – biff! bang! oh! swish! creak! 'Coward!' 'Let him up!' 'British fair play!' and various other sounds … Stones were being thrown through the windows.

When the chairman, Jack McCullough, opened the meeting:

> there was a loud explosion outside, which sounded as if dynamite was being used. The resolutions were moved, seconded and carried, stones coming through the window all the time … The outsiders by this time had secured a battering ram and the side door was besieged, and both door and wall threatened to come down, when the fire hose was discovered and a watery blessing was showered on our gentle would-be defenders from a foreign foe … They then cursed the Socialists, and marched around the city, giving an exhibition of what the people can expect if ever militarism gets a strong footing in New Zealand.[50]

The actual meeting, when resolutions against the Defence Act were carried, lasted only about 30 minutes. The resolutions, moved by Christians D. W. Jones, Mackie and L. P. Christie and two socialists, Reg Williams and Fred Cooke, demonstrated the close cooperation

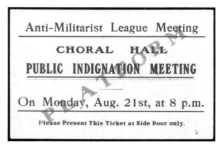

A ticket to the Anti-Militarist League's Choral Hall Meeting, August 1911. (Canterbury Museum)

between the peace movement and the labour movement. McCullough, interviewed the next day, said the worst feature of the night's operations was the fact that a blow had been struck at freedom of speech. Cooke, 'the ardent leader of the Socialist party', thanked the police for their forbearance and tact, and pointed out that the attempt to spoil the meeting was 'an organised rout by the students of the College, the rowing clubs and members of the Volunteer force … We are willing to defend the country, but it is the methods that we object to. Yet people who are supposed to be intellectual lead a rabble that they would not recognise in private life against those who wish only the fair play of the British nation to discuss their grievances.'[51]

The Passive Resisters' Union

The undertaking to prosecute only in special cases came to an end with the return of the Ward government in February 1912. In the same month the Passive Resisters' Union (PRU) was formed in response to the persecution of young men who failed to comply with CMT. The organisation was founded by workers at the Addington Railway Workshops, though its leaders and members came from throughout the community. Socialist beliefs and connections played a strong part in it. The PRU viewed capitalism as 'a harmful global force that could only be challenged by international solidarity amongst the working class';[52] its manifesto stated that CMT originated with the National Service League of England, which was composed 'of the capitalistic and exploiting classes, whose interest it is to keep the worker in subjection'.[53]

Despite the 'inclement weather' the inaugural meeting of the PRU was well attended, and the members pledged 'to resist coercion, conscription and compulsory military training under all circumstances and in defiance of all pains and penalties which may be imposed'.[54] Branches of the PRU were established throughout the country and by the end of the month the union claimed that more than 200 had joined. Membership was restricted only to those eligible for CMT, and their aim was direct resistance. The Christchurch branch produced membership badges, distributed manifestos across the city, and raised money to advertise their weekly meetings in the papers as well as to hire a lawyer to defend themselves in court.[55] With a strategy of direct non-violent action, it became, arguably, the most effective of the anti-militarist organisations in Christchurch at the time, comparable to the more extreme end of the women's suffrage movement in England: 'The boys are doing for our cause what the suffragettes are doing for women's rights in England' wrote David McNicoll in June 1913.[56]

One of the first to be prosecuted was James (Jim) Worrall, a plumber from Linwood. The joint secretary of the PRU was in court in February 1912, charged with distributing 'dodgers', which were pamphlets objecting to CMT. When he was arrested again in March Worrall refused to pay the fine imposed for failing to register under the Defence Act and spent 10 days in Lyttelton prison, after telling the court that he was prepared to go to jail because the Defence Act was 'un-British and unnecessary and the only way to get it repealed was to stand out against it'.[57] In his stand Worrall had the full support of his family, who had arrived in New Zealand in 1901. His father Henry, a labourer and scaffolder, joined the General Labourers Union and become a delegate to the CTLC and was also active in both the Christchurch AML and the NPC.[58]

Jim Worrall's prosecution was one of over sixty initiated in Christchurch, as opposition to the Defence Act was pursued

The Passive Resisters.

Why we will not obey the Defence Act.

Because it is un-British and iniquitous in that it deprives us of our **Liberty**.

Because it is not for the defence of New Zealand, if it **was** it would have been started in New Zealand by New Zealanders, instead of which, it has been originated by the National Service League of England, which is a body composed of the capitalistic and exploiting classes, whose interest it is to keep the worker in subjection. This body through our treacherous politicians foistered this **mis**called Defence Act upon us without the consent of our people. They have already reaped the reward of their treachery by being ousted from office.

Because we are free-born and in spite of all the attempts of the Capitalistic Press, the militarist parsons and other toadies to flunkyism, to forge the fetters of Consription upon us, we will not tolerate serfdom.

Because there are thousands of lads who have as yet no voice or vote in the country, who will not submit to tyranny and who need our assistance against the enemies of the working classes.

We will support these lads to our last breath. Will you join us ? and stand solidly with us against tyranny and oppression.

On behalf of the Christchurch Union—

H. Foote.	C. L. Beary.
F. Hooper.	W. J. Hooper.
J. N. Harle.	A. Duckmanton.
G. Green.	R. Williams.
E. Edwards.	W. Gates.
F. McCullough.	J. K. Worrall.

Christchurch members of the Passive Resisters' Union, including Frank McCullough, Reg Williams and Jim Worrall, explain why they will not obey the Defence Act. (Canterbury Museum)

with renewed intensity. Harry Cooke was arrested at work and imprisoned for a second time for 21 days, and a number of PRU members, including Harry's brother Alex, served sentences in Lyttelton prison. The day Harry Cooke went to prison, the Christchurch branch of the Socialist Party expressed its abhorrence at the cowardly action of persecuting the sons of men who were active in the anti-military movement: 'We are of opinion that this is a deliberate persecution, as there are to our knowledge cases of lads who have not been registered nor have they been summoned for non-registration. We are further of opinion that it is a clear instance of victimisation because of the activity of his father in the anti-military movement.'[59] By late March there were 10 'political prisoners' in Lyttelton prison: Jim Worrall named the others in a letter written from prison as Walter Hooper, Harold Denton, H. W. Hill, H. B. Worsfold, Alex Cooke, Harry Cooke, Fred Hobson, Edward Edwards and Edward Hannam.

In response to accusations of persecution after Cooke was imprisoned for the second time, General Alexander Godley reassured the public 'that nothing is further from the wish of myself or the defence authorities than that men should suffer imprisonment on account of this scheme. In fact, sooner than have it said that the Department wished to persecute anybody, I would like to see the Government release him.'[60]

Godley had recently visited four territorial training camps and had found that attendance had averaged 80 per cent. He was 'thoroughly pleased' with the experience: 'In Otago and Southland I came across men who had been rejected on account of physical unfitness, but who insisted upon attending drills … I decided that we would refuse nobody. We must try to devise some method of utilising the services of such willing and enthusiastic men.'[61] When he was asked if there was any sign of dissatisfaction over the element of compulsion, Godley said he had seen 'nothing except the protests of a small section outside'.[62]

Protest in Victoria Square

At an anti-militarist demonstration in Victoria Square on 9 March 1912 a large crowd of between 500 and 2000 men and women gathered to hear speakers denouncing the Defence Act and calling for the repeal of the compulsory clauses. The speakers included trade union-ists, representatives of the NPC and the AML, fathers of boys in prison, churchmen, members of the Socialist Party and the PRU. There were no women speakers, although Ada Wells was on the list of speakers pub-lished before the demonstration.

A youth who was described as the 'only remaining secretary' of the PRU demonstrated a fighting spirit as he told the crowd that 'he had been to the Lyttelton Gaol, and had seen the boys who were bearing up and quite well'. He added: 'Woe betide Ward or Massey, I say (clenched fists), if they continue to inflict this on us. If they put me in gaol for the rest of my life I would not have anything to do with conscription. They call us cowards. I'm ready to fight anyone, I'm ready for any of the offi-cers at the Drill Shed, but the fight is mental not physical.'[63]

Henry Worrall, who had visited his son in prison earlier in the day, addressed the crowd and advocated the establishment of an effective vol-unteer system. The *Star* reported: 'Cheers were given for Mr Worrall and his son.'[64] The more sensationalist *Truth* newspaper, on the other hand, highlighted the embarrassment his furious words caused to his fellow anti-militarists on the platform on the band rotunda. Worrall, who was doubtless feeling somewhat emotional about the imprisonment of his son, said it was 'he who had inculcated in his son the spirit of resistance to the Defence Act':

> 'Why!' he roared, with an accession of fury; 'Why to –, why the –, why to –, why the HELL didn't they take ME and put ME in gaol?' He was supported on the platform by parsons and wowsers, whose mechanical, brotherly smile froze on their countenances, whilst the ladies present sustained a delightful thrill of shocked surprise. The sentiment was greeted with lusty cheers, for if there is one thing the populace loves above another it is a whole-souled, fervent malediction. It is accepted as conclusive evidence of sincerity.[65]

Fred Cooke 'protested against conscription, but stated that he and his sons would be ready to defend their country if ever the need arose'; James (Jimmy) McCombs, relating some of his own experiences as a

The protest meeting held in Victoria Square, March 1912. (Canterbury Museum)

volunteer and meeting 'with more sympathy from the crowd than any other speaker', said he wanted the Defence Act 'repealed altogether, not to have only the compulsory clauses repealed'; and Dan Sullivan, on behalf of the Trades and Labour Council, also protested against the regulations of the Act.[66] Jack McCullough (since 1907 the worker's representative on the Arbitration Court), Louis Christie from the AML, Revs Charles Murray (Presbyterian) and David McNicholl (Methodist), Mackie (NPC) and Mr Hannam, father of Edward, one of the imprisoned resisters, were also among the speakers.

The following day, extra train carriages were put on to enable a second gathering of several hundred to a thousand people at Lyttelton. The protesters marched from the train, singing 'The Red Flag' and 'We'll Set the Children Free' to the tune of 'John Brown's Body', and then marched several times around the prison before holding a meeting in front of its gates where anti-militarist speeches were given, and a motion was carried by the crowd denouncing the compulsory clauses of the Act.

The range of organisations protesting against the Defence Act were an indication of a move towards greater unity between the labour movement and other organisations, which took another step forward with two meetings held in Wellington at Easter 1912. The aim was to achieve greater unity across industrial workers, farmers, professional workers and other groups, including women's organisations.[67] A Trades and Labour Conference was followed by a Unity Conference, where the United Labour Party (ULP) was formed, replacing the NZ Labour Party, which since its founding in 1910 had demonstrated that a labour party could enjoy success in Christchurch as a political party: in 1911 it had won five seats on the Christchurch City Council. Christchurch delegates to the conference included Elizabeth Taylor and Mrs Green representing the Christchurch Housewives Union,[68] and Jack McCullough, whose son Frank had been released from prison the day before the meetings

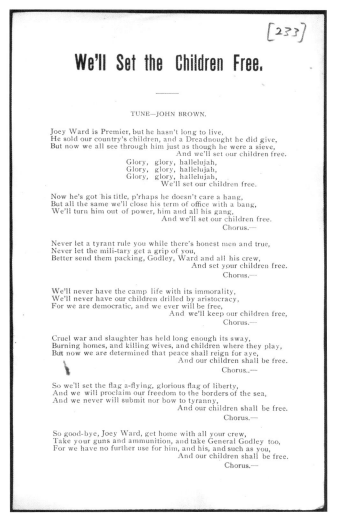

'We'll Set the Children Free', sung to the tune of 'John Brown's Body' in Lyttelton when young resisters were in prison there. (Canterbury Museum)

began. McCullough was well prepared: he had discussed with Atkinson and Fred Cooke the best methods of drawing attention to the 'iniquity of the Defence proposals'.[69] Wanting to ensure that the Defence Act was not forgotten at the meetings Frank McCullough and Mackie also went to Wellington and met with delegates as they made their way into the Trades and Labour Conference. Jack McCullough later wrote in his diary: 'I never attended any conference or meeting where so much unanimity or earnestness has been displayed as there was at this conference.'[70]

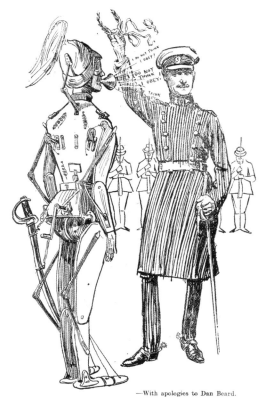

THE PERFECT SOLDIER; OR THE FINISHED PRODUCT OF COMPULSORY TRAINING.

—With apologies to Dan Beard.

The Boss: "You are now ready for any beastly work which Capitalism, Imperialism, or Militarism may require.

"I, ..., do sincerely promise and swear that I will faithfully serve in the N.Z. Military Forces according to my liability under the Defence Act at present in force, and that I will OBSERVE AND OBEY all orders of his Majesty, his heirs and successors, and OF THE GENERALS AND OFFICERS SET OVER ME, until I am lawfully discharged. So help me, God."

Government responds with amended Act

The public and the press had become increasingly uncomfortable with the idea of young CMT defaulters being jailed alongside convicted criminals. The new government, led by Thomas Mackenzie following Ward's resignation in March 1912, lasted only a few months, but just before it was defeated by a vote of confidence in July 1912 it introduced a Defence Amendment Act, based on a report commissioned by Ward when he was still in office. The 'Reform' Government elected in July 1912 was led by the conservative farmer and anti-unionist

A cartoon drawn for the National Peace Council by Len Booth in July 1912. (Canterbury Museum)

William Massey as prime minister, with James Allen as minister of defence. It continued with the amendment to the Defence Act, which came into effect in December 1912.

In the meantime boys were still being charged with failing to render personal service or refusing to take the oath. In a 'batch of prosecutions' in August 1912, for example, 22 were charged in Christchurch, and most were convicted and fined.[71] The amended Act empowered the retrieval of unpaid fines via an attachment order or 'garnishee' placed on an offender's wages, and magistrates were given the power to compel an offender's employer to comply. The Act defined and broadened the rights of religious objectors, and required those who refused to pay the fines to serve time in military barracks as opposed to regular prisons. Magistrates were also given the power to deprive a convicted offender of their civil rights for up to 10 years. In short, the amendments were designed to intimidate young men by hitting them hard with an array of penalties, and incarcerating them in military barracks if they refused to pay their fines.

In response to the proposed amendments the NPC disseminated a letter in which it detailed the ways in which the military had been breaching the existing law, criticised the proposed erection of military prisons, and promised to continue the campaign against the Act until the element of compulsion was removed.[72] The PRU's response to the amendments was to reiterate its determination to resist military training: 'We have refused to obey the Defence Act because we cannot conscientiously comply with it, and we must state that in future, if the compulsory clauses are not repealed, we will again willingly bear the punishment.'[73]

The case of Thomas Nuttall

Thomas Nuttall, a Baptist Sunday school teacher, was another who consistently resisted military training. He was first prosecuted in August 1911 for non-registration; the charge was later withdrawn, although Nuttall had no intention of ever registering. When prosecutions were resumed Nuttall was again charged in February 1912 with failing to register, and the following month he was fined 40 shillings plus costs. When he failed to pay the fine he was sentenced to 21 days imprisonment at Lyttelton, along with four other young men from Christchurch. He did not spend long in prison, however, because within a few days of his incarceration the Liberal government had dissolved and Ward, as a parting gesture, persuaded his Cabinet colleagues to pardon all those imprisoned for breaches of the Defence Act. Nuttall was released on 4 April 1912. His case highlights the problem of religious objectors, because although his objections to military service were based solely on his Christian beliefs, before he could plead his case in court he would have to first register, take the oath of allegiance and be ordered to parade. Like many other resisters he refused to either take the oath or register.

The amended Act was meant to make it easier for religious objectors to gain exemption from military service, but the new clause was hard to interpret and left the decision at the discretion of the magistrate. Twenty-three religious exemptions were granted in Canterbury up to the end of May 1914. In some cases parents, often acting on advice from Mackie, succeeded in getting an exemption by appearing before the magistrate themselves, or by writing to the magistrate.[74]

Frank McCullough was one of the few boys – perhaps the only one – to gain conscientious exemption as a socialist; undoubtedly helped in his case by having the lawyer James Cassidy to represent him. Mackie and Atkinson were also in court, prepared to speak if necessary, and Ellen Howell and Frank's father Jack had written letters to the magistrate. Jack McCullough described his son as a 'genuine conscientious objector':

> I have striven to inculcate in the minds of my five children a
> reverence for human life and a desire to organize society on
> a basis of Brotherhood and equality. I have denounced War
> Militarism as barbarous inhuman [sic]. … Having done this …
> and having taught my family that it would be wicked to train
> and cruel to use any weapon against my fellow man I cannot
> hold it be wrong for my sons to believe and act upon this.[75]

Another issue that arose was that of the 'Illegal oath'. Boys were prosecuted for refusing to pledge an oath of allegiance that was not the one prescribed in the Defence Act. Two issues were involved here: until the 1912 Defence Amendment Act came into force the boys were, in fact, not required to take any oath, but especially not one that was not included in the Act. The NPC's campaign against the illegal oath included sending out 700 letters to members of Parliament, labour unions and newspapers.

There was also the matter of the unfairness caused by inconsistent application of the Act by different magistrates. Why, for example, was one young man fined 40 shillings for refusing to take the oath and to 'perform personal service', while other men charged with the same offence were fined five shillings?[76] Giving advice and support to young resisters and their families throughout the country became a major part of Mackie's work.

More prosecutions, more issues

As more young men were imprisoned the *Maoriland Worker* continued to add to its 'Roll of Honour': by June 1912 it was listing 40 boys as 'jailed anti-conscripts', and 58 three months later: of these, 21 came from Canterbury, 18 from Auckland, six from Waihi, six from Wellington and Petone, five from Huntly, and one each from Nelson and Masterton.[77] With the exception of Harry Cooke's first sentence served in Timaru, Canterbury resisters served their sentences at the grim, mock-Gothic Lyttelton prison.

After the successful meeting in Victoria Square in March 1912 open-air meetings had been held regularly in and around Christchurch, but now PRU speakers were being harassed and arrested for breaches of the bylaws when speaking in a public space – despite the fact that others could speak from the same places with impunity.

For some young men such as Harold Denton, selective and ongoing harassment for offences other than those against the Defence Act seemed to be persecution rather than prosecution, and when Denton's mother died the following year Ada Wells claimed that his ongoing persecution had led to his mother's death:

> The boy … is a marked person under the Defence Act. Warrant
> after warrant has been served upon him. He has been repeatedly
> fined on one pretext or another. He has suffered imprisonment

> … His mother, harried with the constant espionage of the
> police, sickened and drooped with anxiety for her child, and as
> he was setting out on the morning of a recent prosecution at the
> Magistrates' Court, she fell dead.[78]

In October 1912 bootmaker Henry Reynolds, a member of the NPC, was fined five pounds for displaying the *Maoriland Worker* 'Roll of Honour' in his shop window without disclosing the name of the publisher. The whole affair seemed to be a trumped-up case: the court learned that the police had been asked to look into the matter after a complaint from the Defence Department that the list of names could encourage others to break the law. Mackie saw this as 'the first instance of military autocracy … [it was] a deliberate blow at the citizen's rights and usurpation of the duties of the Police, and would have been quite impossible only a few months ago'.[79] Reynolds opted to serve five nights in prison rather than pay the fine. After his release, he followed Fred Cooke's example in exposing the conditions and the treatment of prisoners in Lyttelton prison by writing a long report describing all aspects of prison life. He found that, while the prisoners were 'orderly and respectful to officers', there was 'a tremendous suppressed feeling against the system of punishment. There is no reward, no hope, no encouragement, no brotherly feeling, no sympathy. Everything it appears is done to dishearten them.'[80] Add to this the language, which he found was 'indescribably filthy, disgusting and horrible to listen to', and he felt he was in 'an earthly hell'.[81]

Objectors leave the country

There is no record of the number of individuals or families who left New Zealand to avoid CMT. According to Sarah Page, CMT was responsible for driving from New Zealand young men the country could ill afford to lose – including cartoonist David Low, who was on the staff of the *Lyttelton Times*.[82]

Mackie claimed that hundreds of people had left the country. Challenged by the editor of the *Lyttelton Times* to provide names, he contacted families who, he hoped, would be willing to have their names passed on to the newspaper. At least one agreed: D. W. Jones, his friend from the Oxford Terrace Baptist Church and a founding member of the NPC, had taken his family to British Columbia as the only way to prevent his sons being sent to prison. Others were happy to talk publicly about their experiences. The strongly anti-militarist Sellar family arrived in New Zealand in 1911 to find that their middle two sons were liable for CMT. To their horror the two boys ended up serving time in Wanganui Prison for failing to pay their fines. When fresh summons were issued against three of their sons, the family fled New Zealand in February 1913. Back in England, Mr Sellar was reported as saying that what he complained of most of all was that they were not told before they went to New Zealand: 'I hope our case will be a warning to others.'[83] Peter Thompson, his wife and four children were another family who left: they returned to Scotland after 11 years living in Nelson, because their sons were being prosecuted under the Defence Act. The 'art of war was contrary to the commands of Christ', the boys' father told the court.[84] The Rev Edward Walker was another who told Mackie that CMT was one of the reasons why he and his family had left New Zealand, and would not be returning.

Women promote peace

Mackie had practical and moral support from a core group of individuals, including women who were active in the AML and NPC but were also promoting peace through other organisations. Rose Atkinson, Annie Ensom, Louisa Nuttall (mother of Thomas), Sarah Bradley, Ada Wells and a Mrs Smith attended meetings of the NPC and AML and had connections with other women's groups. Several of them were members of the WCTU.[85]

As the work of the NPC grew exponentially during three busy years from mid 1911 to mid 1914, Rose Atkinson and Ellen Howell were among the highly competent volunteers who helped out in the office. In June–July 1912, for example, they took charge while Mackie and William Ensom travelled to South Island towns. Letters they wrote show that they had strong personal convictions about the iniquities of the Defence Act. Atkinson, who described herself as a 'strong opponent of compulsory military training',[86] said it was barbarous to punish public-spirited, self-sacrificing young men for refusing to participate in the defence scheme: 'In this case the law is wrong not the lawbreaker, the remedy is the repeal of the law', she wrote to the minister of defence.[87] Howell also protested against the Defence Act which, she said, had 'substituted a Continental atmosphere for an English one'. She objected to the loss of parental rights and civil rights: 'it has violated the home; it has fastened the bonds of conscription on mere lads, not men; it has deprived of civic rights the conscientious objector whilst allowing the thief, the drunkard and the debased to retain a vote'.[88] With such competent supporters in the NPC office Mackie turned down an offer of further financial assistance from British Quakers in March 1913: he said he didn't want to employ an assistant in the office as the voluntary workers were willing to meet any extra strain.

Eveline Cunnington, meanwhile, was developing links between Christians and the women's and socialist movements. Her interest in educating young middle-class women in Christian socialism dated from her undergraduate days in London. In 1910, however, she was shocked

Eveline Cunnington. (*The Lectures and Letters of E. W. Cunnington*, 1918)

by the historical ignorance, 'the spite, the pettiness', when she heard a visiting Australian socialist speak, and she decided that the working classes needed to be better educated about true socialism.[89] As well as hosting socialist study meetings and the Fabian Society at her home, she began attending the Socialist Hall on Sunday nights and encouraged the Fabian Society (which had reformed in 1908 under the leadership of Harry Atkinson, with a membership of about forty) to send speakers, including herself, out to working-class suburbs.

'We Socialists are very much worried over the new Defence Bill,'

Cunnington wrote in a letter in October 1911. But while it seemed to her 'to be bringing militarism desperately fiercely into this New Country', she couldn't see her way to agreeing with the majority of the socialists, who were opposing the compulsory training of boys. In her view an army was still necessary for a country to protect itself against invasion by 'the lower races'. Her fellow Fabians were 'very much annoyed' with her for not taking a public stand on the matter, she continued. 'We mean to stamp out war some day but in the meanwhile we must at least have men trained to fight in our defence. War is absolutely against the Christ law, but I suppose the more evolved races must protect themselves against the attacks of the lower races, should they invade our countries.'[90] Cunnington became a popular speaker at the Socialist Hall. In October 1912 she described speaking about Dante to 'an eager crowd of 350 people, mostly men'. The hall was packed full, with men 'standing on the window sills'.[91]

Page and Wells take leading roles

Two women – Ada Wells and Sarah Saunders Page – stand out for their courageous and consistent advocacy for peace. Sarah Page's political awareness came from her father, Alfred Saunders, a maverick politician who had passed on to his children an 'abhorrence of war' – something he learned when living and working with an English Quaker family as a young man. Sarah, too, demonstrated that she was a courageous, energetic and intelligent thinker, and a formidable opponent in any argument. She became head teacher at the girls high school in Ashburton at the age of 21, and this allowed her to further develop her leadership qualities.[92] Initially she did not oppose CMT: she thought that it might do some good, by waking people up to

Sarah and Samuel Page. (Page family)

what war actually meant. Her change of heart came when young men began to be imprisoned: 'when some of the finest lads I knew began to be thrown into the common jails for following the dictates of their consciences in refusing to train for the work of destruction, I realised what militarism entailed even in times of peace, and for the first time publicly and actively joined that despised section of the followers of the Prince of Peace known as "Pacifists"'.[93]

With her elder son Robin already eligible for compulsory training and her younger son Fred becoming eligible the following year, the subject affected her personally. She allowed her boys to drill 'because she could not bear to see them go to prison', but she was scathing about the drill process: they had learned 'no more in two years than an intelligent woman could grasp in two weeks'.[94] After observing a cadet camp in action, she concluded that 'ordinary military training' was 'prejudicial to the best development of our boys'.[95]

Delegates at the Women's Christian Temperance Union (WCTU) national convention in Dunedin, March 1912. The national president of the WCTU, Fanny Cole from Christchurch, is sitting in the front, third from right. (*Otago Witness*, 20 March 1912)

As well as writing letters as individuals, Page and Wells worked through the women's organisations they belonged to. In October 1911 they were at the forefront of a meeting of the Christchurch WCTU on the Defence Act: Reginald Ford addressed the meeting, and Page, Wells and a Mrs Wilson were later appointed to draft and send motions, based on Ford's address, to other women's associations. Page and Wells were also responsible for a leaflet published by the NPC. Addressed to 'the Women of New Zealand: a plea for the repeal of the Defence Act', the leaflet concluded by asking New Zealand women to 'work without ceasing for the repeal of the Defence Act, which will bring disease and death to the moral sense, and in the end to the State we ardently love'.[96]

In March 1912 at the national convention of the WCTU, Christchurch member Lucy Smith delivered a paper in which she set out the pros and cons of the Defence Act.[97] The convention also received a letter from Christchurch WCTU members Ada Wells, Elizabeth McCombs, Elizabeth Taylor and Mrs Hunter, listing 12 reasons why the Defence Act's provisions for CMT should be opposed. While the convention passed resolutions that met some of the objections raised by the peace movement, they did not match the more radical statements made in the letter. An anonymous flyer, printed after the meeting, made this clear by listing the 12 reasons for opposing the Defence Act, followed by the five resolutions actually passed.[98]

When Wells joined the NPC in 1912 as the CWI delegate, she was already well known in Christchurch for her work for women and children through her membership of the Charitable Aid Board, the Children's Aid Society, the WCTU, CWI and the National Council of Women (NCW).[99] Her attitude to CMT was uncompromising and she brought an international and socialist viewpoint to her letters and speeches. In response to a woman who had

Ada Wells, c. 1918. (Canterbury Museum)

THE DEFENCE ACT.

To the Women of New Zealand.

The following reasons were urged against the Defence Act in a letter addressed to the W.C.T.U. Convention and signed by Mrs. T. E. Taylor, Mrs. McCombs, Mrs. Wells and Mrs. Hunter:—

1.—The Defence Act introduces militarism into our schools, and fines, imprisons, and treats as criminals for all time those who, for conscience sake, refuse to take the oath ;

2.—Introduces the principle of conscription, which has proved the curse of Continental Europe ;

3.—Introduces military law and court-martial in times of peace—courts opposed to the spirit and substance of common law and of the British Constitution ;

4.—Introduces a dangerous military caste system ;

5;—Ignores and sets at defiance parental training and authority ;

6.—Violates freedom of conscience ;

7.—Aims at raising a standard army in New Zealand for service abroad ;

8.—Camp and barrack life will be fostered, and the term of service in these will be increased as time goes on ; this will certainly have a demoralising effect upon the nation ;

9.—Confers most dangerous powers of life and death on the military authorities ;

10.—Aims at inculcating in our children the spirit of devotion to brute force ;

11.—Is in direct opposition to the growing peace spirit of the age ;

12.—Is destructive of the principles of democracy.

The W.C.T.U. Convention passed these important resolutions which are worthy of the careful consideration of every New Zealand woman :—

While recognising the necessity of organising and training a citizen army for the defence of New Zealand in the event of hostile attack, we maintain that the citizen shall be paramount to the soldier, and we strongly object to certain provisions of the Defence Act, and urge its alteration in the following direction :—

1.—That no youth under 21 years of age be compelled to bear arms or to undergo military training ;

2.—That any youth over 16 years of age be allowed to volunteer for military training and duty, provided he has the consent of his parents or guardians to his so doing ;

3.—That no man being of age, be compelled to bear arms or perform military duty or undergo military training if he objects on conscientious grounds to so doing, such objections to be declared and signed before a Justice of the Peace, but that he be required to render an equivalent in some other branch of service ;

4.—That no failure to register nor any offence committed during military training, or on military duty after expiration by punishment shall entail forfeiture of the citizen's right of voting or of being employed in the Government service.

5.—That all offences committed by members of the Defence force while on military duty in time of peace shall be tried before a civil court, or in time of war an appeal shall be allowed, if required, from the decision of the military to that of the civil court.

6.—That no commandant of any section of the Defence force shall be at liberty to enter any school at any time to inspect the boys and girls in physical drill unless he has the permission of the Board of Education under whose jurisdiction the school is ;

7.—That no youth under 21 years of age be allowed to volunteer for service outside New Zealand ;

8.—That the convention most emphatically protests against the law which permits youths under 21 years to be imprisoned for refraining from taking the oath and submitting to compulsory military training.

Will you write to your Member and press upon him the urgent need for the modification of the Act in these directions ?

YATES & BULLIVANT, CHRISTCHURCH.

Women's Christian Temperance Union pamphlet, 1912. (Canterbury Museum) defended the necessity of New Zealand having a well-organised military force, Wells argued that New Zealand military forces were not intended to defend the country, but were formed to fight imperial, capitalist wars, which would mean amassing armies, foreign campaigning, and would ultimately lead to national decay, 'which is the antithesis of the ideals of democracy'.[100] Ted Howard wrote that Wells was popular as a speaker, and could draw a crowd any time, 'because she is one of the clearest and most fascinating speakers we have in the Dominion … In addition to her having a splendid knowledge of history and biology, she also has a grip of the history of secret diplomacy.'[101]

The Canterbury Women's Institute takes an anti-militarist stance

Under the leadership of Wells and Page the CWI took a decidedly anti-militarist stance. They were quite probably the organisers of a deputation of women representing the NPC, the CWI, the Housewives Union, the Society of Friends, the Anti-Militarist League (AML), the International Arbitration Society, the Theosophical Society, the Fabian Society and the mothers of boys imprisoned, who met with the minister of defence, Arthur Myers (newly appointed in the short-lived Mackenzie government) in May 1912 to voice their opposition to CMT. Ada Wells spoke first: she condemned the Defence Act as undemocratic and said that, as women had no one to represent them in Parliament, they had to make representations directly to the minister. Speaking mainly from the point of view of a parent, she said the CWI objected to the spirit of militarism that was being inculcated in the young, and believed the 'burden of defence should fall on adults and not on children': 'The present age was recognising the value of the individual, but the military spirit was entirely opposed to the newer and more humane order of things. The Act flouted parental control … [and] made force the basis upon which society was founded, whereas the Institute believed society was based upon interchange of services.'[102] Sarah Page also spoke on behalf of the CWI; Rose Atkinson on behalf of the Fabian Society; Mrs Benson for the Society of Friends; and Louisa Nuttall for the mothers of imprisoned boys. Other speakers not named in the newspaper reports voiced strong protests against the Defence Act as socialists and mothers.

Myers, in turn, urged the women to consider their responsibilities and argued that the training system would not interfere with their rights as mothers: this statement raised a chorus of dissent. The meeting came to an end after one of the women, using a 'strong voice' called out 'Rot' to the minister who regretted that such an expression should be used by any lady in the room. Some of the speakers had spoken with 'volubility and extravagance of language', which took any dignity away from the protest, said another report.[103]

The reporting on this deputation illustrates a tendency for journalists to focus on the women's manners rather than their message. In response to criticism published in the *Evening Post*, Rose Atkinson wrote a spirited defence that drew attention to the minister's dismissive and patronising attitude. The women, she said, had not been allowed to proceed for a few minutes before they were 'impatiently interrupted by the minister, who said that he knew what they were going to say, that he had had no lunch, and that he had to catch a train'.[104]

The number of organisations represented by women in the deputation shows the practical application of cooperation that was the strength of the Christchurch peace movement. As Mackie wrote to a supporter later the same year, the NPC had started with nothing but eight people and 'dogged determination', but 'now are able to command a hearing anywhere'. It was an established organisation with a central city office open daily. As Mackie wrote: 'It is not so much the amount of work that you can do as the mere fact of there being an organization at all to pass resolutions and distribute literature and even the few can do that.'[105]

The Repeal of the Defence Act
Compulsory Clauses.

Public Demonstration
Against Conscription

KING'S THEATRE, Gloucester St.

Sunday Evening Next
at 8 p.m.

Addresses by
Mrs A. Wells, Rev. J. Murray, Rev. D. McNicoll
Messrs E. R. Hartley, J. A. McCullough,
G. R. Whiting, R. F. Williams
and C. R. N. Mackie

Come and help to Free the Child Conscripts. They need
your aid to make them Men, not Marionettes.

Military Barrack Prisons are the newest outrage being
prepared for our boys. Will you, will any of us
tolerate these abominations?

Then Come and Raise your Voice in Protest!
COLLECTION.

[Please Turn Over.

A flyer for a public demonstration against the compulsory clauses of the Defence Act, to be held in the King's Theatre, August 1912. Ada Wells was among the line-up of speakers. (Canterbury Museum)

CHAPTER 3

'A GOOD KICK WILL FINISH THE BUSINESS': THE PEACE MOVEMENT AND THE PASSIVE RESISTERS 1913—14

Two years after it began, the peace movement in Christchurch believed it was closing in on the repeal of the Defence Act. There was a sense of intense activity and excitement in the National Peace Council (NPC) office, and Mackie told an English supporter that he was as busy as it was possible to be: Percy Fletcher, an English Quaker who had arrived in Christchurch in July 1913 to assist with the campaign, was helping him, and a typist was working at 'top pressure'. 'The enemy is on the run here and a good kick will finish the business,' he wrote.[1]

The year had begun with a packed-out public meeting in the Alexandra Hall on 'Women and defence', compulsory military training (CMT) and the penalising provisions of the Defence Act. Despite heavy rain it was a 'glorious meeting', wrote 'The Vag' (the pen-name of Ted Howard) in the *Maoriland Worker*. 'These people are in earnest; it is their children that are being attacked. The speaking was good, the speeches were well chosen and even the local rags could not pull them to pieces.'[2] Despite a surprising comment from Mackie that the women of Christchurch were 'waking up at last', he also noted that the papers were very concerned about the women's protest, as they were well aware that 'when women get on the warpath things will move' – this was probably a reference to the direct action being taken by women in Britain in their struggle to get the vote. [3]

Once again Page and Wells were to the fore, with Page in the chair and Wells moving the first resolution, which pledged the meeting to do all in its power to secure the repeal of the Defence Act. Wells described the Act as introducing a 'reactionary and barbaric caste system of militarism into our lands', and listed her reasons for opposing it, which included the usual concerns of the NPC and Anti-Militarist League (AML): the requirement to take the oath of allegiance; compulsion against conscience and the loss of parental control; the retrieval of unpaid fines by way of a garnishee or attachment order on wages; the loss of civil rights; repeated fines and imprisonment; and military detention.[4] When a small group of young women voted against the anti-military motion they were congratulated by Page for having the courage of their convictions.[5] Other resolutions were moved by Elizabeth McCombs (who later became New Zealand's first woman MP), Louisa Nuttall and Sarah Bradley. The meeting demonstrated that a core group of about 12 women could draw a large crowd from the Christchurch community who were against CMT.

Elizabeth McCombs, c. 1933. (Alexander Turnbull Library)

The increased persecution of the Passive Resisters' Union (PRU) added to public opposition to the Defence Act as the amendments, which came into force in December 1912, were put into practice. In January 1913 Harry Cooke, Thomas Nuttall, Edward Hannam and Jim Worrall

A popular place for street meetings: the Clock Tower at the corner of Tuam, Manchester and High streets, c. 1913. (Christchurch City Libraries)

lost their civil rights for three years for their failure to register for military training. This meant they were unable to vote and unable to be employed in the Public Service: Fletcher and Hills described the harsh penalty as usually reserved for 'treasonable offences in time of war'.[6]

Members of the PRU were still being harassed as they carried out their regular Saturday night street meetings at the Clock Tower on the corner of High, Tuam and Manchester streets. In March 1913 Reg Williams was fined three pounds for using insulting language and one pound for causing a 'wilful blockage of traffic'. Later that month, when Williams had accumulated unpaid fines of 13 pounds and 10 shillings, he was imprisoned in Lyttelton along with Edward Edwards, W. Edwards and William Aaron Chenery. A petition to the minister of justice calling for the release of Reg Williams, signed by more than 1500 people, was unsuccessful.

Leaders in the labour movement took up the fight for free speech in support of the PRU, with the result that Ted Howard, Paddy Webb, Fred Cooke, W. E. J. Maguire and two city councillors, Fred Burgoyne and Jim McCullough (brother of Jack), were all charged with causing an obstruction after they spoke at the Clock Tower, and were fined two pounds. On one particularly action-packed night when a huge crowd, a 'surging mass of humanity', had gathered at the Clock Tower, the police picked up Reg Williams who, because he was wanted for non-payment of a fine, had disguised himself with a false moustache and an 'unusual hat'. As he was taken to the police station the crowd followed him and 'fully a couple of hundred' invaded the building. Williams' fine was paid and he was set free. Meanwhile, back at the Clock Tower, councillors Burgoyne and McCullough 'held forth on the right to freedom of speech'.[7]

A Warning to Anti-Militarists.

Inspector Kiely says he is afraid there may be bloodshed at the Clock Tower.

INSPECTOR : "If you boys ain't careful your blood may be shed here. I am afraid I can't hold my fellows back!"

ANTI-MILITARISTS : "Hurrah! Hurrah! We'll then become martyrs and our cause will win!"

INSPECTOR : "Get along with ye now, or I'll run everyone of ye in!"

Cartoon by Stan Osborn in the *Spectator*, 29 March 1913. (Canterbury Museum)

In the same month the NPC tested the situation by putting Mackie and Atkinson up as speakers. As a result Mackie was charged in the magistrates court with causing an obstruction in Bedford Row: the police sergeant told the court that Mackie had spoken for 20 minutes to a crowd of three or four hundred. Mackie's lawyer James Cassidy, who regularly appeared in court for defaulters against the Defence Act, pointed out that it was the police themselves who had suggested that the peace activists speak in Bedford Row instead of at the Clock Tower, because there was practically no traffic in Bedford Row at night. The charge was dismissed. Atkinson, who had spoken from the northwest corner of the Clock Tower, was convicted but not fined, yet another man who appeared in court on the same day charged with having caused an obstruction at the Clock Tower was convicted and fined three pounds.

Ted Howard described how the mayor, an evangelist and 14 city councillors had all spoken on street corners in the same week as Mackie, with no prosecutions: it was clear that the peace movement was being targeted.[8] Socialist leaders supported the free speech campaign by also speaking at the Clock Tower, and in April 1913 Ted Howard, Fred Cooke and Paddy Webb were fined for obstructing traffic. When they failed to pay their fines, Cooke and Howard were arrested and taken to Lyttelton prison to serve a one-month imprisonment. Later that same night an unknown benefactor paid their fines and they were released, though neither man felt particularly grateful: they had wanted to make a point about the vindictive nature of the punishment being given out for infringements of the Defence Act.

A meeting at the end of May 1913, organised by the NPC with local Independent Liberal MPs George Laurenson, Harry Ell and George Russell, who were at least partly sympathetic with the anti-militarists, lasted from 8pm until midnight. The Canterbury Trades and Labour Council (CTLC) and some fourteen unions were also represented at the meeting. Jack McCullough enjoyed seeing the MPs under attack: 'It was pleasant to me to see the MPs writhing under the scourging they got from our speakers. Who charged them with neglect of their duty in allowing boys to go to jail & the other offences perpetrated by the Police & Military.'[9]

Greater unity in the labour movement

The labour movement, which remained the main ally of the peace movement, was moving towards greater unity during this period, prompted partly by the miners' strike at Waihi in November 1912 in which a striking miner, Fred Evans, had died when he was beaten up by police and strikebreakers. In January 1913 the more radical of the union organisations, known as the Red Feds, invited the United Labour Party (ULP) and the Socialist Party to join them at a Unity Conference in Wellington, where proposals for two new organisations were put forward: one industrial, a United Federation of Labour (UFL); and the other political, to be called the Social Democratic Party (SDP), a merger of the ULP and the socialists. Another conference in July 1913 confirmed the formation of the organisations, and adopted 'the socialisation of the means of production, distribution, and exchange' as the SDP's primary objective.[10] When the Woolston Branch of the SDP was founded in October 1913, Dan Sullivan told the meeting that the aims of the party could be summed up as 'to take the necessary steps to abolish poverty from the homes of the workers of New Zealand'. Jack McCullough, in his address to the meeting, elaborated on the worsening position of workers with the ever-increasing cost of living: 'The land monopolists of the dominion and the various combines were exploiting the people, and the prosperity of the dominion was benefitting the wealthy landowners at the expense of the workers.'[11]

By the end of the year there were two SDP members of Parliament: Paddy Webb had won a by-election in the Grey seat in June, and James McCombs, the leading figure in the Woolston Branch of the SDP, won the Lyttelton seat in a by-election in December. McCombs had been

James McCombs. (Alexander Turnbull Library)

involved with the temperance movement and the Progressive Liberal Association and was often viewed as a labour moderate, a solid, studious man whose 'tinge of "red" is not so rich as some members of the party. Whilst he does not despise the soap-box as a platform he does not rant therefrom.'[12]

The CTLC also acted against CMT by supplying money and speakers for public meetings, passing resolutions condemning the prosecution of the young resisters, and calling for the repeal of the Defence Act. Dan Sullivan took a leading role, as did Fred Burgoyne, president of the CTLC in 1913. The unions within the CTLC that were most involved in the action were the Engineers Union (McCullough and Atkinson were both members), and the Iron Workers and the General Labourers unions, with Ted Howard and Fred Cooke also providing leadership. At times the AML wrote to the CTLC asking it to consider issues such as the persecution of speakers at the Clock Tower, rights to free speech, and the garnisheeing of wages. Opposing conscription, as exemplified by CMT, was a unifying factor in a disparate movement – perhaps the only thing that the different wings of the labour movement could agree on.[13]

Tribute to peace movement

The Christian socialists added their support to the cause. Eveline Cunnington moved from being a 'wavering wobbler' on the Defence Act to being an opponent of CMT because, while she believed a country still needed trained defenders, she also believed they should be volunteers.[14] This brought her into conflict with some of her close friends. She had got into 'more hot water, and quarrelled with more of my dear friends over the Compulsory Act, than anything else in my life', she wrote in October 1913. 'I stand as regards my own particular friends, absolutely alone in this.'[15] In the same letter she praised the work of 'these despised agents' the peace workers, and pointed to the role of the peace movement as the idealists who made people think:

> I consider that the Quakers and Anti-Militarists are doing a
> good work. They are pointing to the hills; they are the idealists
> without whose spur and impetus Humanity would stick on the

low levels for ever … You can't imagine the storm I brought
down on my head (privately, not in the papers) … One thing I
do feel very strongly, that any note, any sound, however feeble,
struck for peace in this hideous uproar and clamour about war,
and armaments and militarism, is to be welcomed. I believe that
Christ is speaking to the world through these despised agents,
the humble Quakers, the wild Socialists, the Idealists – anything
– anything, to make people stop and think …[16]

An Anglican herself, she pointed out (as did the Fabians) that sev-
eral Christian leaders in England had declared that they were socialists.
A Church Socialist League was formed in Christchurch in 1913 with
Cunnington, James O'Bryen Hoare and two Anglican clergymen, John
Mortimer and Humphrey Money, among its members. All became pop-
ular speakers at the Socialist Hall, and the socialists, Cunnington and
the clergy developed a mutual respect for each other. Howard described
Cunnington as a lady 'whom to know is to love'.[17]

The Repeal

The radical young activists, meanwhile, responded to increased persecution by publishing a lively magazine, *The Repeal*: each issue included
20–24 pages of satire, news from anti-militarists in other parts of the
country, editorial comment and articles. It was both serious and humorous with reports of court cases, for example, often treated in a comic
manner. The magazine was produced by the PRU between March 1913
and August 1914. Three members were largely responsible for it: Frank
McCullough as editor, Heathcote Mann as manager, and Reg Williams,
president of the Christchurch PRU, as publisher.

An interview with Williams about his experiences in Lyttelton prison
was a feature of the second issue. Like Fred Cooke and Henry Reynolds
before him, Williams was clear about the need for prison reform. In the
interview, which was interlaced with political comment against the government, he criticised the food, the lack of proper medical care, and the
insanitary conditions that meant he had to clean cells, toilets and the
hospital with no disinfectants, in a place where men with 'loathsome

and contagious diseases' were detained. Williams also gave a vivid account of the personal loss of 'all that they held most dearly' when the gates of the prison 'shut behind them with a bang':

> That meant freedom, friends; intellectual employment, every-
> thing gone! What for? Because we had opinions of our own
> and consciences; because we believed in the sacred right of free
> speech and truth; and last, but not least, because the people of
> New Zealand have been hoodwinked and are slow to repair the
> damage, which is the result of apathy, but a hundred boys have
> been gaoled and New Zealand is waking up, but so slow, and
> the boys must suffer still.[18]

He was scathing about the prison service's aims to reform the character and habits of inmates: 'in practice Lyttelton Gaol is a school of brutality, debauchery, and immorality. It seems to exist to wreak blind vindictive spite and vengeance upon the erring person who lands there. Mental and moral food is lacking and even purposely withheld'.[19]

Lyttelton Gaol, c. 1900. (Canterbury Museum)

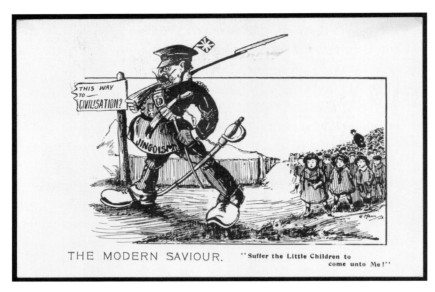

A cartoon drawn by Heathcote Mann for the Passive Resisters' Union's *Repeal* magazine, and later printed as one of a series of postcards. (Canterbury Museum)

Alongside serious articles such as this, humour was always present in *The Repeal*, including cartoons by Heathcote Mann. (A series of post-cards produced later featured 12 of his cartoons.) The magazine was an effective propaganda tool, where PRU members wrote about the impact of CMT on their lives.

The government considered the garnishee order a success, and declared that the defence scheme would be 'wrecked if the clauses allowing the Government to garnishee wages was abolished'. The PRU, on the other hand, considered it 'tricky, subtle, and fraudulent ... contemptible and cowardly ... intended to filch from the earner his earning, from the toiler his rights, and from the citizen his liberties'.[20] When the garnishee was attached to the wages of Thomas Nuttall he evaded it by leaving his employment. Mackie described this as a truly shameful case, because Nuttall was supporting his widowed mother and 'now he is in detention and has lost his civil rights and hope of Government employment'.[21] The PRU seems to have encouraged young men to leave their jobs as a way of defeating the garnishee. Jack McCullough recorded a visit from Cuthbert Beary in May 1913, when Beary told him he had already lost three weeks' pay at 30 shillings a week. McCullough advised him to stay in his job, but recorded that he had 'some difficulty in doing this because he [Beary] was afraid of the criticism which would be levelled at him by his mates in the Union'.[22] But even without the garnishee, some employers chose to sack workers simply because of their stand against the Defence Act. Frank McCullough, for example, was sacked from Strange and Co., where he had worked since the age of 14 and completed his six-year apprenticeship.

Another cause taken up by the NPC and PRU was to do with the free places system in the country's educational institutions. New regulations in 1913 debarred students from taking up education scholarships unless they had complied with the provisions of the Defence Act and had always acted within the law. After a meeting in Auckland, Alexander reported to Mackie that there was a high level of public support for the peace movement on this issue. Defence Minister Allen, who also held the education portfolio, supported the measure. His support for the Defence Act led historian R. L. Weitzel to describe him as 'very much the archetypal Imperialist'.[23]

The 'Ripa Affair'

Rīpapa Island in Whaka-raupō Lyttelton Harbour was used as a refuge pā by Ngāi Tahu in the 1820s, and then as a quarantine station for Julius Vogel's wave of government-supported immigrants in the 1870s. After the 1885 'Russian scare', which arose from Russian and British rivalry in Afghanistan, Rīpapa was commandeered as part of a nationwide defence scheme, and a

OFF TO RIPA ISLAND

'Off to Ripa Island' depicts members of the Passive Resisters' Union being escorted to the boat that would take them to Rīpapa Island in July 1913. (Heathcote Mann, *Maoriland Worker*, 11 July 1913, p. 1)

low-lying fortress, Fort Jervois, was constructed – initially by military labour, and later by prisoners ferried across the harbour from Lyttelton prison. The fort was rendered operational in 1895.

The first orders for military detention under the Defence Act were issued on 11 June 1913 when Walter Hooper and Harold Thackwell were sentenced to 49 days' detention at the Fort Jervois military barracks. On 12 June, four more youths – James Worrall, Edward Hannam, Herbert McDonald and Thomas Nuttall – were taken to the barracks. In an act of pantomimic zeal, the young men were escorted from the local gaol to the wharf by artillery men with fixed bayonets, as if they were danger-ous criminals. But as the launch left for the island 'the waterside workers and others made a demonstration, cheering the boys and hooting the Defence authorities'.[24]

Nuttall's mother Louisa and Worrall's mother Susan both wrote letters to the *Lyttelton Times* denouncing their sons' imprisonment, in which they referred to their British origins and the importance to them of freedom of conscience. Louisa Nuttall also mentioned Thomas's

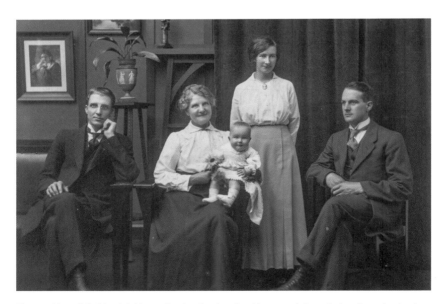

Thomas Nuttall (left), with his mother Louisa, brother Henry and sister-in-law Dorothy. Louisa is holding Henry and Dorothy's daughter Adela, who was named after the founder of the Women's Peace Army, Adela Pankhurst. (Ron Nuttall)

Jim Worrall and his mother Susan. (Worrall family)

Christian convictions, and said that he sincerely believed the Defence Act to be 'contrary to the teaching of our Master, Jesus Christ'. She lamented the fact that he was now branded 'as a criminal' despite having been a 'prohibition worker, a Sunday School teacher, a lay preacher, and has sought all in his power to be a good son and a good citizen'.[25]

Susan Worrall said the young resisters were demonstrating strength of character and an adherence to religious principles that was entirely admirable. She viewed CMT as un-British, and deplored it for its attack on British and family values:

> Today I was the spectator of the most humiliating scene that I
> have witnessed beneath the British flag. My son, in company
> with three other lads, was taken, unarmed, in the custody of
> two conscripts (I cannot say men) armed with rifles and fixed
> bayonets, a superior officer, and one policeman, to Ripa Island
> military barrack prison, there to serve a sentence of twenty-eight
> days, during which time the military authorities, to quote the
> words which an officer said to my son, are to endeavour to
> 'break their hearts'.

> As a mother, I, with all reverence, call on the members of
> Parliament, in the name of God, to stop this iniquitous and perni-
> cious persecution of our lads, and upon the newspapers of this land
> to take up the cause of outraged motherhood and family life.[26]

On 15 June the King's Theatre on Gloucester Street hosted a large anti-militarist meeting, chaired by Cuthbert Beary. Ted Howard told the crowd that the Massey administration would be swept out of office for administering the Defence Act, in the same way as the previous Ward administration had been ousted for passing the Act and for gift-ing a dreadnought to Britain; and Paddy Webb, the first coalminer to enter Parliament, and the first MP for the SDP, urged the audience to join the Labour Party in resisting the government, and denounced the New Zealand press for 'unanimously championing the wrong against the right'.[27] Several of the speakers had already served time in prison or in military detention, including Harold Denton, Reg Williams and a West Coaster, John McTaggart.

An anonymous letter writer, 'Off with the Yoke', was strongly sup-portive of the young resisters, but theirs was a minority voice. Newspaper headlines referred to 'The usual shirkers' clap trap', and the editorials suggested that the rest of New Zealand viewed Christchurch anti-mili-tarism as an eccentric aberration among right-thinking people:

> Extreme anti-militarists are again making a laughing-stock of
> Christchurch, though they are in the merest minority. This
> makes it all the harder for the sensible people of that city … No
> doubt they would be better pleased if the extreme anti-milita-
> rists amongst them were less demonstrative of their eccentricity.
> But that has never been the way with Christchurch's eccentrics,
> who, whatever the cause may be, beat all other eccentrics in the
> Dominion for the persistency and oddness of their exhibitions.[28]

At first things went well on the island. Herbert McDonald, a West Coaster who had just spent five days on Rīpapa, said he had no com-plaints: 'The food was good, the officers treated us well and under other circumstances I should have looked upon it as a good holiday.'[29] Reg Williams, too, wrote that they were living excellently and enjoying themselves: 'We all lived in the barrack room, and a very happy family we were … the work that we did consisted for the most part of cleaning and sweeping our quarters, wash-house, yards, lavatories.'[30]

However, when the young detainees were asked to clean guns, drill and learn semaphore signalling, they protested, and 10 of the 13 went on a hunger strike. Two days later they were sentenced to seven days' extra detention. Williams and Worrall hastily sent a letter off to Fred Cooke, who was in Wellington attending the Labour Unity Conference, demanding a public inquiry. The congress arranged for a deputation to meet with Prime Minister Massey, who attempted to assuage their concerns, assuring them that the 'Minister of Defence and the Government will institute a most searching inquiry into the statements made'. Bob Semple, the leading trade unionist working as organiser for the New Zealand Federation of Labour, demanded that 'the boys … be taken off the island immediately', but Massey refused to budge on the issue of conscientious objectors (COs): 'My difficulty is finding who the conscientious objector is. The reason we did not include the conscientious objector in the Act last year was because we thought a great many shirkers might pose as so-called conscientious objectors, and we did not wish to let the shirkers go.'[31]

Characteristically – and perhaps not altogether incorrectly – James Allen complained that the 'regular young anarchists', encouraged by their parents, were out to 'break down the Act altogether' and were willing 'to adopt any means to attain their end'.[32] On 25 July, the Rīpapa Island resisters published a manifesto in the *Maoriland Worker*. 'We are determined and united; we are pledged to uphold to our last breath the honor of our cause.'[33] Some of the men were released at the end of July and embarked on a speaking tour of New Zealand, attracting over a thousand people to meetings in Wellington and Auckland.

English Quakers respond

One outcome of the affair was the publication of a booklet by English Quaker Samuel Bracher, called *Ripa Island: A lesson for conscriptionists*.

Bracher's purpose was to warn the British public of what could happen if CMT, as advocated by the National Service League, was introduced in Britain. 'New Zealand seems to be regarded by the National Service League as its own little experimental farm,' the booklet began.[34] More particularly, by telling the story of what had happened on Rīpapa Island, Bracher was keen to open up the subject of compulsion: 'If a lad does not want to drill how shall he be made to do it?' Freedom of belief and freedom of conscience were hard-won rights and Bracher's conclusion was that: 'The dearest rights and liberties of Englishmen must be destroyed if conscription is to have a chance of success … conscription in a modern British community simply cannot be enforced.'[35] Even the *Lyttelton Times* was of the opinion that military detention was 'serving no good purpose. … The situation, in fact, is becoming absurd.'[36]

The NPC added to the debate between the militarists and anti-militarists when it published a series of letters between Henry Worrall as secretary of the AML and James Allen, minister of defence. The correspondence arose from a request from Worrall, dated 27 August 1913, that the Defence Department launch make two trips to Rīpapa Island each visiting day, or that the number of visiting days be increased so that each of the detainees could receive his allocated one visit per week. The request was refused. When Allen asked Worrall, 'Why do you not help these lads to comply with the law and thus get rid of all difficulties?', Worrall replied, 'our reason for not endeavouring to persuade the boys to break with religion, conscience and principle, is that we believe they are right and that you are wrong'.[37] By 25 September some of the boys at the island had served a continuous term of 91 days, and one had served 98 days. The exchange of letters continued throughout September culminating in a long letter written by Worrall on 8 October, where he pointed out that his views were shared by thousands of earnest citizens, and that the United Labour Conference in July, the largest ever held in the country, had condemned CMT. He argued that 'such an Act would not be tolerated in the Homeland of the British race' and admitted that, as a parent, he held a biased view:[38]

> What parent would not be [biased], if, after bringing up a son
> to years of discretion, that son, by reason of his standing by the
> principles instilled in his youth, by reason of his having some
> character, and by reason of his remaining true to that relation-
> ship between God and man which we call conscience, had been
> cast into the common gaol, had been subjected to that outrage
> upon British freedom – deprivation of civil rights – had endured
> the rigours of a military gaol, and at the outset had had his
> career threatened with ruin.[39]

Worrall's views highlight once again that the leaders of the resistance
had the full support of their parents whose world views, often encom-
passing Christian and socialist beliefs, were implacably opposed to those
of the government.

Despite the publicity that arose from the 'Ripa Affair', young men
were still being sent into detention on the island. West Coaster James
Nuttall wrote from the island near the end of September that 'seven boys
were discharged last week … McTaggart goes out next Friday … and I
will be released in a fortnight, after serving three and a half months'.
He struck a resolute note at the end of his letter: 'We are fighting here,
and hope you are doing likewise outside, because we realise that New
Zealand must at all costs be freed from the clutches of this jingoistic
monster, conscription.'[40]

Street speakers from the peace movement were still being harrassed.
In September Percy Fletcher was arrested, fined and imprisoned for
non-payment of fines: his offences were posting handbills, and 'obstruction' while speaking in Sydenham. Mackie predicted that he too would
probably end up in prison: he wrote to Ford that Fletcher had gone to
prison 'for experience', adding, 'Your humble servant will no doubt have
to go too.'[41] From October 1913, when the NPC office moved to the
Dominion Buildings on the northwest side of Cathedral Square, the
regular Saturday open-air meetings in the square that had started earlier
in the year with good attendances and no opposition, were held outside
the building.

In the same month Mackie, Reg Williams and Jim Worrall gave evidence to the Joint Defence Legislation Committee, set up at the request of the NPC to inquire into the Rīpapa Island affair. The committee's report quoted military officers in charge of Rīpapa Island: Colonel Heard said, 'We are placed in a humiliating position; we are open to all kinds of insults, to all kinds of insubordination, and we are perfectly helpless'; and Lieutenant Macdonald told Allen, 'under the present conditions I cannot maintain discipline at the fort. I cannot do it.'[42]

If the government had acted on the committee's recommendation that it consider placing religious and COs on the same footing, and allow exemption to both groups provided they agreed to give alternative service under civil authorities, the steam may well have gone out of the resistance movement. The Defence Department was clearly eager to be rid of its role in detaining offenders, and welcomed the recommendation that detention should be restricted to military offences committed while on duty; other offences against the Defence Act would be dealt with and punished by the civil courts. But in the absence of such changes to the legislation, the prosecution of resisters continued.

Support from the peace movement

One way in which members of the NPC and AML could show their support for the detainees on Rīpapa Island was to visit them – often standing in for parents who were not able to do so. Charles Murray, Rose Atkinson, Ellen Howell, Charles Mackie and Sarah Bradley were regular visitors to the island. Like many in the NPC, Sarah Bradley and her daughter Ida were motivated by their Christian beliefs. They attended meetings of the Society of Friends, and Sarah became a member in 1916. She began attending meetings of the AML in October 1912, and she and Ida became members of the NPC in March 1913. Both Sarah and Ida had regularly attended meetings at the Clock Tower to hear young objectors speaking, and Ida was one of a women's deputation to the mayor in January 1913 to ask him to convene a public meeting at which the women of the city could discuss the Defence Act. The request was declined.[43]

It was Ida's idea to form a Children's Peace League, which met at first in their home but soon had to move to larger premises. Members wrote to the newspapers, performed at public concerts and made a 'fine show' with a 'number of very pretty banners' at the first United Peace Day Demonstration in May 1913, organised to mark the establishment of the first Court of International Arbitration, and which attracted more than 200 people to Victoria Square.[44] Ida Bradley died suddenly when she was struck by a taxi in Cashel Street on 24 July 1913, as she and Sarah were cycling home from a peace meeting. The funeral procession from the Bradley home in Matheson's Road, Linwood was led by children of the Peace League, carrying a banner that the Bradleys had made for the recent demonstration. Between 2000 and 3000 people attended the funeral.[45]

Mackie was still urging Christchurch's church leaders to take an interest in the peace movement. He invited them to attend the magistrates court at 10.30am on Fridays when young resisters were being charged, and he sought opportunities to address Baptist, Methodist and Quaker conferences; only the Quakers were unwavering in their support. When H. H. Driver, editor of the *NZ Baptist*, advised that he wouldn't publish a letter and other material sent by Mackie, he noted that the Baptist conference had not endorsed Mackie's contention, and he added his own view that a 'bit of military discipline is not likely in any case to do our easy going colonial youths any serious harm'.[46] He also declined to publish a letter from Louisa Nuttall about her son's detention.

When David McNicholl took a notice of motion to the 1913 Methodist Conference protesting against CMT and supporting the use of arbitration in all international disputes, the conference approved only the latter part. While this was no doubt disappointing to McNicholl and to Mackie, the NPC never wanted to be seen as an organisation that was concerned only with the repeal of the Defence Act. In his invitation to the United Peace Day Demonstration in May 1913, for example, Mackie made it

The Children's Peace Society
request the pleasure of
Mr Mackie & Friends
Company at a Social Evening to be held in
the Manchester Chambers, corner Gloucester
and Manchester Streets, on Thursday,
October 23rd, 1913, at 7.30. p.m.

After Ida Bradley's death the Children's Peace Society continued to meet, as may be seen from this invitation to 'Mr Mackie and Friends' to attend a social evening in October 1913. (Canterbury Museum)

clear that there would be no reference made to the Defence Act during the demonstration, as the aim was 'to bring before the public the broad principles underlying the great peace movement'.[47] At the second Peace Day gathering, held in the Alexandra Hall in May 1914, the speakers included Margaret Lloyd, Charles Murray, MP James McCombs and Charles Mackie.

The anti-militarist movement was still seen as a Christchurch 'fad' however. Mackie told a supporter in October 1912 that 'the general opinion in the House seems to be that there is no opposition outside of Christchurch', despite there being active movements in other parts of the country, particularly in Auckland.[48] Leaflets published in August 1913 listed peace organisations in Auckland, Wellington, Petone, Dunedin and Christchurch.

In March 1912 Mackie began a correspondence with Egerton Gill, a young Auckland Quaker who was secretary of the Auckland International Arbitration and Peace Association, and in March 1913 Gill founded the Auckland Freedom League, whose aim was the repeal of the compulsory clauses in the Defence Act. Gill's letters show that there was considerable activity in the city: by July 1913 a meeting called at short notice to condemn the Act could draw 1000–1500 people. However, Auckland was still not sufficiently in touch with other organisations to

The First General Meeting of the New Zealand Society of Friends, held in Auckland in 1914. Included in the group are Margaret Lloyd (third row, fifth from left), Elizabeth Rutter (bottom row, second from left, holding baby) and Percy Fletcher (bottom row excluding children, sixth from right with baby). (Auckland Libraries Heritage Collections)

be able to organise effective deputations to politicians.[49]

In Wellington P. Josephs, secretary of the Wellington Anti-Conscription League, told Mackie it was impossible to get a proper meeting together in that city. He mentioned as an example a meeting organised by the Society of Friends: the Quakers had failed to notify the league of their meeting, and had never attended any league meetings. Similarly, when the Quaker William Alexander visited the city, he found that the Freedom League there had never organised anything but meetings. When Mackie sent Alexander a 'parcel of dodgers', Harriette Alexander posted them to workers they had met in other parts of the North Island because 'there is no way of getting them around Wellington as yet'.[50] In Mackie's view it would be more difficult to build

DOMINION SERIES, No. 1.

CONSCRIPTION
OR
FREEDOM?

"THAT NO MAN IS A SOLDIER AGAINST HIS WILL IS THE BADGE OF FREEDOM IN ENGLAND AND AMERICA."
—Prof. D. Starr Jordan.

"There is not a responsible Trades Union leader in England behind Lord Robert's campaign. Conscription would elevate the Military Cause and put more money into the pockets of the "armour-plate" manufacturers who, in case of war, would be making a dividend out of the deaths of both sides."
—W. C. ANDERSON, Chairman Independent Labor Party.

" The principle of aristocracy has everything to gain, the principle of democracy has everything to lose, by the militarisation of the country: and more especially by the military capture of our schools. Nothing more need be feared from labor, nothing more need be hoped for by labor, if only the laborer can be made a Conscript by compulsory subjection to military training."
—J. A. Farrer.

New Zealanders !
The Conscript's Uniform is your Badge of Servitude.

Come and join those who are working to abolish CONSCRIPTION.

AUCKLAND : Freedom League, 45 Victoria St. West.
CHRISTCHURCH : Anti-Militarist League, P. O. Box 897.
       National Peace Council, (consisting of representatives of organisations in favour of International Arbitration and the repeal of the Compulsory clauses of the Defence Act), Dominion Buildings, Cathedral Sq., P.O. Box 733.
       Passive Resisters' Union, 98 Lichfield St,
DUNEDIN   ...   Peace League, Mr. Silvester, Gt. King St.
NELSON   ...   Freedom League, T. Harris, Tasman St.
PETONE   ...   Mr. Whittaker.
RUNANGA   ...   "   R. Knight.
WANGANUI ...   "   C. Goldsbury, Manuka St., Castlecliff.
WELLINGTON   ...   "   67 Webb St.

Repeal Print

This pamphlet, c. 1912, includes a list of peace organisations in New Zealand at the time. (Canterbury Museum)

a strong movement in Wellington because it was the seat of government. Christchurch had the strongest peace movement of all the cities – and it was the continued butt of accusations of faddism and mischief-making, or, as McNicoll put it more positively, 'Christchurch is our hope of success.'[51]

Rural stronghold of militarism

The contrast between Christchurch as a stronghold of anti-militarism and the country town of Ashburton, 72 kilometres to the south and probably typical of other country towns, was vividly illustrated in

August 1913 when Mackie, Fletcher, McCombs and Reg Williams went to Ashburton to address a public 'anti-conscription' meeting. Despite valiant efforts by the Ashburton mayor, Henry Davis, the meeting was completely taken over by a well-prepared audience, almost entirely male, who had come along to disrupt. Many had brought whistles and motor horns with them, and they drowned out the speakers with hooting, shouting, shrill whistling, horns and lusty singing of well-known songs. It was later revealed that young men had been promised sixpence if they prevented the speakers from being heard. Determined to try and get their message across, Mackie, Williams and Fletcher wrote a four-page leaflet that they had delivered to every home in Ashburton.

Later in the year the anti-militarists made another attempt on Ashburton: they held a women's meeting in the afternoon, followed by a men's meeting in the evening. Sarah Page, Ada Wells and Louisa Nuttall addressed the noisy afternoon meeting, which was attended by about one hundred and fifty women, held under the auspices of the Canterbury Women's Institute (CWI). The meeting was not sympathetic to the speakers, however: 'Every mention of the Act was applauded and anything said against it was hostilely received.'[52] The resolution passed by the meeting, put forward by the secretary of the local branch of the mothers' union, Mrs W. G. Roberts, fully supported the principle of universal military training as being 'in the best interests of the dominion of New Zealand'.[53] Only four of the women in the hall voted against it, along with those on the platform. The *Lyttelton Times* reported the addresses given by Page and Wells in some detail; the Wellington *Evening Post*, on the other hand, rejoiced at the rebuff that was 'administered to the skirmishing party from Cathedral Square by the good sense of the unsympathetic women of Ashburton'. The report went on to say that the CWI, 'like others in Christchurch, appears to have been entirely captured by the anti-militarists'; it concluded: 'For the present the moan of the martyrs of Ripa Island is silenced, and a broad smile radiates from Ashburton all over the country.'[54]

The men's meeting that evening fared no better than the August meeting had; in fact reports described it as 'an even worse failure than before … short of actual violence being perpetrated on them, a worse reception than this evening's could not well be imagined.'[55]

'Alternative service' causes division

Mackie and the NPC fully appreciated the assistance that William Alexander had given to the peace movement, but just before Alexander left the country in February 1914 their good working relationship became strained over the issue of 'alternative service'. The government, when it made it possible for religious objectors to be exempted from CMT, had also endeavoured to introduce 'alternative service' so that objectors to CMT could be put to work in some non-military form of employment. It even invited local bodies to set up avenues for 'alternative service' – with a marked lack of success. Just before he left New Zealand, Alexander wrote a private letter to Allen in which he put forward proposals for alternative service.

Mackie was deeply disappointed by this. Concerned that Allen would see Alexander's letter as representing the views of the NPC, Mackie and the New Zealand Quakers acted quickly to make it clear they disagreed with Alexander – mainly because the 'alternative service' would still be performed under military control.[56] Percy Fletcher, who had been elected president of the Christchurch AML at the 1913 annual meeting and was still in office in 1914 on the outbreak of war, also disagreed with Alexander on this issue. Fletcher's contribution to the movement included launching and editing a *Monthly Circular* for the NPC, which ran to 10 issues from October 1913 to August 1914, starting with a circulation of 400, which had risen to 700 by the outbreak of war.

New tactics in 1914

The Christchurch Magistrates Court was still hearing large numbers of cases brought against objectors to CMT on Fridays – a day that became known as 'Crucifixion Day'.[57] In February 1914, 400 cases came before the courts in Canterbury alone. *The Repeal* responded to this situation with a humorous notice alleging to be from General Godley OC of the New Zealand Forces: 'Seeing that the parades at the various drill sheds are a failure, and those at the magistrates court are so popular, it is hereby notified that the former are abolished as from this date and in future all parades will be held at the various magistrates courts at 10am.'[58]

A change in tactics then becomes apparent: presumably to try and prevent publicity for the resisters, cases in the Christchurch Magistrates Court were conducted in whispers. 'Following the usual custom, the proceedings were quite inaudible,' reported the *Star* in April 1914. 'The officers of the Defence Department whispered confidentially to the Magistrate; the accused made their explanations sotto voce, and an air of mystery and secrecy pervaded the entire scene.'[59] This did not prevent court reporters from publishing lists of names and the amounts fined; often they noted that this information had been gained after the court hearing. The sheer number of cases was causing delays, too. A report in the *Sun* described the 'irritating loss of time' to numerous people, while twenty or thirty young fellows were being charged in court that morning. The report balanced the small number of people who found the proceedings of interest – which included the 'two ladies, who sat in the body of the Court and took notes in the interests of anti-militarist and peace organisations' – against the solicitors, police officers, the truant officer, firemen, detectives and prisoners who were among those kept waiting.[60]

It would appear that in order to try and avoid making 'martyrs' of the resisters, and attracting publicity for them, a new approach aimed to keep lads out of military detention. Instead they were hit with high fines, the garnishee of wages which could then be used to pay the fines and, most damaging of all, the loss of their civil rights. Rose Atkinson, who apparently attended all the court hearings, kept a notebook in which she recorded the cases brought before the court in 1914. She listed the names of 21 young men who had lost their civil rights in 1913, and another three in 1914. Her notebook shows there were still numerous cases going through the courts in June and July 1914: for example, there were 48 listed for 31 July 1914.[61] Some of the fines imposed were as much as 20 or even 40 shillings – although, as always, the punishments were inconsistent; some young resisters were convicted and discharged.

The peace movement found itself in a difficult situation with the inconsistent treatment of resisters to CMT. While they knew the names of some who had not attended any drill session and had not been prosecuted, they did not want to reveal the boys' identity in case it exposed them to prosecution. Percy Fletcher tackled the issue in a letter to the editor where he listed 12 cases, all members of the PRU, and, without naming the individuals, detailed for each one how many times they had been prosecuted and the penalties they had incurred. All had been summonsed more than once, and seven had served terms of imprisonment. But in the more recent past some had been summonsed several times; others not at all.[62]

Surprisingly, Atkinson made no mention of resisters going to prison or military detention in her 1914 notebook. Evidence from various sources, however, shows that at least twenty of Canterbury's resisters were detained in the first half of 1914. Peter Robert Basher of Marshlands, who was released on 11 March 1914, reported that nine young men from Temuka had been brought in while he was in detention; and 'Cox', writing from Rīpapa Island in April, named 10 fellow detainees.

In March, Arthur Whale and Albert Duncroft reported feeling abandoned by the peace movement as they described the confinement and punishment they were enduring as a result of their refusal to work or drill while being incarcerated in the Lyttelton barracks. They were the only two out of six detainees who were refusing to work, and their punishment was to be locked up all day apart from at mealtimes and half an hour of exercise time:

> The two of us are locked up practically all day. Even the mattresses and blankets are taken away. Also all our civilian clothes. There is no fire in the room, and it is bitterly cold some days. The windows are only open a few inches at the top and bottom and can't be opened further. The jailer is particularly strict and exercises every authority in his power. If we walk about the room keeping ourselves warm, we are told to 'shut up that row', and are threatened that they will take away our boots. Not even books or magazines are allowed us to read. Have the visitors deserted us? Kindly send us a 'Repeal'. You can publish this if you think fit.[63]

Collision of views

Meanwhile six leading members of the Christchurch peace movement – William and Annie Ensom, John and Ellen Howell and Henry and Susan Worrall – had embarked on overseas travel, including visits to England. In keeping with the cooperative nature of the Christchurch movement their farewell gathering – a garden party at the home of Sarah and Samuel Page – was convened by the NPC, the AML, the Fabian Society and the CWI, and was 'well attended by quite a nice crowd of Anti-Militarists & Socialists', Jack McCullough recorded.[64]

When he arrived in Bristol Henry Worrall was interviewed by the *Daily News and Leader* about his son Jim's experiences as a CO on Rīpapa Island, and a sensationalised article was published that included the theoretical situation of a boy who continued to refuse to register on his release and was therefore rearrested: 'a lad convicted at the age of 14 might spend the next 16 years of his life in the fortress'.[65] New Zealand High Commissioner Thomas Mackenzie was understandably upset by the article and accused Worrall of trying to convey that his son had been imprisoned in a 'lonely island fortress far away from civilisation', whereas the island was in Lyttelton Harbour. In Mackenzie's view, 'The bulk of the so-called objectors are entirely unfit for our vigorous country.'[66]

Percy Fletcher, as president of the Christchurch AML, waded into the debate with two long letters to the editor disputing the *Press*'s figures (for example, it had cited prosecutions for non-registration and refusal to take the oath, but had not included the number of prosecutions for other offences, including 'absence from, or obstruction of, parades'), and citing a private letter from Henry Worrall in which he wrote that the report in the *Daily News* was: 'most unsatisfactory' … 'I wrote a fifteen page letter to the "Daily News", giving my version of the interview but it was cut down to a few lines'.[67] The affair brought into sharp relief the ongoing dispute between the peace movement and the authorities about the accuracy of official statistics – which was the subject of innumerable letters written by Mackie in the pre-war period.

The *Press* also attacked Fletcher as a recent arrival to the country, and queried where the funding for the peace movement had come from – a question that Fletcher avoided by writing about the international nature of the peace movement and, by extension, its funding. Neither the government ministers nor the press seemed to be aware of the inconsistency between their fervent British patriotism and their accusation that the trouble-makers were 'recent arrivals'. The *Press* declared that the number of 'shirkers' in Canterbury was thanks to Fletcher and a 'gang of mischief makers': 'We admit, however, with shame that Canterbury occupies a most unenviable position of notoriety in regard to the number of shirkers brought before the Court, and that this is largely due to the efforts of Mr Fletcher, and the gang of mischief-makers with whom he is associated, to induce weak-minded youths to be false to their duty as citizens, and to defy the law.'[68]

Yet the peace movement, far from being a 'gang of mischief-makers', continued to present a broad front of opinion in its dealings with politicians. The previous month the leader of the Opposition, Sir Joseph Ward, had agreed to meet with a deputation at the NPC rooms in Cathedral Square. About fifty women and men were waiting there with well-prepared speeches, each one representing a distinct perspective. Harry Atkinson reminded Ward that in 1908 he had opposed CMT and had asked for the compulsory section of the Act to be struck out. Ada Wells spoke about the ways in which the Act had compromised the education system and was causing harm to the boys; she was applauded when she said, 'The women would never, never, cease to fight against the Act.' Louisa Nuttall spoke on behalf of her son Thomas, who had suffered indignity and injustice by being imprisoned, but she also spoke on behalf of the mothers of other boys. Rose Atkinson spoke from her experience of sitting in court and of the 'disgraceful cases' that young boys had been forced to hear while waiting for their case to be called. Trade unionist Hiram Hunter, representing the SDP, said the party favoured a volunteer defence force, and that those who served their country should be paid the 'ruling rate' of wages fixed by an industrial agreement. Reg Williams argued that New Zealand's army could not repel an invasion but was an army of aggression: the opponents of the Act were 'against it for principle'.[69] Ted Howard argued that an army could not be made out of those who were compelled to train against their will.

The following month the MP James McCombs introduced a similar deputation of about fifty anti-militarists to Prime Minister Massey, seeking repeal of the 'un-British' compulsory clauses of the Defence Act. Percy Fletcher, representing the AML, pointed out the danger of fostering a military spirit, and on behalf of the NPC he advocated the setting up of a government department to promote international good feeling and peace.[70] Ada Wells, speaking for the CWI, said the Defence Act was fostering a spirit of hostility and was injuring the health of the boys. Visiting English Quaker Margaret Lloyd advocated the establishment of a department of peace in every country. Charles Mackie said the NPC stood absolutely for the repeal of the Defence Act, which was a menace to New Zealand, rather than a protection.[71]

The range of speakers in the deputations and their concerns are a reflection of the strength of Christchurch's ebullient and effective peace movement, which felt it was on the brink of defeating CMT. They had been further encouraged by an unexpected editorial in the *Manawatu Evening Standard*, which spoke of 'very serious doubts … as to the wisdom of the expensive and disorganising system … There are signs of a revulsion of public opinion in favour of the old volunteer system.'[72]

Two months later, Atkinson's warning that the government had the power to 'plunge New Zealand into war at a moment's notice' as a catspaw of English militarists came to ghastly fruition when New Zealand joined Britain in the European war.[73] Massey, addressing a crowd outside Parliament on 5 August, pledged that New Zealand would do its duty in a whole-hearted manner:

> That we shall be called upon to make sacrifices goes without
> saying, but I am confident that those sacrifices will be met
> individually and willingly, and in a manner worthy of the
> occasion, and the highest traditions of the great race and
> Empire to which we belong.[74]

Any anti-militarist sentiment in New Zealand fell very suddenly and very decisively out of favour.

CHAPTER 4

THE 'CONSCIENCE OF SOCIETY': THE PEACE MOVEMENT 1914–16

With the outbreak of war the National Peace Council (NPC) endeavoured to remain an effective voice for peace while working within the limitations imposed by military censorship and the war regulations. Acting in cooperation with a number of allied groups, some of which at times urged more radical action, the NPC steered a middle course. At the same time it attempted to stir up groups such as the Christchurch Ministers' Association (CMA) to do more.

Despite a small membership and the disapproval, if not downright hostility, of the press and religious, educational and city leaders, the NPC continued to promote the peace message during the war years. Elsie Locke, a historian of the peace movement, applauded it for being the conscience of society: 'regardless of the hostility which surrounded it … the messengers could not be silenced'.[1]

Initially the NPC decided it was inadvisable to hold public anti-militarist meetings that might contravene the war regulations and stir up hostility against them: they believed they could do more good if they stayed in existence rather than being shut down altogether. The Anti-Militarist League (AML) made a similar decision: they declared that they were opposed to any action that might encourage local strife, and felt they could afford to remain silent because 'the general outbreak of war, with all its horrors, [was] sufficient proof of the rectitude of their purpose and endeavour and ample evidence also of the fallacy of the faith built upon the old pagan motto, If you want peace prepare for war'.[2] Unfortunately for the peace groups this withdrawal led some newspapers to think that the anti-militarists had seen the 'folly of their campaign'.[3] The AML met only a few more times in 1914 before it ceased activities altogether: the final minuted meeting was held in November 1914 to welcome Henry and Susan Worrall back from overseas.

The first objective of the NPC had always been to 'create and educate Public Opinion and to organise, throughout New Zealand, in favour of Peace in the settlement of International Disputes, by the substitution of Arbitration for War'. While this objective had been overshadowed by its work towards the repeal of the compulsory clauses of the Defence Act in the pre-war period, this now became its core activity.[4] Initially it took the form of a study circle which, from September 1914, discussed the 1912 book *Evolution and Empire* by John W. Graham, an English Quaker academic and peace activist. The study leader was Margaret Lloyd, who had been helping Mackie in the office. As Mackie said in a letter to the Methodist Conference, there was 'immense work to be accomplished in educating the populace along definite peace lines. We now have the future confronting us, and should prepare our plans for the settlement, whenever that may be.'[5] Throughout the war Mackie never lost sight of the pacifist belief that: 'This war will not crush militarism any more than the 8000 previous wars have crushed it: this war will no more end war than all the wars of the past have ended it! … WAR WILL NEVER END WAR!'[6]

'People have lost their heads'

At first the peace movement felt isolated and abandoned. 'People have lost their heads,' lamented Dunedin pacifist J. A. Forbes in a letter written in the first month of the war, and he noted in particular the clergy who had 'put Christ's teaching in the background'.[7] There was also 'great grief' over friends who 'went off to the war as soon as the "CALL" came.'[8] To another correspondent, Mackie commented on the way the war had drawn many supporters away 'in the fever which took possession of the people'. It was strange, he reflected, 'to notice how many who were most against militarism went quite mad when the war came and were prepared to banish all their love of pacifism and take up a gun and rush off to slay Germans!'[9]

The enthusiastic reaction of crowds in the street to the news that New Zealand would join Britain at war gave the impression that four years of vigorous campaigning by the Christchurch peace and anti-militarist groups had made little impact. The *Lyttelton Times* reported that a 'pleasing feature' was that among the first volunteers were several anti-militarists who had previously been fined for not attending drill.[10]

The Passive Resisters' Union (PRU) seems to have quickly faded away. Mackie hinted at dissension in the organisation in November 1913 when he noted that it was not as strong as it had been, due to disruption in the ranks.[11] Historian Herbert Roth, who collected much valuable first-hand information from peace activists, including Harry Atkinson, wrote: 'Lacking a clear understanding of the issues involved the PRU fell to pieces. Some of its members volunteered for active service overseas and lost their lives in battle, while others fled to Australia or the United States. ... or became COs in New Zealand.'[12]

Because the existing lists of the thousands who resisted military training generally give only initials and family names, sometimes inaccurately, it's difficult for the historian today to check their names against those who served during the war. It's also difficult to establish how many of the much smaller cohort of about fifty Canterbury resisters who served time in prison or detention pre-war, later served in the military; there were possibly eight, but without further personal information most cases cannot be verified.

One who can be identified is Harold Denton, who enlisted in May 1915 and was reported as saying that 'he had fought hard against compulsory military training, but was now "up against" the intrigue of Germany and her system of conscription'.[13] The *Press* congratulated Denton for 'publicly admitting that he had been mistaken in his anti-militarism', though, as both the *Star* and the *Maoriland Worker* pointed out, Denton had admitted no such thing.[14] The *Star* reminded readers that Denton was voluntarily going to help Britain in its contest against Germany, while the *Maoriland Worker* made the point that if Denton returned home to New Zealand to find conscription still in place he could be jailed again for his opposition to what he went to fight against in Europe.[15] Denton served in Egypt and on the Western Front before suffering from dysentery, and he then went to work in the New Zealand stores at Southampton Docks. On his return to New Zealand in 1919, he was declared physically unfit for further service.[16] Another of the pre-war resisters, Harold Thackwell, also served in the military, and died of wounds he received in France or in Belgium, on 11 September 1917.[17] But at least four of the pre-war detainees – Edward Hannam, Jim Worrall, Thomas Nuttall and Reg Williams – stayed true to their pre-war ideals and were conscientious objectors (COs) during the war.

The number of resisters leaving the country for Australia or the United States is difficult to establish because they avoided publicity.[18] In 1915, for example, it was reported that an exceptional number of young men were leaving the dominion by each steamer bound for America. Fifty-two men, a great number of whom were allegedly of military age, were said to have left New Zealand for San Francisco on the *Moana* in November. Another report, which was immediately challenged, said that 70 Irishmen had arrived in San Francisco: they had left New Zealand because they were afraid of conscription.[19] Two who are known to have left for San Francisco from Christchurch are Frank McCullough and Heathcote Mann. Meanwhile Frank's brother Roy McCullough was one of an unknown number who went on the run for the duration of the war.[20] (Other Canterbury men known to have 'gone bush' are discussed in later chapters.) But it was not just young men who left the peace movement. Other supporters, including Reginald Ford, while they were still supportive of the peace movement in general, believed that 'Britain had no option but to enter the war'.[21]

It also became apparent that some people in the labour movement who had worked alongside the peace movement during the campaign against the compulsory aspect of military training were opposed to conscription, rather than militarism. Dan Sullivan, for example, who was now

THE FLIGHT OF THE SHIRKERS.

The Government is taking steps to prevent an exodus of young men from New Zealand to escape military service. A number of men of military age sailed in the Moana for San Francisco last week, and it is the opinion of the authorities that there were shirkers among them. Regulations under the War Regulations Act have been made and gazetted, requiring all men over the age of 18 years to obtain a permit before leaving New Zealand.
—*Daily paper.*

Zealandia (to Premier Massey): Let the chicken hearts go, William. We're far better without them. They're no good to us.

'The Flight of the Shirkers'. 'Zealandia (to Premier Massey): Let the chicken hearts go, William. We're far better without them. They're no good to us.' (Edward Brodie Mack, *New Zealand Free Lance*, 19 November 1915, p. 1)

president of the United Federation of Labour (UFL) and stood for the SDP in Avon at the 1914 election, advocated voluntary recruitment, and became a member of various patriotic organisations.[22] Hiram Hunter, secretary of the Drivers Union and president of the SDP, became an enthusiastic supporter of the war effort when war was declared. But as secretary–treasurer of the UFL he worked strenuously against conscription from 1915 to 1919, and in 1918 he was sentenced to three months' imprisonment for sedition (he was released after 19 days). Ted Howard was more consistent in his views – and too old to be conscripted: he condemned the war as a capitalists' war and was uncompromising in his opposition to militarism.[23]

Peace movement under attack

Shirkers, COs and representatives of labour groups who agitated against conscription were seen as marginalised, solitary outcasts from the mainstream. Perhaps this was more evident in Christchurch than in other cities: historian P. S. O'Connor wrote in 1968 that 'the strong anti-militarist and anti-conscription tradition in Christchurch' meant that 'political passions and class hatreds, at least insofar as they were likely to be exacerbated in wartime, were more violently expressed in Christchurch than elsewhere'.[24]

Sarah Murray, in her study of cartoons published in the *New Zealand Free Lance* and the *New Zealand Observer*, found that cartoonists consistently 'criticised men who shirked the system of compulsion or agitated against conscription, questioning their manliness and patriotism'.[25] The men were depicted as being weak, disloyal and evasive, 'malnourished men with poor posture, unable

THE SHIRKER.—IS HE TO BE THE FATHER OF THE FUTURE?

'The Shirker – Is he to be the father of the future?' The unhealthy-looking shirker lurking in the shadows is depicted in strong contrast to the manly soldier striding to war. (William Blomfield, *New Zealand Observer*, 2 October 1915, p. 1)

to stand without support, and with their hands in the pockets of their dishevelled suits … New Zealand shirkers smoked cigarettes, drank and sometimes were distracted from their duty by the frivolity of sport.'[26]

Cartoon depictions of objectors as 'shirkers' and the vitriolic attacks made on the peace movement in newspaper letters and editorials all contributed to it feeling under attack throughout the war. The institutions of government, the leaders of the mainstream churches, the educational institutions and the newspapers all seemed to speak with one voice in support of the war effort. Meanwhile, the views of many of the working class and ordinary citizens remained unvoiced and unacknowledged. This was something that CO Archibald Baxter also discovered. Many people opposed or had doubts about the war, he wrote in his account of his treatment as a CO, 'but fear usually prevented that opposition from being at all effective'.[27] Jack McCullough wrote in 1917 that he was afraid to express his pacifist views: 'I feel they are unpopular and that I am in a hopeless and helpless minority.'[28]

J. A. McCULLOUGH
(Workers' Representative, Arbitration Court.

He represents the working man and
  working woman, too.
The sweated factory girl or boy, their
  cause he'll always woo.
He toils with might for what is right
  to benefit his neighbor;
And so with zest he does his best to
  help the cause of Labor.

Jack McCullough. (*NZ Truth*, 9 October 1915, p. 5)

The threat of open hostility and violence was very real. The NPC and PRU had for some years been under attack when speaking in public places. Earlier in 1914 the NPC had been systematically prevented from speaking in Cathedral Square by a group calling themselves the 'Reform Club': on the last occasion Mackie and Fletcher spoke they were pushed off the platform and prevented from remounting it. 'Our people did not support us quite as well as we expected and we had to abandon the meetings for a time,' a disappointed Mackie reported.[29] Just a few days before New Zealand joined the war the mayor of Christchurch told the NPC he had cancelled their use of the band rotunda in Victoria Square for an anti-war demonstration, planned for 1 August 1914, because he had been told personal

THE SLACKER AND THE SHIRKER.

Britannia : Bring them in, David, with the long arm of the law—the Slacker and the Shirker both—and we'll deal with them. Better an open enemy than a selfish waster.

'The Slacker and the Shirker'. 'Britannia: Bring them in, David, with the long arm of the law – the Slacker and the Shirker both – and we'll deal with them. Better an open enemy than a selfish waster.' (Ken M. Ballantyne (unsigned), *New Zealand Free Lance*, 2 June 1915, p. 1)

violence would be perpetrated on members of the peace party. The NPC proceeded to hold a peaceful meeting on the grass at Victoria Square, and they later protested that they were being prevented from holding lawful public meetings by people who objected to their beliefs.[30]

Education becomes the core activity

Gradually the NPC gained confidence about what it could and could not do. By the end of November 1914 it had prepared a series of questions for parliamentary candidates, and Mackie was working on a leaflet about the current situation. With education still in mind, the NPC opened a circulating library with some 'excellent' books that were available for loan to anyone who was interested. The nucleus for the library was books donated by Ford when he moved to Whanganui.[31]

Early in 1915 the NPC and the Canterbury Women's Institute (CWI) affiliated to the newly formed Canterbury Workers' Educational Association (WEA), and the first meeting of the WEA in April 1915 was held in the NPC's rooms. The WEA was another product of the close connections between Christchurch's progressive thinkers. Eveline Cunnington, who had been running study and discussion classes in her home (attended by Percy Fletcher, among others), was one of the instigators, and the provisional committee included several people who were already active in the peace movement, including Ted Howard, Jack McCullough, John Howell and Harry Atkinson. When the WEA council met for the first time in April 1915 three pacifists – Mackie, Howard and Sarah Page – were present as delegates from the NPC, the General Labourers Union and the CWI respectively, and there was probably an anti-war influence on the WEA's education programme, despite the organisation's stated determination to remain non-sectarian and non-political.[32]

In June 1915 the NPC agreed to became a subscriber to the Union of Democratic Control (UDC), a group that had formed in England to provide a means for working towards a permanent peace. The intention was that a set of four principles, adopted by the UDC, should inspire any peace settlement. The first two principles dealt with the need for democratic decision-making in any transfer of a province from one

Canterbury Workers' Educational Association foundation students in 1915. Anti-militarists in the group include Reg Williams, standing in the back row, third from left; Ted Howard, back row, second from right; and Fred Cooke, standing at far left. (Canterbury WEA)

government to another, or in any treaty agreed to by Britain. The third principle advocated the establishment of an international council and a foreign policy for Britain that worked towards an abiding peace; and the fourth principle said Britain should propose a drastic reduction in arms by all the warring nations as part of the peace settlement. Mackie saw the principles as the basis for concrete plans that peace groups could work towards. In an effort to spread the word about the UDC, the NPC published a leaflet that included the UDC's platform, to be distributed to trade unions and societies in New Zealand, and they ordered 250 copies of 'The Morrow of the War', a UDC leaflet that laid out its policies and principles.[33]

Receiving regular news from the UDC was one way the NPC kept in touch internationally with those who held similar viewpoints. Another was through international visitors such as Mrs Allen and Mr Harvey, visiting Quakers from the United States in April 1915. They also kept up a correspondence with supporters such as the English Quaker Alfred Brown, who was instrumental in establishing a Japanese Friendship Bureau that was 'heartily endorsed' by the NPC in June 1914.[34] The aim of the bureau was to foster good relations and to counter scaremongering about the threat to Australia and New Zealand of invasion by China and Japan.

But despite knowing there were groups in New Zealand and overseas who were in sympathy with their work, a comment by NPC stalwart William Willmer at the August 1915 meeting reflected the group's feelings of smallness and isolation. There had been nine people present at the meeting a year earlier, and there were nine people present now: 'nine persons who had not lost their head,' said Willmer, a former Methodist home missionary who, along with Harry Atkinson, was a delegate to the NPC from the Engineers Union.[35] The meeting passed a resolution regretting that after 12 months of war there had been no serious efforts made towards reconciliation.

'Nothing but reading will cure the world'

Education remained the mainstay of the NPC's operations, and Mackie noted a move in the public from being 'in no mood to be educated' in January 1915, to settling down to the inevitable once news was received 'as to the real state of affairs in England and elsewhere'.[36]

Mackie had observed a decrease in hooliganism and the disruption of peace movement meetings in Christchurch before the war, and put this down to the peace groups' educational work.[37] NPC supporters shared his views: one wrote, 'I hope the Peace Council is selling tons of stuff. Nothing but reading will cure the world of its present diseases.'[38] Because of the restrictions of the war regulations the NPC decided not to print their own newsletter; in the main, they distributed literature sent from Britain. In 1915, with the help of William Ensom, who was then in England, the NPC managed to import several parcels of literature from the Independent Labour Party, containing more than 1600 items.[39] By December 1915, however, censorship had become more evident and all correspondence sent to the NPC was being read by the military censor – even Mackie's private correspondence. In the same month a large parcel of 'mischievous anti-war literature' sent to Mackie from England was detained.[40] In some cases literature originally detained was later delivered wholly or in part, as for example in March 1916 when the deputy chief postal censor forwarded a packet of a dozen each of six pamphlets, from the contents of three large parcels. Two months later the New Zealand solicitor-general advised the censor to detain all correspondence and documents sent to the NPC by the UDC.[41]

Mackie wrote several letters of complaint about this interference with his mail. In one case a private letter inviting him to give a lecture on 'Mission work in India' had arrived three weeks after the event. In a letter to the chief military censor he drew attention to the more liberal attitudes in Britain, where all the literature he was receiving was allowed to circulate freely.[42] Yet despite the 'severe restrictions on the importation of literature',[43] the NPC later reported it had purchased a surprising amount during the four years of war, including 15,590 leaflets; 4483 pamphlets; 184 books for sale; two reference books; and three reports – much less than in the first years of their existence, but still adding up to 25,722 items.[44] To some extent they were able to get around the restrictions of military censorship with help from friends in the movement: a parcel that arrived in March 1916 had come from Quakers in England via Quakers in the North Island.

Meanwhile the NPC's representative in Wellington, the English Quaker Elizabeth Rutter, lost a quantity of papers in a raid on her home in November 1915. Among the items taken for inspection were two years' worth of cheque butts, her receipt book, a letterbook with duplicates of private and business letters, copies of her letters home to England at the beginning of the war, and the minute book of Wellington Quakers. 'They must have expected I think to discover that we were engaged in some plot against the Government, & that cheques &c would be able to reveal the secret payments. If so they must have felt somewhat disappointed as a result of their enquiries!' Rutter commented.[45] As a precaution the NPC decided to remove from its shelves 'all literature of a Christian character objected to by the authorities'.[46] On one occasion, detectives visited the NPC office looking for a leaflet the NPC had circulated 18 months earlier.

Lack of finance was another constraint. By June 1916 the NPC was in deficit and no longer able to expect financial support from the Quakers in England, who were working to combat conscription and engaged in extensive relief work. The NPC needed £65 per annum to function – almost double the £35 that regular donors gave each year.[47] Individuals were still helping, however: in 1915 Elizabeth Rutter offered to pay half, and she applied to the Quakers' Peace Fund for help with the cost of printing 5000 copies of Alfred Salter's 'Christianity and War' pamphlet.[48]

By mid-1916 the NPC felt sufficiently confident to hold a series of 'open' educational meetings. These began by looking at the present crisis, then delved into historical aspects of war and the peace movement, before discussing how a peaceful future could be achieved. One of the first speakers was Charles Murray, who addressed an audience of 32. Others included Robert Laing, who spoke about Norman Angell, author

Rev Charles Murray, c. 1910. (Presbyterian Research Centre (Archives))

of *The Great Illusion*; Mr Wills on 'Education and militarism' in April 1917; and William Ensom on 'The effects of humanitarianism upon future peace' and Ada Wells on 'The influence of the suffrage movement on the movement towards peace', both in July 1917. Mackie spoke on 'The effect of international law upon future peace' in August, and Harry Atkinson spoke on 'Economic and social influences on future peace' in September. Only members and friends were invited to the meetings, which continued to attract about thirty people. The time was 'inopportune for public meetings', Mackie wrote.[49]

Robert Laing, sitting front right, a leading New Zealand botanist and science master at Christchurch Boys' High School, seen here on a field trip with Workers' Educational Association students. (Canterbury WEA)

Women add strength

Women played a vital part in the NPC throughout the war. Those who regularly attended meetings included Rose Atkinson, Ada Wells (who occasionally chaired the meetings), Sarah Bradley, Louisa Nuttall and Margaret Lloyd (until she returned to England at the end of 1914). Others who attended less regularly included Mackie's wife Ethel, Annie Ensom, and Naomi Macfarlane, who joined the council with her husband John in June 1915. In the same year Sarah Shillito joined, as representative of the Society of Friends.

Sarah Page, who attended very few of the NPC's meetings, was nonetheless a strong supporter who, like Mackie, felt deeply upset by her compatriots' response to the war: 'But New Zealand as a whole seems so absolutely obsessed by the idea of fighting evil with the devil's weapons that I must confess to a feeling of hopelessness,' she wrote.[50] Despite this she still advocated strongly for peace, mainly through the CWI but also in a personal capacity. Thanks to the leadership of Page and Ada Wells who, throughout the war, were secretary and president respectively, the

CWI became increasingly outspoken in its advocacy for peace while still commenting on a range of social and local issues to do with the wellbeing of women and children. Their monthly meetings were well reported in the newspapers of the time.

In contrast the Women's Christian Temperance Union (WCTU), whose support for the resisters pre-war seemed to strengthen over time (their 1914 conference resolution protested strongly against the disenfranchisement of conscientious objectors (COs) to military service), seems to have predominantly agreed with the war effort while continuing to support a system of international arbitration for the settling of disputes.[51] Thus, in the same paragraph, the editor of the *White Ribbon* wrote in 1915, 'as true patriots [we] are prepared to do all to assist in driving back the menace of German militarism. But it is equally the duty of patriots to strive that in future international arbitration take the place of war.'[52] A pattern developed at the WCTU national conventions whereby the resolutions introduced by the superintendent of the WCTU's peace and arbitration department would be watered down

Mackie and his wife Ethel, fourth and fifth from the left, on a tourist trip in April 1914: the date suggests it was taken on their honeymoon. (Canterbury Museum)

by the meeting. In 1917, for example, a resolution that condemned war in a general way was passed, while a second resolution calling for COs to have the same right to be exempted as religious objectors was withdrawn, in order to avoid dissension. The following year a resolution was passed that showed support for internationalism, but a second resolution about 'liberty of conscience' was amended to read '[that] no resolution on the conscientious objectors be passed by this Convention of the W.C.T.U'.[53]

It was clear where the sympathies of a majority of members lay, judging by the amount of money raised for the patriotic fund. Tribute was paid to Mrs Stewart who, as secretary of the Christchurch Branch of the WCTU, had done 'yeoman service during the first years of the Great War in collecting clothing, packing, and sending it off for Belgian refugees, and also in organising efforts to raise money for the Union's war funds'.[54]

Earnestly working for universal peace

The CWI, which included in its objects 'earnestly working for the cause of universal peace', consistently advocated for improved international relations, often with an emphasis on women's special responsibilities as mothers and educators of the young.[55] In April 1915 it sent a call for unity to the International Council of Women (ICW): 'the women of the world must arise in their strength to put an end to the savagery of war, the bitterest foe to every noble inspiration of womanhood … We women realise that the people have no quarrels one with another but what may be settled by sane and wise counsel, that federation, not Empire, is our goal.'[56] Conscious of the war conditions abroad, the same statement expressed solemn sympathy with the women of Europe and Britain. The CWI was pleased when the Education Board approved addresses to school children on international friendship, given by Margaret Lloyd: this tied in with their belief that children needed to be educated from an early age in kindness and justice to all.

In Europe, meanwhile, a group of women organised an independent women's peace congress at The Hague in April 1915, chaired by Jane Addams from the United States. The congress was attended by more than 1100 participants from several European and Scandinavian countries, including Germany, and they articulated demands that were already familiar to women in the NPC and CWI: for 'international arbitration, democratic control of foreign politics, general disarmament, free trade and pacifist education'.[57] Women at the congress have been described as subtly combining 'ideas about well-accepted social norms of motherhood … with radical political demands', a stance that sounds very like that of the women activists in Christchurch.[58]

One result of the congress was the establishment of an International Committee of Women for Permanent Peace (ICWPP), and reports from the congress fed into CWI meetings later in the year: the report of a British delegate to the congress was read to the July 1915 meeting and friends of the CWI were invited to join the discussion on the topic, 'What women of other lands are doing to encourage goodwill among the nations'.[59] A later meeting took up the issue of peace and equitable commercial relations in the Pacific. The CWI urged an international conference of Australasian and all other countries who had 'possessions' in the Pacific: this, they said, would be preferable to sending representatives to an imperial conference to discuss Pacific problems.[60]

In 1916 the CWI sent a request to the British Dominions Women's Suffrage Union that the question of the establishment of international courts for the furtherance of permanent peace should be placed on its conference agenda. The CWI later learned that the conference had resolved: 'That … in order to prevent future wars, an international council with an equal number of men and women should be established, to regulate all disputes between nations by means of reason instead of force.'[61]

National Registration Act

The behind-the-scenes discussions that went on for about two years within government as to how the volunteer system of registration for military service could be improved, and the pros and cons of having a compulsory rather than a voluntary system, have been thoroughly described and discussed in other publications.[62] It is a complicated, confusing and constantly changing picture that led ultimately to the introduction of conscription with the passing of the Military Service Bill in 1916.

As a first step a national register was proposed. The CWI and NPC both protested against this. The CWI's 'Memorandum' of protest focused, in a long-winded way, on three main issues: the loss of democracy in wartime; the financial burden of war falling unfairly on working people; and the fact that the suffering and hardship caused by military service and militarism affected women most heavily. The statement began by drawing attention to a 'sinister power of the Armament Rings of the World', which was attempting 'complete domination of the world through control of press and parliament'; and it protested against 'the surrender of our political life to the most sinister ideals of Europe'.[63] There was little response to the statement. Other letters the CWI wrote in the same month about the quality of movie shows, and about whether school holidays should be delayed to allow children to help with harvesting, provoked a greater response in local newspapers.

A meeting called by the NPC in September 1915 to discuss the proposed National Registration Act expressed regret and consternation at the move already underway to introduce conscription and send men to Europe or elsewhere for war service. It protested against such moves, and asked Parliament 'not to wantonly sacrifice the freedom and future well-being of this Dominion'.[64] The resolution was forwarded to trade unions and other 'advanced societies throughout the Dominion', and was published in some newspapers. The NPC also sent a letter to all MPs. Once again a newspaper columnist saw the protest as the work of Christchurch 'faddists': a representative of the labour movement who styled himself as 'Veteran', writing in the *Evening Star*, was scathing about those 'few misguided people' in the NPC who had annoyed the unions in the pre-war period with their communications about the Defence Act. 'We thought that the outbreak of the present war had shown this small number of faddists how really foolish they had been, and that they had quietly obliterated themselves from the public view, but no such luck.'[65]

The NPC, evidently feeling it could take a more public stand on its beliefs, albeit in a sympathetic publication, published a lengthy peace manifesto in the *Maoriland Worker* in December 1915, urging that wartime was an opportune time to discuss and prepare for peace,[66] and it published similar manifestos in December 1916 and 1917. By focusing on general statements about the importance of ending the war, uniting to work for an abiding peace, and listing the changes needed in governments and international relations, the NPC was able to avoid breaching the war regulations. They did, however, add a warning that any letters addressed to the NPC would be subject to examination by the military censor. The CWI also started publishing an annual manifesto which appeared on the same page of the *Maoriland Worker*. Under the heading 'For humanity' the CWI manifesto focused on social justice as the way to end war: the need for an end to poverty, destitution, ill-treatment of children, insanitary dwellings, unhealthy workplaces and underpaid workers. It ended with a call for governments to be inspired by 'Good will to all mankind'.[67]

The Social Democratic Party (SDP), which by the first year of the war had at least six active branches in Christchurch, also issued a peace manifesto which it distributed to 10,000 residences in November 1916.[68] As well as discussing the policies that had led to war and the devastation it had caused, the manifesto concluded that: 'The War has settled nothing. It will settle nothing. Negotiations for Peace must take place sooner or later. Why not now?' The SDP called on the New Zealand Government to urge the imperial government to initiate a free and frank discussion of peace terms with Germany.[69] The SDP in Christchurch had a firm foundation of working-class support and an energy that came from their involvement in the wider community. At the 1915 local body elections Woolston Borough Council had gained an SDP mayor and majority on the council.[70]

Impact of war regulations

The arrest of Egerton Gill, Quaker and secretary of the Auckland Freedom League, in October 1915 for distributing circulars likely to prejudice recruiting came as a warning to Mackie, who was in close correspondence with Gill. Closer to home, NPC member Henry Reynolds was prosecuted in January 1916 for 'publishing matter likely to interfere

[721]

Social Democratic Party

PEACE MANIFESTO

Two years ago Europe was plunged into War. The events which immediately preceded the outbreak would have been too trivial to produce such a gigantic catastrophe if the conditions favourable to war had not been in existence.

An examination of the Diplomatic Policies of the various European Powers, of the operations of the Balance of Power Policy, of the intrigues of the various national groups of capitalists, of concession hunters, of Armament Rings, inevitably brings the conclusion that, unless the policies of the nations had been altered considerably, warfare on a gigantic scale was inevitable sooner or later; and that the murder of the Austrian Heir Apparent, the tearing up of treaties, etc., were but the sparks which set the world ablaze. The material for the conflagration—clashing economic interests, and the suspicion, jealousy, and militarism engendered by such— were already on hand piled up. Alone among the peoples, the Socialists of the world realised this. They tried to point it out and to rouse the workers of all countries so that war could be rendered impossible. Before they could succeed the floodgates of bloodshed were opened and there was no time or opportunity for reason to be heard.

For two years War has raged. Millions of lives have been sacrificed. Millions of pounds have been wasted. Devastation, Disease, Death have swept over immense areas, and wrecked homes, ruined lives, maimed men, widows and orphans, misery, unhappiness, tears and distress have been its bitter fruits. Liberty of speech, thought, liberty of the most elementary kind, has been trampled underfoot, and Military Autocracy and despotism has acquired a new lease of life in every country involved in the struggle.

The War has settled nothing. It will settle nothing. Negotiations for Peace must take place sooner or later. Why not now?

The German Chancellor, Herr Bethman-Hollwegg, speaking on April 5, declared :—

"Europe must be for all the peoples that inhabit it, a Europe of peaceful labour. The peace which ends this war must be a lasting peace. It must not contain in it the seeds of new war, but the seeds of a final, peaceful regulation of European affairs."

Page 1 of the Social Democratic Party peace manifesto, 1916. (Canterbury Museum) with recruiting'. This arose from a display in his shop window that included a placard, picture, postcard, calendar, article and pamphlets. The most offensive, from the Crown's point of view, were the additions Reynold had made to an article from the *Maoriland Worker*, proclaiming in large type that more than 34,000 New Zealanders would not kill or help to kill their fellow men.[71]

HENRY WILLIAM REYNOLDS
(Who Was Fined £50)

A sketch of Henry Reynolds in court.
(*New Zealand Truth*, 29 January 1916, p. 7)

Reynolds was fined £50: the magistrate commented that he was entitled to his views as long as he kept them to himself and did not attempt to spread them. A letter written by Reynolds in 1915 was read to the court and reported fully in the *Truth* newspaper, giving good publicity to the pacifist cause. Reynolds said he had no intention of prejudicing recruitment – his aim was to 'bring people to realise the stupid, cruel and hellish uncivilised action by declaring war on each other … My sole desire is to promote PEACE amongst my fellows, whether German, French, or any nationality.'[72] While the NPC continued to support Reynolds, a note of exasperation is evident in a resolution passed in January 1916: while it expressed sympathy for him, it hoped that he would refrain from exhibiting material in his shop window.

Later the same year Reynolds was sentenced to three months' hard labour for evading the censor by enclosing a letter inside another letter. Reynolds, whose business letters and invoices were being opened, read, and sometimes detained for up to fourteen days, later described the incident:

At that time I was selling Socialist and Anti-Military literature. A correspondent whose letter had been censored wrote concerning some books. In order to expedite my reply to him I enclosed it in an envelope addressed to another person asking him to hand it to the correspondent. My handwriting was known to the censor … He opened it with the result that I was charged with attempting to evade the Censorship Regulations.[73]

He was discharged from Lyttelton prison in December 1916 after serving most of his sentence.[74]

Even NPC stalwart William Ensom was a person of interest to the censor. A 'very close watch' was kept on his correspondence; his correspondents in America had been noted, and the censor was aware that Ensom was receiving his letters via fellow NPC member George Wells. A letter Ensom wrote in October 1917 to Edmund Morel, secretary of the UDC, who was serving time in prison for his anti-war activities, was retained by the military censor even though Ensom had taken the precaution of addressing the letter to Arthur Ponsonby, a British member of Parliament (and member of the UDC). A report by the New Zealand censor's office about Ensom, labelled 'secret', was dismissive of him as someone who carried no weight in any matter, and who was considered to be a 'crank'.[75]

Responding to conscription

When the Military Service Bill introducing conscription was published in 1916, both the NPC and CWI responded with public statements. The NPC's rather wordy protest, prepared by a committee of four, condemned the bill and pointed out that conscription had not been 'placed before the country': 'Members of Parliament are betraying the trust of the people by not consulting them or allowing time for protest.' The leaflet also criticised the harsh penalties in the bill, and listed the pre-war measures taken to 'dragoon' the country into a militarist state. The issue of conscience, defined as 'the higher law residing in each individual', was at threat according to the NPC.[76]

The CWI resolution, which similarly opposed conscription and which expressed concern at the loss of civil freedoms and democratic decision-making, was sent to all MPs and widely published in the country's newspapers, alongside responses from the prime minister and the minister of internal affairs. The CWI argued that: 'The supply of large armies for the slaughter of men and the infliction of suffering on other peoples are not the methods that will tend to bring an early or enduring peace';[77] instead they proposed the building up of a universal or world democracy. The letter provoked some strong editorial responses, such as the *Sun* newspaper's 'Pretentious futility', and the *Marlborough Express*'s 'The latest Christchurch cranks'. Once again Christchurch's strong anti-militarist movement was ridiculed and

MAKING THE SHIRKERS SIT UP.

The Military Service Bill, giving the Government the power of conscription, is before the House and will come up for its second reading this week.—*Parliamentary news, May 30th.*

Prime Minister Massey: By Jove, James, she works well. The shirkers are lively at last.

'Making the Shirkers Sit Up', a cartoon about the Military Service Bill, 1916. 'Prime Minister Massey: By Jove, James, she works well. The shirkers are lively at last.' (Edward Brodie Mack, *New Zealand Free Lance*, 1 June 1916, p. 1)

dismissed as a 'Christchurch fad', while the CWI was dismissed as a few 'female busybodies':

> Christchurch is notoriously the home of fads and faddists, and within the last few years quite a number of silly and mischievous agitations have found their principal centre of activity in the Cathedral City. We cannot, however, recall any more stupid and in its way, more mischievous movement than that of which the so-called Canterbury Women's Institute has constituted itself … In all probability, the body in question, like so many of the Leagues and Associations which spring up in Christchurch suddenly achieve a temporary celebrity or notoriety, and then fade away into the limbo of silly things deservedly soon forgotten, consists of some half dozen female busybodies, inflated with an idea of their own importance, and quite negligible as representatives of the great mass of the community …[78]

Another editorial writer referred scathingly to the CWI as an organisation that 'seeks to stem the current of opinion with a resolution'.[79]

In fact, the CWI was a group that had carried out effective education and lobbying for more than twenty years. The publicity achieved by the April 1916 letter and the response it provoked from government leaders and newspapers indicates that the CWI was being taken seriously, perhaps more seriously than the NPC, and while the leader writers in a few newspapers tried to destroy the CWI's credibility, they also had the effect of giving it increased publicity. Sarah Page's response to the prime minister clearly stated the pacifist position – using capital letters for added emphasis: 'INCREASINGLY LARGE ARMIES ARE INEFFECTIVE TO BRING ABOUT AN ENDURING PEACE', she wrote. 'Our contention is that war is all atrocity. It is the supreme national and international crime. It is the insanity of the age which regards brute force as the deciding power.'[80]

The proposal to introduce conscription was opposed by many in the labour movement, too. A 'no-conscription' conference, called by the UFL and attended by representatives from 82 labour organisations, issued a manifesto that included a call for the conscription of wealth. The conference, held in Wellington in January 1916, was dominated by Christchurch delegates.[81] Despite these protests, though, conscription was approved by the NZ House of Representatives on 31 May 1916.

Adela Pankhurst's visit and the founding of the Women's International League

A visit to Christchurch by Adela Pankhurst in the winter of 1916 added to the visibility of the anti-militarist cause. A daughter of the leading English suffragette Emmeline Pankhurst, Adela was founder of the Women's Peace Army and was living in Australia at the time. She credited the CWI with having 'prepared well' for her visit, with its determined opposition to the Defence Act and its cooperation in the anti-conscription campaign. The *Maoriland Worker* reported a 'brave reception' and 'packed meetings with crowds turned from the doors'.[82] Pankhurst's published 'Notes of a tour' were similarly enthusiastic about the success of her visit: she noted in particular the large number of people who turned out to her 'no conscription' meeting on Sunday afternoon in the Socialist Hall, and to her farewell lecture on 'Church and Empire', held in His Majesty's Theatre: 'The Christchurch campaign was wonderfully successful. The crowded halls and enthusiastic audiences prove that the people are war-weary and longing for peace. … The No-Conscription meeting on Sunday afternoon necessitated a large overflow gathering, and in the evening the largest theatre in Christchurch could have been filled two or three times over.'[83] She also held a crowded afternoon women's meeting, and commented that the most remarkable feature of the campaign had been the part played by women, many of whom had never before entered into public affairs. The *Press* report of her visit was much less sympathetic, though it agreed that the Alexandra Hall had been crowded for her talk on 'Women and war', with many turned away. It dwelt disapprovingly, however, on her side-tracking into socialist doctrine.[84]

Pankhurst was invited to New Zealand by the newly formed Auckland branch of the Women's International League (WIL), the body originally established as the International Committee of Women

Adela Pankhurst, holding flowers, with a group of women during her visit to Auckland in May 1916. Some of the women are wearing badges of the Women's International League. (Auckland War Memorial Museum Tāmaki Paenga Hira)

for Permanent Peace (ICWPP) at the Hague Congress the previous year. It went through several name changes in its early years before settling on the Women's International League for Peace and Freedom (WILPF). Early statements of objectives show that the league aimed to unite women around the world in a common cause of political equality for women, and peace and justice for all. In 1915 and 1916 the league had written to several Christchurch women, including Kate Sheppard, Christina Henderson, Ellen Howell and Ada Wells, in the hope that at least one of them would take the lead in establishing a New Zealand branch.[85] In March 1916 the CWI received a similar letter and replied that it was prepared to affiliate to the ICWPP, if the committee would accept the proposal.[86] Presumably nothing came of this.

It was probably Pankhurst's visit that prompted a different cohort of women to establish a Christchurch branch, sometime before October 1916 when a meeting was held in the Socialist Hall. Later events show that members of the WIL were more aligned to the socialist and labour movements than with the NPC or CWI, but it quickly became yet another group with whom the NPC and CWI could cooperate.[87]

Founding of the Anti-Conscription League

A second group also dates from Pankhurst's visit. A preliminary out-doors meeting in June 1916, addressed by speakers 'standing on a table in the open air', deeply offended an indignant bystander who described socialist speakers 'preaching sedition, treason and anarchism, while the best of our manhood are sacrificing their lives for a cause that we all hold sacred'.[88] The meeting ended with an invitation for volunteers to gather at the Socialist Hall and pledge themselves to do all they could to stop conscription from being enforced. The Anti-Conscription League was formed a few days later at a meeting addressed by Pankhurst, with membership restricted to men between the ages of 20 and 46. Once conscription was introduced the league changed its name to the Conscription Repeal League.[89]

A few months later George Thomson was fined 50 pounds for breaching the war regulations by refusing to display a military service poster at his office. Thomson told the court he had destroyed the poster. He was president of the Conscription Repeal League and had a conscientious objection to displaying it. When his 'harangue' against militarism was cut short by the magistrate, Thomson shouted: 'I am an International Socialist and object not only to war but to conscription, one of the things that is getting down the working classes.'[90]

By November 1916 Peter Scott Ramsay was president of the Conscription Repeal League. While he refused to give details to the press – it was difficult for the league to do anything in public that would not breach the war regulations – he confirmed there had been a good attendance at a meeting where 'a definite pledge towards conscription was adopted, and the lines of the campaign of the league were mapped out'.[91]

For the same reason the organisers – and the police – took precautions when a league meeting was held in December 1916. Tickets were issued in advance, and when the door was cautiously opened to allow ticket holders to enter there was a rush from the crowd of about three hundred men who had gathered to oppose the anti-conscriptionists, many of them wearing the 'red badge of honour' of a wounded soldier, while others wore the 'khaki badge' of uniform. This segment of the crowd sang patriotic songs, but although there was a threat of violence between the different elements present, the police kept tight control. The organisers later explained that, because the league had been told the meeting would breach war regulations, they had gone ahead with a meeting in a private room nearby, attended by 50 men. Charles Webber, an executive member of the Conscription Repeal League, urged the attendees to agitate for repeal of the Military Service Act.[92]

Mackie may have considered the organisation to be running too close to breaching the war regulations for his comfort. While the WIL was happy to participate in a joint meeting with the Conscription Repeal League, an invitation to the NPC to join them 'in the fight for the preservation of civilisation' evoked the reply that the NPC felt 'it must leave the latter to the individual members'.[93]

The effects of the war on workers

One thing that everyone in the labour movement could agree on was that war was bad for the working class. After August 1914 there was an immediate rise in the number of unemployed in Christchurch, and an increase in the cost of living, which was not controlled by the government and became the dominant issue of the labour campaign that year. There was a strong belief that the burden of war should be equally shared, and this later developed into an anti-conscription campaign on the grounds that wealth should be conscripted before men were. Moderate labour leaders began calling for a 'conscription of wealth' – a term coined by a British Labour MP when he advocated confiscating enough wealth to raise military pay and pensions, while also eliminating war profiteering and reducing economic inequality.

As the war progressed it became obvious that some sectors of the community were doing very well out of it. Farmers benefited from the imperial requisitioning of most of New Zealand's agricultural produce. Middle men profiteered from the prices they charged for on-selling agricultural products such as butter. The government's tax policies also benefited the wealthy. 'What equality was there,' asked McCombs, 'when a volunteer sacrificed half his income (and perhaps his life) while a man with £100,000 paid only .75 per cent in tax?'[94] In effect, as Paul Baker has noted, whether by neglect or design, the government was 'presiding over a considerable redistribution of wealth between workers (especially those on fixed incomes) and their traditional enemies, farmers and capitalists. Moderates and militants united in a chorus of complaint about prices and profiteering.'[95]

Despite the increasing hardship for working people, many of those in the moderate labour camp responded to the war, as did so many of the population: they saw it as a war that had to be fought. It was a tumultuous period for all who were on the left in politics, as they made personal decisions about where their loyalties lay.

'Fat and the Profits' shows the capitalist profiting from the war while the wives and families of soldiers suffer from a rise in the cost of living. (Credited to Colborne in the *Edinburgh Socialist*; *Maoriland Worker*, 16 June 1915, p. 1)

In the end, however, it was the issue of conscription that led to the formation of the New Zealand Labour Party in July 1916. It came about when the SDP invited delegates from the UFL and labour representation committees to attend its conference to discuss the advisability of forming a New Zealand Labour Party. Leading labour figures had called for this move: Dan Sullivan was concerned that some conscriptionist Liberals might form a Labour Party; and Dunedin's Tom Paul, a Liberal member of the Legislative Council, had warned that 'it was dangerous to leave the name Labor party lying around'.[96] The conference referred the proposal to a subcommittee, which drew up a new constitution. The party was to be based on labour representation committees, which represented unions, trade councils and SDP branches. SDP branches in Christchurch, however – the stronghold of the party – decided not to join.

PETTICOAT COVER.
The Shirker: "Ye cannot harm me now!"

'Petticoat Cover'. 'The Shirker: "Ye cannot harm me now!"' depicts a shirker getting married in order to avoid conscription. To ensure that marriage could not be used as a means of evading conscription, the Military Service Act in 1916 provided that men who married after 4 August 1914 were in the First Division and were therefore liable to be called up as soon as conscription was introduced. (William Blomfield, *New Zealand Observer*, 11 December 1915, p. 13)

By this time conscription had been approved. Initially it covered unmarried men, widowers with no children, and men who had married after 4 August 1914 (the First Division). The men would be called up by a monthly ballot. All other men would be in the Second Division; but no second division man in any district would be called up until all the first division men had gone. Where a family had two or more eligible brothers and none had enlisted, they would be liable for immediate conscription, without the ballot, but they still retained a right of appeal. Individuals, or their employers, could appeal for exemption on the grounds that their service would be contrary to the public interest, or would cause undue hardship to themselves or others. Civilian military service boards were set up to hear appeals against military service. Māori were initially excluded from conscription altogether.

In October 1916, on the day that Allen announced that the first ballot would be held in November, the news came through that conscription in Australia had been defeated by a referendum. Believing that many Australians had been led astray by anti-militarist orators, and seeing a danger in free speech in wartime, the government moved quickly to try and silence any opposition to conscription. A few weeks later Cabinet approved further war regulations that extended the definition of sedition to include 'inciting disaffection, disorder, and class hostility; interfering with recruiting, production, and transportation of essential goods; and discouraging the prosecution of the war "to a victorious conclusion"'.[97]

While some in the labour movement had hoped that a widespread strike would see conscription defeated, this did not eventuate; instead, industrial action against conscription got away to a faltering start. Coalminers at Blackball on the West Coast were the first to strike over conscription at the end of November 1916. They were not joined by other unions, however, and went back to work on 11 December. Coalminers throughout the country began a 'go-slow' against conscription in January 1917: this placed the government in a difficult position because coalmining was an essential industry. An agreement was finally reached, with better conditions for the miners, in April.[98]

Meanwhile fears that the government aimed to silence any opposition to conscription with the threat of imprisonment were confirmed before the year's end when socialist labour leaders, including four from Christchurch, were arrested. A 'Conscription Repeal' conference called by the Labour Party at short notice in January 1917 was smaller than the conference held the previous year, and began by moving into committee. Discussion could only be very general, hampered as they were by the war regulations. The NPC sent as delegates William and Annie Ensom, Charles and Ethel Mackie and George Wells, all of whom may have witnessed the arrest of a future prime minister, Peter Fraser, as he was about to enter the hall; Thomas Brindle was arrested when he took Fraser his breakfast in prison the following morning.[99]

The peace movement had gradually become more assured about what it could and could not do in wartime, assisted by a change in the public mood as wounded soldiers returned home and news from the battlefields became widely known. Now, with friends and supporters facing terms of imprisonment, attention shifted to these individuals who were prepared to sacrifice their freedom for matters of principle.

CHAPTER 5

'THE ONLY PLACE FOR A DECENT SOCIALIST … WAS GAOL': SEDITIONISTS AND OBJECTORS 1917–19

The Canterbury men who were arrested for speaking out against conscription in December 1916 and January 1917 – and indeed about half of Canterbury's conscientious objectors (COs) arrested later in the war – were all socialists. Some were imprisoned more than once: Reg Williams and Henry Reynolds were imprisoned both as seditionists and as COs, and at least three socialist COs had served prison terms before the war for refusing to do compulsory military training (CMT). A fourth man, Peter Ramsay, after serving a sentence for sedition, seems to have evaded imprisonment as a CO by going into hiding.

As had happened with the anti-militarists in the pre-war period, the men who risked imprisonment by their actions were supported by the peace and labour movements. Indeed some of the earlier ebullience of the combined peace and labour movements once again came to the fore in demonstrations of support for the anti-militarists. In many cases, including after the trials or court-martials of Tim Armstrong,

Reg Williams, Peter Ramsay, Arthur Borrows and Charles Warden, the courtroom was crowded with supporters who, at the end of the trial, marched outside singing 'The Red Flag' and cheered the prisoner as he was driven away in the police vehicle. Such demonstrations of support were not possible, however, for those who were court-martialled at Trentham or Featherston military camps.

In 1913 the New Zealand Socialist Party (NZSP) ceased to exist as a national organisation, with all bar the Wellington branch transferring their allegiance to the Social Democratic Party (SDP). But during the 11 years that the Christchurch branch had been active the NZSP had been strongly anti-militarist. The party's 1908 conference had agreed that 'this Conference of socialists in New Zealand recognises the workers of the world have no quarrel among themselves and affirms the principle of universal peace as in the best interests of humanity'.[1] A few years later the party condemned war and declared that international disputes should be solved 'by reason and arbitration'. It urged workers in every country to take action with workers in other lands 'to counter militarism and promote peace and social justice'.[2] Between the two conferences held in January and July 1913 (and just months before the demise of the NZSP), Ted Howard and Fred Cooke, as president and secretary, had issued a manifesto that included a strong anti-militarist statement: 'We, the Socialist Party, are uncompromisingly hostile to all forms of militarism, recognising that while the Class State exists the armed forces will be used to buttress up Capitalism and to hold down the workers.'[3]

Internationally, socialists had come together in the Second Socialist International and at their recent congresses had debated the use of a general strike to prevent war. In 1910 at Copenhagen the congress had debated an amendment proposed by Édouard Vaillant and Keir Hardie that called for a general strike in case of war. A decision to continue discussion of the amendment at their next congress in 1914 was overtaken by the outbreak of war.[4] Fred Cooke was one who supported the amendment, and was 'bitterly disappointed' when war broke out because he'd cherished hopes that 'the workers of the world would, by a general strike, halt the war in its tracks'.[5]

While the government tended to label all socialist objectors as 'defiant', unpatriotic and 'non-genuine', the objectors saw themselves as true patriots with the best interests of the country at heart. They were the upholders of the British tradition of freedom of conscience, freedom of belief and free speech, who were opposing the tyranny of conscription. Statements made in court by seditionists and by COs incorporated a wide-ranging mix of beliefs that included socialist, Christian, moral, humanist, ethical and political viewpoints. All the objectors were prepared for the punishment they knew would follow.[6]

Frederick Riley (Fred) Cooke, c. 1920s. (Alexander Turnbull Library)

Bob Semple, organiser for the New Zealand Federation of Miners, was the first of the labour leaders to be targeted by the government for speaking out against conscription. Although he was not a Canterbury resident, Semple was arrested and tried in Christchurch and served his term of imprisonment at Lyttelton. 'I believe that if the wealth of the wealthy in this country had been conscripted and better provision made for the married men who desired to enlist, but were prevented by economic difficulties, there would have been no need for a conscription policy,' he told the court. 'Conscription was a Prussian method; a policy borrowed from Germany', and the people of New Zealand had been given no chance to accept or reject it.[7]

A few days later, on 19 December 1916, Fred Cooke was arrested and tried for seditious intention. In January 1917 it was the turn of Tim Armstrong, Reg Williams and Peter Ramsay: all four were found guilty of sedition and sentenced to a year's imprisonment with hard labour, which they served alongside Semple in Lyttelton prison. Their trials, when their 'seditious' statements were read to the court, were fully

Ticket to the United Federation of Labour reception for Bob Semple on his release from prison in 1917. (Canterbury Museum)

reported in the *Maoriland Worker* alongside the defendants' statements made at the trial. The trials were also (though less fully) reported in other newspapers, and in this way their views were widely disseminated.

'I cannot obey that law'

Fred Cooke was typical of other Canterbury socialists in that he was a relatively recent emigrant from Britain, where he had been a foundation member of the British Independent Labour Party (ILP). His arrest arose from a speech he gave in the Socialist Hall on 10 December 1916 to a large and attentive audience of men of military age. His seditious statement included the assertion that he would not fight for the 'Old Land' or the aristocracy: 'for the Duke of Devonshire, of Westminster, of Richmond, of St Albans'. He also spoke strongly against the War Regulations and the 'Conscription Act', and defended his right to speak against them: 'The War Regulations are framed for slaves, and no free men will tolerate the conditions imposed by those War Regulations. We Socialists at this side of the world have to oppose all the tyranny that is to be levelled at the workers here. There is twice the population on the side of the Allies, and they want to conscript a little country with one million population.'[8] Cooke told the court he had much to say, if the court would tolerate a pacifist. He defended his right to protest, and to criticise any government that went beyond the rights it had when it took power. Despite the magistrate telling him that no one could criticise the government 'to the detriment of recruiting requirements of the country', Cooke said that 'as a Britisher' he protested: 'while the Conscription Act prevails, I shall make speeches … I cannot obey that law.'[9]

After his release Cooke continued to campaign on behalf of other prisoners of conscience, and he published a small magazine, *Punchi*, which 'gave detailed coverage of the cases, imprisonments and sufferings of the young men who refused to fight'.[10]

'War is an utterly ineffective weapon'

A few days after Fred Cooke appeared in court, James Thorn, who was born and bred in Christchurch and had become a leading trade unionist when working at the Addington Railway Workshops, was arrested in Wellington and tried in Auckland for seditious utterances made in that city. Thorn, too, addressed the issue of freedom of speech and claimed the freedom to discuss conscription, which was permitted in Australia and Britain. His opposition to conscription was based 'not on merely sentimental objections to the inhumanity of war, but upon the perfectly rational objection that war is an utterly ineffective weapon in settling the relations between different peoples'.[11]

After serving a one-year sentence in Mt Eden prison, Thorn was immediately presented with his call-up papers and appeared before a military service board in March 1918. His appeal for total exemption on the grounds that he was extremely valuable to the Agricultural and Pastoral Workers Union because of his extensive knowledge of the awards affecting rural workers was dismissed. He was granted leave until 4 June but instead went into hiding, thereby managing to avoid another prison sentence. Thorn was welcomed 'back to civilisation and active work', by the *Maoriland Worker* in November 1920.[12]

Conscription armies used against workers

Trade unionist Hubert Thomas (Tim) Armstrong had moved to Christchurch in 1916 where he worked on the Lyttelton wharves and immediately became active in the local labour movement. He was arrested for sedition in January 1917 on a charge relating to a speech he had made in Christchurch on 21 December, which according to the Crown Prosecutor, used words of a very seditious character and was a serious breach of the regulations.[13] Part of his speech was about the way conscription had been used in 'conscription countries' to keep working people in subjection:

> when the working classes rise in revolt against the damnable conditions that prevail, asking for a little more of that which their labor produces, the conscript army has been used in every instance by the money burglars of those countries, and against the working class … I want to say as far as I am concerned I am not going to be a soldier and no power on earth will make me.[14]

Hubert Thomas (Tim) Armstrong, c. 1922.
(Alexander Turnbull Library)

Armstrong said that, as the father of a family, if he did not speak against the 'infamous legislation' (the Military Service Act), he 'would not only be a traitor to my own country but to my own children, who will inhabit this country after I am gone'.[15]

Described by *Truth* as a 'man of striking personality and a quiet, convincing speaker', Armstrong addressed the court with a well-organised statement that drew attention to the way some employees had been exempted from conscription. The miners, seamen and railway men had all been exempted, he said, because 'the Government was frightened of their combined kick'.[16]

There was a poignant moment at the end of his sentencing when one of his six children called out from the courtroom, 'Goodbye, Dad'. Armstrong buried his face in his hands for a moment before replying 'Goodbye'.[17]

'I am an Internationalist'

Reg Williams, a seasoned campaigner as a leader of the Passive Resisters' Union (PRU), was charged with having expressed a seditious intention at Victoria Square on 7 January. The case was heard before a crowded courtroom on 24 January 1917. Conducting his own defence, Williams affirmed his right to question the reasons for conscription

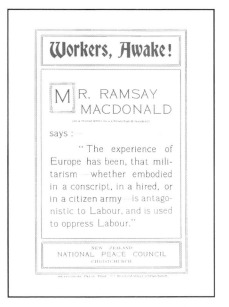

'Workers, Awake!' – a card produced by the National Peace Council quoting from a letter written by English Labour politician Ramsay Macdonald. (Canterbury Museum)

and to stand up for the rights of free speech. The extracts cited in court might appear seditious – but were not if read in context:

> any intelligent working man has a right to question why he should give his life. He was more of a patriot standing in the dock to defend the working class against a blind Government … than the howling flag-waggers who week after week got up in different places in the city … I have nothing to apologise for. I have spoken what I believe to be the truth. I am an Internationalist, opposed to war, and I shall oppose it as long as I have a tongue in my head.[18]

Williams was released in October 1917. In April 1918 he successfully appealed against being called up on the grounds that, at the time when his name had been drawn in the ballot, he had been in prison. After he was balloted again, and failed to parade for a medical examination, he was arrested in June 1918 and taken to Trentham Military Camp where he was court-martialled on 1 August 1918 and sentenced to imprisonment with hard labour for two years.[19]

A ringing endorsement for a defiant socialist

Peter Scott Ramsay was a socialist, president of the Christchurch Grocers Assistants Union and the Christchurch Conscription Repeal League. When his name was drawn in the first ballot after conscription was introduced, he said it would be a farce for him to go before a military service board. He had always been opposed on principle to war; he had made this clear on his registration form, and he could not under any circumstances accept service.[20]

When he addressed a 'glorious crowd' in the Socialist Hall in December 1916, 'The house rang when he said, "Come weal or woe, I am not going to the front"'.[21] Instead he was arrested in January 1917 for making seditious utterances on two occasions.

Ramsay was clearly a popular figure in the movement as, while the courtroom had been described as 'well filled' with members of the public for previous similar cases, for Ramsay the Christchurch Magistrates Court was crowded: 'people standing in the alleyways and even in adjacent passages, so as to be within earshot of the proceedings'.[22] Many people, including women, were standing in the courtroom. A reporter described Ramsay as clean-shaven, well dressed, 'an earnest and virile speaker, though somewhat given to drifting from his real subject'.[23]

In court, Ramsay defiantly echoed the statements of PRU members before the war: 'We are not going to go. They cannot make us go. We are prepared to take all the penalties of the law and all the punishment

Peter Scott Ramsay, c. 1920. (Canterbury Museum)

they can fix on us rather than break our principles for which we have stood up for so many years in the Labour movement.'[24] His reference to his long-standing membership of the peace movement in Britain was unusual for objectors in New Zealand: 'I have the courage of my convictions. I have been a member of the peace movement since I was fourteen and a half, and I am not going to give up the principles for which I have fought for so many years for the class to which I do not belong.'[25]

Ramsay told the court it was 'the height of hypocrisy for men to be punished for preaching peace in this so-called Christian country. (Applause which was at once suppressed.)'[26] He protested against the 'unconstitutional process' which deprived him of a jury trial, and pointed out that anti-conscription speeches were permitted by law in Britain. Defending his right to free speech, he said, 'what ideas he possessed he had the right to express, and those who prevented him doing so were intellectual robbers. A twentieth century government ought to know that they could not make people believe anything by force.'[27]

In sentencing Ramsay to 11 months in prison, the crown prosecutor, eager to counter the 'impression that some of these men believed that it would be safer in gaol than in France', made it clear that Ramsay was still considered a soldier of the Expeditionary Force and could at any time be taken into camp.[28] Sure enough, when he was released from prison the following year a warrant was issued for Ramsay's arrest for failing to parade, and he immediately went 'to a little known part of the South Island'.[29] According to a later report he had been spotted with other objectors at Glenorchy, at the head of Lake Wakatipu. When he returned to Christchurch in May 1918 he was unwell and was given leave by the military authorities until he was well enough to be examined.

Ramsay was one of a group of six men who had been living in the rugged bush-covered country near Lake Wakatipu, surviving mainly on birds and fish that they caught. About seven months after Ramsay left the group, the four remaining members – including William Wallace Yeoman, who was described as secretary of the Socialist Party in Christchurch, and William Douglas Pearston, a butcher of Christchurch – were arrested at Elfin Bay, Lake Wakatipu. They were described as having been driven 'near the haunts of men': they had no provisions whatsoever, and were 'almost in rags and tatters'.[30] They did not resist arrest: they were court-martialled in Dunedin and sentenced to two years' imprisonment as military defaulters, after the war had ended.[31]

The five labour leaders imprisoned for sedition early in 1917 were all well-known figures in Christchurch who intentionally took a stand. But the short prison term served by Walter Brown, a labourer from the small rural town of Rakaia, shows how easy it was to commit a breach of the war regulations. Remarks he made at the Methven saleyards about returned soldiers not receiving fair treatment, and the misuse of money by the Patriotic Societies and the government, were judged to be 'calculated to interfere with recruiting and the raising of patriotic funds'.[32] Brown's conviction might have been less severe if it weren't for the fact that he had earlier been discharged from camp on account of misconduct.

'I ignore militarism, which is murder'

Henry Reynolds was undeterred by two stints in prison in 1912 and 1916, and also resisted his conscription – which, as it turned out, was illegal. Throughout his court-martial at the King Edward Barracks on 2 June 1917 Reynolds, who had failed to attend a medical examination, displayed complete indifference to the proceedings: he first said a few words about the 'military farce' and protested about the cell where he had been confined for nearly a week with no opportunity to get out on bail. He then asked for a chair, and settled down to read a copy of the *Maoriland Worker*. He refused to pay attention to the proceedings because, as he put it: 'It doesn't matter. I don't want a hearing.' He also refused to plead: 'I don't plead anything. I ignore the Military Service Act; so you put down what you like.'

Reynolds had returned the letter he received ordering him to attend a medical examination, and this was solemnly produced in court – still unopened. He had also been sent a telegram, and on both the letter and telegram he had written 'I ignore militarism, which is murder.'[33] Asked if he'd like to make a statement bearing on the trial, Reynolds replied: 'I wish to tell the court that I'm an anti-militarist, and have been an anti-militarist for the last six or eight years – since they started with boy conscription. I'm against all military power and military rule. I look upon it as the curse to a nation … I'm willing to take the punishment that is going to be meted out to me, in the hopes of breaking down military power.'[34]

Because of Reynolds' indifference to the proceedings it was left to National Peace Council (NPC) member William Ensom to testify to Reynolds' good character: he spoke of him as a family man who was bringing up his three children in an exemplary way. While Reynolds said he refused to establish anything for the court, he did volunteer the information that his youngest child was 12, which meant he was clearly in the Second Division and should not have been balloted. He failed to tell the court that he was over-age for a soldier. This meant his punishment of one year's imprisonment with hard labour was wrong. Despite *Truth* arguing that, if it could be clearly established that Reynolds was in the Second Division, the government should set him free, it was three months before Charles Mackie and others in the peace movement succeeded in obtaining his release from Lyttelton prison.[35] 'I feel convinced that had you not persevered and done all that was possible to gain my release, I should not be enjoying my liberty,' Reynolds wrote to Mackie in October 1917.[36]

Reynolds later explained his continued opposition to militarism: 'The war was progressing and the slaughter of lads was going merrily on. I could not stand by silently and I thought if I could but save one lad that it was worth my efforts.'[37] His ongoing display of 'seditious matter' in his shop window led to a conviction and a warning in December 1917, followed by another court appearance in May 1918. One of the documents he'd displayed drew attention to the implications of New Zealand having annexed Sāmoa in the opening days of the war: 'When nations go to war they are gangs of robbers. They are out for plunder. We have stolen Samoa. If we are going to keep it we shall have to drench it with our children's blood. Take your choice; your children or more Empire.'[38] On this occasion Reynolds was ordered to pay the costs of the prosecution but would not incur further penalties as long as he refrained from putting objectionable material in his window for the next 12 months.

Worrall brothers tried in the North Island

Unlike the trials of the seditionists, which were heard in the magistrates court in Christchurch and were fully reported, only some of the court-martials of Canterbury's COs were held in the city; many were held at Trentham Military Camp near Wellington, and unless the individuals concerned kept a record of the proceedings, it's almost impossible to know what was said. In the case of Jim Worrall, very little is known about his court-martial. His father, who was in attendance, later read Jim's address to the court at an NPC meeting, but unfortunately the content of his statement was not included in the NPC minutes.[39]

Jim had been arrested in September after ignoring his call-up in May 1917 and failing to have a medical examination. He was court-martialled on 6 November 1917 and sentenced to two years' imprisonment, initially at Kaingaroa.[40] His case shows how easily a CO's experiences can disappear from the public record. Because he did not appeal to the military service board and his court-martial was held at the military camp, there are no newspaper reports of his court hearings, and there is also no personnel file in army archives.

James (Jim) and Marion Worrall who married in 1921. (Worrall family)

We know more about the experiences of Jim's older brother William because of letters he wrote to his family while he was in prison as a CO. William, an accountant who worked for the New Zealand Refrigerating Company, was called up in February 1917, soon after his marriage to Beatrice O'Donohoe.[41] Canterbury's No. 2 Military Service Board found he was 'fit for home service only' and dismissed his appeal against service. He was arrested for refusing to enter C Camp and was escorted to Featherston Military Camp, where he was brutally treated when he refused to put on uniform

William and Beatrice Worrall on their wedding day in January 1917. (Worrall family)

(see chapter 7). His court-martial was held at Featherston on 14 February 1918, with his father in attendance. In a letter written the following day William said he had made a statement 'setting forth my conscientious objection to taking any active part in war and describing in part how my objections are deep-rooted', but although 'every word was typed' as he spoke, the record of his trial does not seem to have been kept.[42] While he was known to be a socialist, a family letter from before the war shows that his Christian beliefs were probably at the root of his objections to military service. William had resigned as a Sunday school teacher at the Richmond Methodist Church in 1913 because of the church's attitude towards the Defence Act. 'I personally cannot reconcile the teachings of Christ with the form of militarism which persecutes those who take to heart the Sunday School teachings of their youth,' he wrote. He went on to say that while he was 'in perfect accord with what I believe to be Christ's true doctrine and God's true religion,' he couldn't serve as a Sunday school teacher for men who upheld the Defence Act, which he saw as 'the forces of evil'.[43]

Edward Hannam, a carpenter, had also been involved in resistance to the Defence Act before the war. He served time in Lyttelton prison in 1912 and was detained on Rīpapa Island in July 1913. When he was conscripted in April 1917 he refused to undergo a medical examination and was court-martialled at the King Edward Barracks on 31 August before 'a considerable gathering of spectators'.[44] Hannam told the court 'he was not a soldier, being an anti-militarist and having been in gaol for that … I'm against militarism in any shape or form.'[45] After his discharge from Paparua prison in May 1918 he was rearrested and received an initial 28-day sentence and, on 22 July 1918, a two-year sentence. At war's end he was in the Invercargill Borstal.[46]

'Human life was sacred'

Among the socialist COs jailed in 1918 were five men who were identified as members of the Woolston branch of the Social Democratic Party (SDP). Four of them were well known in the Christchurch labour movement. The fifth, Aucklander Louis Ross, appears to have had no connection with Christchurch: we can only surmise that he joined the group while he was in Paparua men's prison, alongside brothers John and James Roberts, George Samms and Frank Robinson.[47]

The fact that the men were recorded as being members of a particular political party branch is unusual, and is a reflection of the strength and the level of activity of the Woolston Branch of the SDP. This has been attributed to a core group who had previously been members of the British Independent Labour Party (ILP), and who replicated many of the social activities of the ILP after they moved to New Zealand: 'there were holiday camps for the families and friends of supporters, a dramatic society, a choir modelled on the British Clarion Choir and an energetic round of festivities, sporting fixtures and socials as well as the normal business of party branch activity'.[48] When Peter Fraser visited Christchurch on behalf of the SDP in December 1915 he found that: 'In Christchurch the Social Democratic Party is a force. It is recognised by the workers as the political party of their class.'[49] The Woolston choir received special mention: 'Woolston Branch, more wonderful than all … a choir – and a successful choir too. The Social which I attended on December 4 along with the National president, was splendidly organised'.[50]

In March 1918 John Roberts, a recently elected councillor for the Woolston Borough Council, was the first of the Woolston SDP members to be court-martialled, followed a few months later by his brother James.[51] John Roberts, a presser in the clothing trade, had arrived in New Zealand with his future wife, Agnes Farrar, in 1908 and joined the Christchurch Socialist Party in 1909. He belonged to the Christchurch Tailoresses and Pressers Union, and

John Roberts, secretary of the Canterbury Clothing Trades Union and NZ Clothing Trades Federation 1929–59. (Macmillan Brown Library)

became secretary of the Woolston Branch of the Christchurch Socialist Party. He was elected to the Woolston Borough Council in April 1917, after running on an anti-conscription ticket.[52]

His experience as a councillor was short-lived, however, as after his call-up in November 1917 and his refusal to attend a medical examination, he was court-martialled at the King Edward Barracks in March 1918. While Roberts willingly pleaded guilty to refusing a medical examination, he would not plead guilty to disobeying the command of a superior officer, because he recognised no superior officer. He had nothing to say in mitigation, because he did not admit that he'd done anything wrong. Speaking to the court, he said that as a humanitarian, 'he believed that human life was sacred'.[53] His statement, which covered moral and economic issues and the primacy of freedom of conscience, was greeted with applause from spectators in the courtroom:

> He believed killing to be murder, even if the blessing of the Church and the sanction of the State were appended. As a Socialist he believed that all wars were waged for economic ends, for the capture of new markets, and he had no desire to

assist such ends. In New Zealand today no man was allowed
a conscience unless his conscience had the hallmark of State
approval. It was futile to put conscientious objectors into gaol or
to punish or torture them otherwise, as that could not kill their
consciences … violence applied in matters of conscience was a
plain confession of a bad case … He was a married man, and the
penalty would press heavily upon his family and himself, but he
would submit to any penalty rather than violate the dictates of
his conscience.[54]

Roberts was sentenced to 18 months' imprisonment. In later life he said
that, during World War I, 'the only place for a decent socialist … was
gaol'.[55]

Four months later John's older brother James Roberts, an electrical
fitter married to Nelly Dawe, was court-martialled in Christchurch as
a CO. Appearing in court 'with a child standing by his knee', James
emphasised the moral nature of his stand and made special mention of
the impact on families of the loss of a father and husband:

in judging between right and wrong his standard was that of
morality and not of legality. Parliament could make 'any old
thing' legal, even an immoral thing but that did not make it
right. That explained why he stood there. Since the war began,
it had been constantly put forth from Press, pulpit and platform,
that British militarism was vastly different from Prussian
militarism. Recently The Sun had said editorially that the two
were as unlike as water and wine. If that were so, now was the
time to prove it, and to show that only in Germany was it that
men were dragged off to fight, or thrown into prison. The court
had married men before it that day …[56]

Classed as a 'defiant' objector, James was sentenced to one year's
imprisonment. The Roberts brothers had grown up in Leeds, and their
early socialist influences had come from their father, a union secretary
and foundation member of the ILP. John had attended the first Socialist

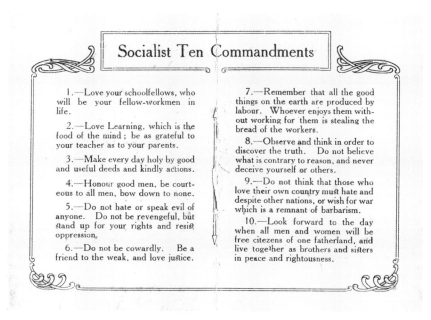

Socialist Sunday Schools, such as the one attended by John Roberts in England, taught a strong commitment to world peace. Pictured here is Lincoln Efford's 'Socialist Ten Commandments' card from the Christchurch Socialist Sunday School in the 1920s. (Efford family)

Sunday School in Britain and recalled hearing the ILP leader Keir Hardie speak. The ten commandments of socialism that were taught in the Socialist Sunday Schools included a strong commitment to international peace. The ninth commandment read: 'Do not think that those who love their own country must hate and despite [sic] other nations, or wish for war which is a remnant of barbarism'; and number 10 read: 'Look forward to the day when all men and women will be free citezens [sic] of one fatherland, and live together as brothers and sisters in peace and rightousness [sic]'.[57]

'He stood … for Socialism'

James Roberts's fellow SDP member, George Samms, was court-martialled on the same day. Samms made a strong statement for socialism as an anti-militarist movement, and he explained to the court how his beliefs that wars were fought for private greed had been formed as a result of his experience in the South African War when he was 17 years old:

He stood, he said, for Socialism and all that Socialism stood for against militarism. … He believed in the spirit of internationalism against the spirit of nationalism. Therefore he must refuse to become a soldier. To show the foundation of his views, he said that when the Boer war broke out he had been a boy of 17, longing to serve and to help towards crushing the Boers, whom they were told were a most cruel people. He ran away from home and enlisted, as he honestly believed the enemy to be one that must be crushed. So he went to South Africa with the 3rd Battalion of the Duke of Wellington's West Riding Regiment. When he returned, his views on war had greatly altered. He had seen none of the glory that the Press was so fond of talking about. He had seen nothing but suffering and misery. In his native town he had seen a procession of returned soldiers, all out of work, at the same time that thousands of Chinese coolies were being imported into South Africa. Then he saw that wars – all wars – were fought only for the greed of the exploiting classes. For the past 15 years he had been a consistent advocate of the cause of the workers, and he had sworn never again to shoulder a rifle or to shoot one of his own class.[58]

Another report said that Samms ended his statement by warning that countries that lived by war would perish: 'To try and kill men he now held was not only criminal but insane … War cut into the very vitals of a race, and the list of the fallen did not tell half of war's effects. Every country that tried to live by war must perish.'[59] Samms was sentenced to one year's imprisonment.[60]

Samms and his wife Lily Bamford had followed a friend, Frank Robinson, in emigrating to New Zealand in 1911. After looking for work in Christchurch and Wellington, Samms was happy to return to Christchurch where Robinson had found him a job as an iron moulder at Scotts Iron Foundry in Christchurch. The two families lived together while they saved money to buy two sections on Tilford Street in Woolston, where they eventually built.[61]

Robinson, who was also a member of the Woolston SDP, was court-martialled in Christchurch in September 1918. Evidently considering

Conscientious objectors at Paparua prison. Robin Page is sitting centre front on the ground. The four men sitting at the back from left to right are Frank Robinson, George Samms, James Roberts and John Roberts, all members of the Woolston Social Democratic Party. (Patricia Smith)

it a waste of time to try and argue or present a statement to the court, he simply pleaded not guilty on the grounds that he didn't acknowledge any military authority, and that following his conscience was paramount to him: 'he was quite satisfied that the course he had taken was the right one, but he did not expect to affect the views of the Court by what he might say any more than he would be affected by what the Court might say. He would obey his conscience.'[62]

'So-called patriots – were profiteering'

James Walker, a labourer from Christchurch who was court-martialled on the same day as Robinson, argued he was a civilian, not a soldier, and he objected to a military court having jurisdiction over him. His comprehensive statement to the court explained why he refused to recognise a military authority; he denounced the immorality of the Military Service Act, and criticised those who were profiting from the war: 'Men were being forced to leave all that they held dear, and to make heavy financial sacrifices, while others – so-called patriots – were profiteering in all directions, even from the dependents of those who had given their lives for the Empire …'[63] He also criticised farmers who, while calling for the conscription of labour at soldiers' pay, were refusing to grow wheat except at high prices.[64]

Walker was allowed to continue reading his statement, despite the prosecutor saying it was irrelevant. He went on to denounce the use of force to settle disputes: 'the time was past for all that. Militarism against militarism would never set things straight. Only by the masses seeking out the evidence and realising the causes of war, and then refusing to sanction the rush of armaments, could there be justice for all and the full rights for men.'[65] In conclusion he said he was prepared to pay the price for having a conscience. He was sentenced to 12 months' imprisonment.[66]

'I shall not in any shape or form acknowledge militarism'

Arthur Borrows was a former railways employee who was working for Booth, Macdonald and Co. as a labourer when he was called up in November 1917 at the age of 39. He was married but had no children, and lived in the same street as Samms and Robinson. When he and another CO, Charles Warden, appeared before a court-martial in Christchurch in January 1918, the court was adjourned because both men – who wore red roses in their buttonholes – had refused to have a medical examination before the trial. The president of the court explained that the reason for the medical examination, which was required under the King's Regulations, was to satisfy him that the men were fit to stand trial and serve time in prison, if necessary: it was not to be confused with the medical examination required under the Military Service Act. Both men had refused because the doctor who came to examine them was a military doctor. As Borrows said: 'I shall not in any shape or form acknowledge militarism. I will not. I would rather face death … The doctor who came to examine me was in uniform.'[67] When the two men appeared again a few days later Borrows told the court he was a CO who was against all militarism. He had the Rev James Chapple with him to assist, but when Chapple was invited to give evidence to the court he said he wanted to make a statement 'to interpret Borrows' mind to the court; to show the reasons for his conscientious objection'. This was refused because it was not evidence; nor was Chapple permitted to speak after Borrows was found guilty. When Chapple jumped to his feet and asked: 'Have I no right to speak in mitigation of sentence?', the president of the court silenced him 'in a stentorian voice'.[68]

When George Quartermain, a house painter who was married with one child, appeared before the Second Military Service Board in July 1918, he was given short shrift. He had no grounds for appeal, said the board chairman, Magistrate Helyar Bishop. Quartermain, who was willing to serve in any civil capacity, said, 'I simply apply for exemption because I do not believe in military service.'[69] A reporter commented that 'a record must have been established this morning when an International socialist, holding conscientious objections, was sent on his way in just about thirty seconds'.[70] It is not known what Quartermain did for the next few months, but he arrived at camp under escort on 26 October 1918; he was court-martialled at Trentham Military Camp in December and sentenced to two years' imprisonment with hard labour.[71]

'If Jesus Christ was now on earth he would be tried for sedition'

In May 1918, Unitarian minister Rev James (Jim) Chapple was tried for sedition in Christchurch at the age of 53. Chapple, his wife Florence and 13 of his 14 children had moved to San Francisco in 1915 to avoid the war. From there Chapple sent back articles to the *Maoriland Worker*, which were published under the heading 'A New Zealander in Exile'.[72] In one of his articles he explained, in stirring literary style, why he felt optimistic about a socialist future: he argued that millions of soldiers who were fighting in the 'inhuman military machine' would come out of the war ready to fight 'our only real enemy – "Capitalism"':

> Comrades, there are stirring times ahead. I feel the snap of it in the air, I feel the tang of it in the brain. My teeth are clinched. My fingers just itch for the coming world-wide struggle against that unholy trinity of Monarchy, Capitalism and militarism. Forward! Line up for the Co-operative Commonwealth and the destruction of Imperialism.
>
> Optimism, not Pessimism![73]

It's not clear why Chapple returned to Christchurch in February 1917, two months before America entered the war, but as a Unitarian minister he continued to speak provocatively on topics such as 'War enables profiteers to stand on velvet whilst the poor stand in queues'.[74] His arrest came after a public meeting in the Greymouth Opera House on 29 March 1918, organised by the Labour Representation Committee and attended by more than 120 people.

The first charge arose from a speech in which he said he hoped there would be no victory in the war:

Rev James (Jim) Chapple. (Alexander Turnbull Library)

> You are under the heels of the War Lords. … I am hoping with a fervent hope that in this war there will be no victor. To pray about a war is blasphemy. A woman goes down the valley of death to bring a child into the world; she nurses it, sends it to school, sees it through the sixth standard; then comes a call to arms, and it goes away to war. What for? To die for its country? No. To die for the profiteer.[75]

He also attacked the churches in his speech:

> If Jesus Christ was now on earth he would be tried for sedition. The churches are the recruiting agent for the world's greatest tragedies. Some of the clergy were now known as the black militia. We are weeding out the best of our manhood and leaving the weeds. Where will it land you?[76]

Chapple was 'a dangerous man to be at large' according to the magistrate, who sentenced him to 11 months in prison.[77] His crowd of supporters, however, mostly women, shook his hand as they filed past him on their way out of court. One woman, who was described as shrieking in a 'strident' voice, expressed her condemnation of the court for convicting a man with 14 children.

Chapple's earlier career as a Presbyterian, then a Unitarian minister, had been no less colourful. Jim and Florence were both Salvation Army officers in Australia, and had been transferred to Invercargill in 1893. Over the next 10 years they served in numerous towns in the South Island until, in 1903, Jim was ordained a Presbyterian minister at St

"THOSE ARE THE SWINE I LOST MY LEG FOR!"

The number cited here as unwilling to serve came from a 1915 government survey.
(William Blomfield, *New Zealand Observer*, 18 December 1915, p. 1)

Andrews, south of Timaru. But the socialist views that he preached from the pulpit eventually led to his resigning from the church in 1910. He went on to found the Timaru Unitarian Church.[78]

'Aliens' argue they are not eligible

There were other reasons given by COs for their refusal to fight. Two objectors argued that they had been wrongly conscripted because they were American citizens.

Hope Whitfield Horne, a 21-year-old variously described as an iron-monger and a hardware salesman of Duncan Street, Spreydon, appealed against conscription in August 1918 on the grounds that he was an American. When he failed to appear for a rehearing of his case, his appeal was dismissed and in November 1918 a court-martial was held in Christchurch. Because of the influenza epidemic the court was closed to the public.

An editorial in *Truth* presented a sympathetic view of the case: it argued that 'Horne is fighting for a principle', and, in order to dispel any idea that he was endeavouring to shirk, it spelled out the circumstances of the case:

> Horne has fulfilled and complied with all the requirements of the constitutional laws of America to retain his citizenship. That the Military authorities regarded Horne as an American is supported beyond dispute, because when Horne went to America some time back the passport issued him by the New Zealand government classed him 'American', while Horne also was given alienage papers.[79]

In the view of the Christchurch *Star*, however, the case had:

> all the appearance of being the excuse of a transparent shirker. Horne showed no desire to serve the country which he is so anxious to claim. The whole history of his actions in reference to military service betrays the fact that his one end and aim was to avoid the camp and the firing line.[80]

Despite the advocacy of *Truth*, Horne was sentenced to a year's imprisonment with hard labour and served nine months before his release at the end of August 1919.

Richard Gadd, who had worked as a blacksmith and a storeman, was married to Annie Gadd, secretary of the Christchurch Women's International League (WIL) and a prominent anti-militarist. Gadd, who was born in America, appealed against his conscription on the grounds that he was an alien and therefore ineligible for service with the New Zealand forces. The chairman of the military service board, Helyar Bishop, disagreed: he said that because Gadd's parents were British subjects, so was Gadd. The *Sun* newspaper described him as an 'emphatic American', and it reported that when his appeal was dismissed, 'the true born American expressed his sarcastic thanks for the "learned decision," swung defiantly on his heel and strode down the room'.[81] His court-martial in the King Edward Barracks two months later was fully reported in the local newspapers because of the complexity of the arguments produced in court. Gadd's mother confirmed that her son had been born in Philadelphia during the four years she lived there, and was registered as American-born. Gadd was sentenced to one year's imprisonment, and at the war's end the religious advisory board (RAB) labelled him as socialist and anti-militarist.[82]

Irish nationalists would not support Britain's war

Some of the Irish settlers living in New Zealand were Irish nationalists who in no way wanted to support Britain's war.[83] South Canterbury farmer Gerald Connor evaded arrest by going into hiding in the West Coast bush after he was called up. As his daughter later wrote, 'He [and] one or two other local Irishmen, including his cousin Campbell Houston, had made no secret of the fact that they would not fight in Capitalistic English wars and on no account would they be responsible for the death of another man in war or otherwise.'[84] Her description of the night when her father, wearing a 'very fine Donegal tweed suit, a heavy coat and slouch hat and carrying a bag',[85] was driven to Temuka in a gig with padded wheels, drawn by the heroic 'Tartan', conveys all the drama and emotion of the enterprise:

The gig lights were not burning and in the gig was Tartan, fit and well fed. He had need to be. During that long, cold, winter night he travelled close to 70 miles, first through Albury, using grass tracks and with leather boots made to go on over his shoes to deaden the sound.

Here and there other horsemen joined them. Below Albury an elderly farmer on a black horse came out of the shadows and wished them well and God speed and almost frightened them to death. Near Sutherlands they were joined by a cousin, also on a horse. At just after midnight they rested Tartan. Just out of Pleasant Point they took a short cut and by three o'clock they were in Temuka, waiting in a side street for a goods train that passed through at 4am. They clambered aboard and slept all the way to Rolleston. From there they caught a train to the West Coast and disappeared into the bush for the duration. The horses that were ridden were planted all over Temuka in the yards of sympathisers or relatives and left to be picked up innocently at some future time. Tartan went home in the frost and dark with still no lights. He had a very short rest and a small feed at 5 a.m. By daylight he was back in the stable at Cricklewood, still lively … his driver slept like the dead, physically and emotionally exhausted.[86]

Connor's flight to the West Coast is an example of what several sources mention as an 'underground railway' which successfully smuggled hundreds of evaders to the West Coast and sometimes out of the country, but because of the secretive nature of the enterprise there are few definite facts to go by. In 1919 it was reported that about 1200 men evaded service by keeping out of the way. Connor's family suffered greatly as a result of his refusal to fight, according to his daughter, being on the receiving end of white feathers in 'neat white envelopes with no name attached'.[87]

Three other Canterbury COs – Edward Mortimer Murrane, William Michael Ryan and Henry Jordan – who were labelled as Irish, either by the RAB or in Henry Holland's *Armageddon or Calvary*, were treated as political or defiant objectors. They said nothing of their Irish allegiance at their military board hearings or their court-martial. This may have been simply prudence on their part – it's impossible now to know what their beliefs were.

Socialist objectors to military service often cited freedom of conscience and their strongly held beliefs as their reasons for objecting. But how did a strongly held humanitarian or ethical belief differ from a religious belief? The intersection between the two was raised by NPC member Ellen Howell after the court-martial of John Roberts. Citing Thomas Carlyle's description of religion as 'the thing a man does practically believe … the thing a man does practically lay to heart and know for certain concerning his vital relations to this mysterious Universe and his duty and destiny there', Howell argued that Roberts was one of those who were 'recognised as sincere by those who knew them and members of a church outside the church'.[88] Howell was advocating for COs to have the same right to successfully appeal against military service on the grounds of their beliefs, just as some religious objectors were able to do.

CHAPTER 6

'LOVE YOUR ENEMIES': RELIGIOUS OBJECTORS 1917–19

With the exception of the few Irish Catholic objectors, none of Canterbury's 36 religious objectors who were imprisoned came from the four largest churches in New Zealand at the time (Anglican, Presbyterian, Catholic or Methodist), whose combined membership comprised 89 per cent of the population. The mainstream churches all saw World War I as fitting into the 'just war' theory initiated by St Augustine in the fifth century and adopted by all the major Christian traditions since that time.[1] The just war doctrine held that war could be justified if it was 'required, as a final resort, to put right or prevent some clear wrong; and where just means are employed, that is, the violence used is strictly limited and highly targeted (aimed only at enemy combatants) and intended only to prevent them from perpetrating further injustices'.[2]

Within the broad doctrine of the just war, church leaders in Christchurch tended to see the war as a holy mission. In September 1915, for example, the Christchurch Anglican dioscesan paper *Church*

News described the war as a righteous cause: 'No nation or group of nations ever had a more holy and rightful and inevitable task than ours today.' Future generations would bless those who 'set the world free from an unholy doom.'[3] The *New Zealand Methodist Times* also developed a view that the war was a holy war: 'the war was a barbarous anachronism which had been deliberately started by a German nation in league with Satan'.[4] Church leaders whose views differed from those of their church received little support from their peers. When the Rev Charles Murray, as convenor of the Presbyterian Church's International Peace Committee, took a report to the Christchurch presbytery advocating an international agreement that all disputes in future be settled by arbitration and conciliation, not one of his colleagues supported him. It was necessary first to crush Germany to obtain peace, argued Rev J. Dickson: 'England could not do otherwise than go to war in defence of the cause of the Empire and of justice and of the smaller nations of the world. She was in the war for peace and justice and righteousness.'[5] The general feeling of the presbytery was that this was not the time to be framing the means of preserving peace, and the report was shelved, Murray reported to Mackie. He felt 'beaten but not overwhelmed'.[6]

Some church leaders offered comfort to the families of soldiers who had been killed by arguing that there was the reward of eternal life for those who lost their lives in war, and for those who 'had made the great sacrifice of sending them forth'.[7] But some Canterbury Christians, notably those from small, fundamentalist sects, took a different view: they argued that the teachings of the Bible prevented them from going to war. About 60 per cent of Canterbury's imprisoned religious objectors came from two little-known sects, the Testimony of Jesus and the Richmond Mission: the former was an import from Northern Ireland, and the latter was an indigenous group founded in Christchurch.

The biblical basis for religious objection

Most people at the time would have been familiar with the King James version of the Old Testament where, in the book of Exodus, Moses, leader of the Israelites, is described as receiving the Ten Commandments directly from God. The commandments gave guiding principles on how people of God should worship, and how they should live with each other, including: 'Thou shalt not kill'.[8] Christians would also have been familiar with the Old Testament prophetic book of Isaiah, which included a vision of peace in the 'last days'. The passage talks about beating swords into ploughshares and pruning hooks, and continues with: 'Nation shall not lift up sword against nation, neither shall they learn war any more'.[9]

But in contrast to these passages the God of the Old Testament often encouraged his people into battle, promising victory to those on his side. World War I conscientious objectors (COs) were more likely to follow the New Testament teachings of Jesus, who was believed to be the son of God and who preached a peaceful way of living. In the 'Sermon on the Mount', for example, Jesus said the peacemakers and those who are 'persecuted for righteousness' sake' are blessed.[10] The fact that Jesus himself had been treated as a criminal when he was arrested, found guilty and put to death was a comfort to the religious COs. Douglas Day, when facing a prison sentence, confirmed that identifying with Jesus helped him cope with the ignominy of being seen as a criminal and imprisoned:

> Surely it is apparent that men with good reputations suffer
> keenly to be numbered with criminals, and were it not that
> our blessed Lord Jesus was numbered with the transgressors
> primarily to make atonement for sins and secondarily suffering
> for righteousness' sake, we could not bear it. But he says 'Blessed
> are they that suffer for righteousness' sake,' and we are still fully
> convinced that we are amongst that number.[11]

Members of the military service boards were well versed in the Bible and at times they challenged objectors with verses that apparently supported the use of violence. In January 1917 the chairman of the Canterbury Military Service Board, J. S. Evans, cited both the Old and the New Testament when hearing the appeal from Thomas Nuttall. There was nothing in the scriptures to support the argument of the religious objectors, said Evans: 'God not only enjoined war in the Old Testament, but instances were recorded in which he had taken part in battles on behalf of the children of Israel. In the New Testament Christ said: "I come not to send peace on earth but a sword."' Nuttall, who had already served several prison sentences and lost his civil rights in the pre-war period, was quick to respond: 'I think that is perfectly true. I have felt the sword of persecution for the past five years.'[12]

The New Zealand Government was not entirely unsympathetic to genuine religious objectors, but it did not want to make exemption too easy, or to encourage shirkers. The Military Service Act provided for some Christians to successfully appeal against military service on the grounds of their religion, but only if they belonged to a religious body whose doctrine held 'the bearing of arms and the performance of combatant service to be contrary to divine revelation'.[13] In fact only two small churches – the Society of Friends and the Christadelphians – met the criteria, although Seventh-day Adventist leaders successfully argued in 1917 that their members should be exempted under the Act.[14]

But members of such churches did not necessarily take advantage of their exemption. The Military Service Act of 1916 said that Christians who were exempted would still be required to do non-combatant service, either in New Zealand or in the Medical Corps or the Army Service Corps overseas. Quakers, who did not want to be given preferential treatment over other equally sincere objectors, advocated that civilian, not military work should be offered to all genuine objectors.[15]

Realising that nearly all religious objectors would end up in prison, the Defence Department first decided to extend its offer of non-combatant overseas service to any objector who attended his hearing and whose religious beliefs were 'genuine' and long-standing (from before the outbreak of war); and it later agreed, informally, that agricultural work could be offered to genuine objectors.[16] This study of religious objectors focuses on those who served time in prison, many of whom were offered non-combatant work with the military, which was rejected.

The 'shirkers' section of the Act

After the introduction of conscription in 1916, in an effort to obtain recruits as quickly as possible the government turned to section 35 of the Military Service Act, sometimes referred to as the 'shirkers' section, which provided for the calling up of brothers in a family of two or more eligible men, if none of them had enlisted. Such men were liable for immediate conscription but could appeal to a military service board. This was the case for brothers from two South Canterbury farming families in 1917.[17]

David Gray appeared before the military service board in Ashburton on 7 February 1917 alongside his brothers John, Samuel and William. They all lived in the Hinds district: John was a blacksmith from Coldstream, and Samuel, William and David were farmers and shearers from Lowcliffe. The four brothers, described as 'diffident young men', belonged to the Testimony of Jesus sect and were appealing solely on religious grounds. Their case was weakened when one brother said they had adopted their 'non-combatant' religion after the war had started. The decision was that two of the brothers would have to serve, and as David and John did not own land, their appeals were dismissed. William and Samuel, meanwhile, were allowed to stay on their farms and take their chances in the ballot: William was later conscripted and began a 14-month sentence in 1918.[18]

Named in the New Zealand Census as 'Christian Assemblies', and referred to by some as 'Cooneyites', the Testimony of Jesus had been brought to New Zealand by evangelists from a schism of the Faith Mission in Northern Ireland in 1905. By 1917 there were 700–800 members in New Zealand, with 24 ministers or evangelists. The sect had no written constitution but followed New Testament teachings and believed, among other things, that the bearing of arms was forbidden by Christ. Membership was dependent on a willingness to observe the teachings of Christ in everyday life. The evangelists, who were required to have given away all their possessions to the poor, were chosen at annual conventions and were dependent on voluntary contributions. There was no formal structure to the sect and it did not own any property; the weekly meetings were held in members' homes.[19] Their evangelism seems to have been particularly effective in rural mid and south Canterbury, as nearly all of Canterbury's 13 Testimony of Jesus members who were imprisoned were agricultural workers from Lowcliffe, Coldstream, Claremont, Mt Somers and Greendale. Together they accounted for almost half of the 28 members from throughout New Zealand detained during the war.[20]

Deported to Europe

David Gray's experiences were probably the most horrific of any of Canterbury's COs. His first sentence was unusually long at 84 days and, apparently due to a clerical error, he was classed as a 'defiant' objector.[21] On 14 July 1917 he was one of 14 COs who were plucked overnight from prisons in Wellington (in his case from Mt Cook Prison) and transported to Europe. The New Zealand Government wanted to demonstrate that if COs were placed in the frontline of battle they would capitulate and join the forces. But the intention had been to send only defiant or non 'genuine' COs; as a religious objector, Gray should never have been sent. When this was realised he was allowed to remain at Sling Camp in the south of England before being sent back to New Zealand.[22]

As one of the 14 deported COs, David Gray appears in Archibald Baxter's 1939 memoir *We Will Not Cease*. The two men first met in the 'clink' of the transport ship *Waitemata* – a single room that soon became stuffy and smelly after bad weather caused most of the deportees to suc-

cumb to seasickness. Those in charge tried to force them to wear a uniform, but when they refused, their own clothes were returned to them. There was a measles outbreak on the ship; Baxter and two others stayed in South Africa to recover, while Gray and the remaining deportees continued their voyage on ships of the Union Castle line.

Soon after Christmas 1917 Baxter came across Gray at Sling Camp in England, where he was heating up something in an oil drum over a fire. Gray explained that he was in uniform because the authorities were communicating with New Zealand in order to decide what to do with him. He'd been told he was different

David Gray, seated left, watching another CO being dressed in uniform. (Archives New Zealand Te Rua Mahara o te Kāwanatanga)

175

from the other deportees because they saw him as a 'genuine' objector, and he was doing some gardening around the camp. Gray's account of his time on the *Norman Castle* between South Africa and England made Baxter feel he had been fortunate to have had measles:

> They were forcibly dressed in uniform, their own clothes taken away and not returned to them. When they took the uniform off and went about in underclothes, their underclothes were taken away. They were hosed down and then dressed only in uniform. Though they had been brought out on deck in front of the passengers, they took the uniform off and went naked. After a while they managed to get underclothes again and went about in them. Before landing they were dressed in uniform again and some of them who refused to walk were dragged off. We had certainly missed hardships through having measles.[23]

Gray was discharged from the NZ Expeditionary Force in England on 21 May 1919.[24]

'The teaching of Jesus was binding'

Isaac Aicken, a labourer, and his brother John, a farmer, both of Lowcliffe, were also called up under section 35 on 17 February, and they too appealed for exemption on religious grounds as members of the Testimony of Jesus. Isaac's appeal was dismissed and he served almost two years in prison. John was allowed to take his chance in the ballot.[25]

Other members of the Testimony of Jesus were called up by ballot: Robert Clayton Patton, a contractor from Mt Somers, was called up in the first ballot and appeared before the military service board in January 1917. When he was questioned about the Testimony of Jesus, Patton confirmed that: 'The teaching of Jesus was binding. The whole of the teaching of Christ had been contrary to the taking up of arms.'[26] Asked if the group had any actual churches, he replied, 'We make our own body. We are taught not to carry arms to destroy our brother-men.'[27] When asked if he would undertake military service other than fighting Patton replied emphatically that he would not.

Patton, John Gray, Isaac Aicken and several other members of the Testimony of Jesus who were already in Details Hut 19 at Trentham did not receive their first prison sentence until 31 August 1917, while the authorities determined whether members of the Testimony of Jesus could be eligible for exemption. Because of the change in the regulations regarding non-combatant service, a rehearing on behalf of about eighteen appellants, most of whom were already 'in camp', was heard in July 1917. John Findlay KC appeared for the appellants and attempted to demonstrate that not bearing arms was a cardinal doctrine of the group, despite the fact that it had no written charter, rules or constitution. But while Findlay confidently stated that all the appellants were willing to sign an undertaking to perform non-combatant work, it would appear this was not the case, and most of the men listed at the time of the appeal went on to serve prison terms.[28]

Membership of the Testimony of Jesus was not formalised and some 'members' preferred to say they belonged to no particular church. James (Jim) Vallance, for example, came from a farm at Coopers Creek, near Oxford. He belonged to a small evangelistic church there, started by Adam Hutchison and Joe Williamson, who had arrived at Coopers Creek from Northern Ireland in 1906. The church had sent Vallance as a missionary to South Australia in 1908, though as a travelling evangelist he was in Auckland when he was balloted for military service in December 1917.[29] He told the military service board in May 1918 he was not ordained or attached to any particular church, but was a 'a member of Christ' who received no salary but lived on what Christians gave him, and occasionally worked on farms in return for his keep. He later refused non-combatant work on religious grounds.

James Vallance as a young man. (Vallance family)

Fellow evangelist Bertie Morgan, who accompanied Vallance to his military board hearing, had been working as a farmhand in Canterbury. He told the board their denomination had no particular name and that he had not lodged an appeal because he thought it would be useless. He lived by voluntary offerings and tried to preach the Gospel as Christ had done.[30] Similarly John Ernest Holtham, despite giving evidence in court as a member of the Testimony of Jesus, preferred to say that he 'did not belong to any particular sect and recognised no body or head. He was an undenominational preacher and did evangelistic work in the streets or in public halls. His religion was simply what came out of his own brain or experience.'[31]

Draughtsman, artist and photographer Arthur McIntyre was another religious objector who 'did not state what sect' at his court-martial in November 1917.[32] It was the religious advisory board (RAB) which, after interviewing him in Rotoaira in February 1919, described him as a member of the Testimony of Jesus. With eight other members of the sect in Rotoaira at the time, it's possible his first association with the sect occurred while he was in prison.

'Treasure in heaven'

Adherents of the Richmond Mission, based in the Christchurch suburb of Richmond, lived by a literal reading of the New Testament and, like other sect members, came in for harsh criticism from military board chairmen and the newspapers. Twelve members of the Richmond Mission are known to have taken a stand against military service during World War I, and nine were imprisoned.[33]

The group was founded by David Smith and his wife Florence (née Pashby), who came from a Methodist background. David had been converted to Christianity during the voyage from England to Sydney in 1897. After their marriage in 1900 they began holding bible study and prayer meetings in their home, and as the meetings grew in size they met in the Linwood Library, and then in the Druids Hall in Avalon Street. In 1911 one of their members bought an acre of land on the corner of Petrie Street and North Avon Road, and it was here that the mission built its first – and later – halls. Eventually Smith, a gifted teacher and preacher, gave up his job in order to work full-time as an evangelist.

Smith did all he could to try and persuade the authorities that mission members should be exempt for military service on religious grounds. By June 1917 the sect had four members in detention at Trentham, three of whom had been exempted from CMT pre-war. In a letter to Colonel Robert Tate, adjutant-general of New Zealand's military forces, Smith argued that the Richmond Mission fell within the definition of the Military Service Act: 'We are truly a religious body and the tenets and doctrines held since the inception of the Mission declare the bearing of arms and performance of any military duties whatsoever to be contrary to Divine Revelation.'[34] The members in detention were prepared to do civil work under civil authority, he said, and if members became eligible for this under new regulations, the sect would consider withdrawing the petition that they had sent to James Allen.

Tate was evidently convinced by the Richmond Mission's case. In a memo to the solicitor-general he argued that sects such as the Richmond Mission, despite not having any written doctrine or tenets, could still show evidence that they had consistently held the sincere belief that bearing arms and engaging in combatant service were against divine revelation. The conscription of their members would lead to the 'making of martyrs and the causing of infinite trouble to the Military Authorities', he concluded.[35] But despite Tate's views, an application from Smith for a rehearing for two of the members in detention who had pre-war exemptions was unsuccessful. Smith was told the only way he could appeal was to Parliament.[36]

The military service board hearing of brothers Albert and Herbert Church, farmers of Greendale, called up under the 'shirkers' section, is a good example of the complete lack of understanding between sect and military board members. It also shows up the differences in interpretation that could be applied to the teachings of Christ on the subject of personal wealth. The board chairman cited scriptural teaching that said followers of Christ should 'sell all you have and give to the poor and lay up for yourself treasure in heaven' – to which Herbert Church replied, 'It all depends how you look at it.' Further discussion led to the chairman declaring Church's attitude was 'too absurdly ridiculous for anything'.[37] The appeal of the older brother, Albert, was dismissed and he received his first prison sentence on 23 April 1917. Herbert's appeal was allowed, and when he was later called up by the ballot he said he was prepared to serve in a non-combatant capacity.[38]

The issue of religious objectors owning property was brought up again when farmer Keith Hamilton Broughton of Waireka, Homebush, appealed on religious grounds, and on the grounds that his being called up was against the public interest because of his occupation. His statement about his religious belief relied chiefly on the Sermon on the Mount. Because he lived in the country, he said, he belonged to no particular denomination, but was 'in fellowship' with the Richmond Mission. When the chairman of the military service board commented that he saw no logic in 'a follower of Christ having so much property', Broughton's father, speaking for his son, replied, 'I think it is because I am a follower of Christ that I have so much property.' Broughton senior went on to contend that 'the scriptures did not mean that a man should not hold property'.[39]

'Would not fight "in this world"'

Two brothers, Percy Dodge and Charles Wilfred Forest Dodge, both members of the Richmond Mission, received very different treatment as religious objectors, probably because they were called up 18 months apart. Percy was the first to appear before the military service board, in March 1917, where he declared he would 'not render non-combatant service', and would not fight 'in this world'. He served two prison sentences: one for 11 months and the second for two years.[40] In September 1918 his older brother Charles said he was not prepared to serve in the medical corps because he believed in Jesus 'and it is contrary to His teachings'. The chairman of the board, Helyar Bishop, was frustrated by this: he told Dodge he was 'absolutely hopeless. There is no use talking to you. You set up standards to follow, and won't let anybody else have standards.'[41] Although Dodge told the military service board he was quite prepared to suffer for the stand he took, there is no record of his being in prison at the end of the war, nor does he have a military record.

'Snuffling "conscientious objectors"'

Ernest Munns. (Canterbury Museum)

Two other Richmond Mission members, Ernest Edward Munns and Douglas Day, were imprisoned after refusing to serve in the medical corps because it was under military authority.[42] Day's refusal to do 'ambulance' work' was reported in the press as an 'uncompromising reply'. Day disagreed: he wrote that it had been a respectful 'No sir', and he had felt no need to enlarge on his reasons for his conscientious refusal, given that members of the mission had previously given 'a complete statement of our reasons from a Scriptural standpoint'.[43] Religious objectors had become used to disparaging remarks from the chairmen of the military service boards, but Day's letter prompted a blistering attack on the Richmond Mission and COs from the editor of the *Sun* newspaper:

> If our correspondent chooses to throw in his lot with a sect which interprets Scripture in such a way as to absolve him from the duty of striking a blow for freedom and civilisation, he deserves no sympathy whatever. Brave and gallant fellows are giving their lives by the thousand to protect snuffling 'conscientious objectors' from the fate of the inhabitants of northern France and Belgium, and any man who would rather be enslaved by the Huns than lift his little finger in resistance to them is unfit to be a citizen of a free country.[44]

The few letters that Douglas Day wrote to his family from Lyttelton and Paparua prisons show that he was sustained throughout his incarceration by his intense religious faith. From Lyttelton he wrote: 'Here

I am alone so far as Christian fellowship is concerned but "He abideth faithful and in Him I have perfect peace".[45] He gained great comfort from being among other members of the Richmond Mission when he eventually arrived at Paparua, and informed his family in December 1918 that though there had been times of acute spiritual suffering, the last six months had been 'at times the best I have ever known'. He went on to slightly misquote from John Bunyan's poem 'Prison Meditations':

I am indeed in prison now,
in body, but my mind,
Is free to study Christ and know
Unto me He is kind.

For though men keep me outward man
Within their locks and Bars,
yet by the faith of Christ I can
Mount higher than the stars.[46]

Douglas Day (left) with his sisters Margery and Muriel and brother Arthur. (Author's collection)

The stigma against COs seems to have influenced former members of the mission even 80 years later. A history of the mission published in 1995, written using information gained from interviews with former members, acknowledges that many members of the mission were COs in both world wars, but mentions only three of the World War I COs by name. (Others are mentioned in the text but are not identified as COs.) 'Although there were accusations made about the mission "making people conchies", this was not true,' former members are quoted as saying. There was never any preaching for or against war: 'It was always left up to the individual and not one sermon supported or opposed such a stand.'[47]

The Exclusive Brethren was another sect that had no written creed or articles of faith. Members lived according to a literal reading of scripture, and while this led some members to oppose military service, others volunteered.[48] Exclusive Brethren member Frederick Ernest Dodge, brother of Richmond Mission members Percy and Charles Dodge, was called up in January 1918. He later told his son he would not have passed the medical test and had objected to military service 'as a matter of Christian principle'.[49]

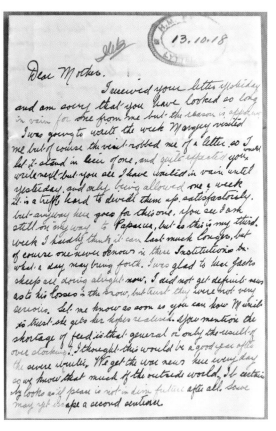

Douglas Day's letter to his mother from Lyttelton prison, 13 October 1918. (Author's collection)

'These fellows are all mad'

Even the objectors who belonged to churches that fitted the strict criteria for exemption came in for harsh public criticism. Many of them refused to co-operate with the military altogether.[50]

Canterbury Quaker Noel Goldsbury came from a family who had made a considerable contribution to Quakerism in New Zealand. As might be expected, his objection to military service was based on the Quaker peace testimony, which dated back to the founding of the group in the 1600s. It was a doctrine of conscience, not a commitment to absolute pacifism, and had been publicly reiterated by New Zealand

Noel Goldsbury, c. 1913. (Canterbury Museum)

Quakers in several statements. In 1915, for example, the General Meeting of the Society of Friends in New Zealand had declared their belief in the full revelation of God being in Christ. Their actions must therefore be guided by the tenor of Christ's teachings:

> Since He has said 'Love your enemies, do good to them that hate you' … and since the whole tenor of His teaching is that loving-kindness, and mercy, and a generosity that has little regard for selfish interests should be the mainsprings of our actions, we cannot but believe that war, which involves the wilful infliction of sorrow and suffering upon our fellows, is the very negation of His Spirit; and not only war, but all that causes or tends to cause feelings of distrust and bitterness between man and man.[51]

In July 1918 Goldsbury refused to undergo a medical examination because to do so would be to obey a military order. His first appearance before the military service board concluded with the chairman of the board making the derogatory comment: 'These fellows are all mad, I think.'[52] By the time Goldsbury appeared before a district court-martial in Christchurch he had appealed to a higher appeal board, and he claimed that he should not have been arrested while an appeal was pending. He objected to being tried by court-martial, refused to plead and refused to give evidence on oath. He was found guilty and sentenced to 11 months' imprisonment.[53] In a letter he wrote requesting leave of absence until his release from prison, he cited the teachings of Christ: 'As I have been imprisoned by the military authorities for obeying what I conceive to be the Divine Will revealed by the teachings of Jesus Christ, I beg to apply for leave of absence ...'[54]

Goldsbury was employed as a secretary, registrar and part-time teacher at the Christchurch Technical College, and when the college board granted his requested leave of absence by one vote, a furore erupted in the Christchurch press. 'Goldsbury can have no claim on our sympathy,' said the *Sun*, and it called for the decision to be reversed.[55] Letter writers joined in: one said Goldsbury was not 'a fit and proper person to have the remotest connection with the education of our young people in such times as these'.[56] Board member B. Seth Smith announced his resignation. The chairman of the board defended its decision, and Goldsbury's wife Jennie drew attention to the inconsistent way in which the Military Service Act was being interpreted.[57] Organisations that granted funds to the technical college, including local bodies, the School Committee Association and the Agricultural and Pastoral Association, discussed the issue, and some said they would withhold funding if Goldsbury's position was held for him until his release.[58]

With the financial viability of the college under threat, the board rescinded the motion that had approved Goldsbury's leave of absence, with only four members voting against this. Just two board members – Ada Wells and Henry Worrall – spoke in support of him. By this time Goldsbury had resigned from his position, but this was not enough to stop the Canterbury Chamber of Commerce withdrawing its support for the college in January 1919, and its representative on the college board resigned.[59] Despite the furore, there may have been some concession to the fact that Goldsbury was a Quaker, in that he served just eight months in prison.

Walter Edward Robinson and Joseph McMillan were members of the Seventh-day Adventist Church, one of the few religious groups that met the criteria for religious exemption under the Military Service Act. The church had been active in New Zealand since 1885, and by 1916 it had 1534 adherents, all of whom took seriously the Old Testament commandment not to kill. Yet the appeals of both Robinson and McMillan were dismissed, probably because they had joined the church after the war had begun. Robinson, a farm labourer, declined to serve in the New Zealand Medical Corps; and McMillan, a fruiterer, argued unsuccessfully that he should be exempt because he was Australian, and there was no conscription in Australia. Both men received prison sentences.[60]

Other Seventh-day Adventists agreed to perform non-combatant work, including Clarence Amyes, a farmer from Prebbleton who went to work on a 'state farm'; and two Christchurch men, David Barlass and John Thompson, whose cases had been reheard after the church received new documentary evidence.[61]

Disillusioned Baptists

The published histories of the Oxford Terrace Baptist Church make no mention at all of the strong pacifist stance taken by some of its members. Baptists, like Quakers, put an emphasis on freedom of conscience,

THE SHIRKER'S LAST REFUGE.

New-born Conscientious Objector Shirker:—
Other refuge have I none, hangs my useless soul on Thee,
Leave, ah leave me not alone, still support and comfort me,

'The Shirker's Last Refuge' depicts a 'new-born' CO seeking refuge with the Society of Friends, which was one of the few religious groups to meet the criteria for religious objection under the Military Service Act. The Act got around this by requiring religious objectors to have belonged to their churches for at least two years. (William Blomfield, *New Zealand Observer*, 1 July 1916, p. 16)

and they brought to New Zealand a long history of critique of the state and dissent from state interference in religion. For a number of radical Baptists this aligned with anti-militarist conviction, but opinion varied and the church did not develop a strong peace tradition;[62] instead, it tended to discourage discussion of contentious political issues because of the division this could cause in congregations where individual conscience and belief were respected.

Charles Mackie, who was 45 when the war began, was not called up. Thomas Nuttall, however, appealed against military service in January 1917, basing his objections on the New Testament. While the military service board was satisfied that Nuttall held a genuine 'conscientious objection', his appeal was dismissed because the Baptist Church did not have a doctrine against war. His case prompted about twenty people, mostly Baptists, to meet a few days later and plan an appeal to the minister of defence. [63] Whether this appeal eventuated is not known, but Nuttall does not seem to have served a prison sentence. Nuttall himself did not understand why he was not in prison: he wrote to his friend Frank Money in Trentham Military Camp that he felt almost ashamed that he was still free and comfortable, but he was still convinced that

Thomas and Maud Nuttall, who married in 1919. (Ron Nuttall)

it must be part of God's plan: 'I should be by your side up there, but we can never fully understand God's providences. I feel sometimes it is because of my work at Bromley, because Sunday School, Services, and Guild are mainly dependent upon me, and it's possible it would collapse if I were taken away for a long time.'[64] Nuttall had been sent four medical notices, the last one served by a man in uniform. He was out of work and had prepared himself for prison or camp. He was seeing a great deal of Mackie, and was supported by his Christian faith: 'Things work together for good to them who love God,' he told Money.[65]

We can only speculate about why Nuttall did not, apparently, serve a prison term. Was it due to the appeal made to Allen? Was it fear of a public demonstration in Christchurch? Or did he develop health problems that meant he was unfit for service? Nuttall himself speculated that it might have been due to fear of insurrection in the military camps: 'the presence of such a number who are not under discipline, does not inspire greater discipline to those who are training for service'.[66]

In 1917 a special meeting was held at the Linwood Baptist Church to consider the conscience clause in the Military Service Act. The meeting was called by 12 members of the church, and 26 members were present. The first motion put to the meeting thanked Thomas Nuttall for his work at Bromley: it was carried unanimously. The second motion, moved by Charles Mackie and seconded by Nuttall's mother Louisa, was a long statement asserting the primacy of conscience in the life of the Baptist Church, protesting against the persecution of one of its members, and asking that all such people should be discharged from being military reservists: 'That every Christian is bound by the dictates of his or her conscience absolutely in matters of conflict, we wish to express, as a church of the Baptist order, our hearty agreement with this view … We believe that the forcing of conscience by whatsoever authority is contrary to Divine revelation and amounts to persecution of the grossest kind'.[67] The resolution was to be sent to the prime minister. Twelve people supported it, and 13 were against.

The split in the congregation threatened the church's existence. Membership declined from 69 to 35 in 1919; those who left included Charles and Ethel Mackie (who started attending the Quaker meetings instead) and Thomas Nuttall. Historian Laurie Guy has noted that, given that 11 of the church's members were serving in the armed forces, the motion could not have done other than split the church.[68]

'God alone is the giver of life'

The only Christchurch member of the Baptist Church who is known to have been imprisoned as a CO in World War I was Frank Money. In 1910 Money had left the Salvation Army and moved to the Oxford Terrace Baptist Church, where he got to know Mackie.[69] Like Mackie he became disillusioned with the church.

In a letter to the Defence Department written in January 1917, Money explained that his objections were religious, and a closer study of the New Testament had strengthened his beliefs: 'I find it impossible to take part in a struggle which has for its object the killing of men. God alone is the giver of life … I have no right to take a life, or even assist other men to do so. I know this action to be contrary to the laws of the land, nevertheless I am fully persuaded this action is right in the sight of Almighty God.'[70]

His faith stayed strong while he was in prison, but he felt alienated from the church. Hearing church bells ringing on Sunday prompted him to write: 'This however does not concern me as I only look upon such institutions as social centres. I believe the true Christian of today is to be found outside her walls.'[71] Later the same month Money received a letter from Ethel Mackie, who told him that she and Mackie had had to relinquish their work at Linwood and were praying for God to open up the way for them: 'I cannot understand the Ministers of Religion at all,' she wrote, 'they are the people, who should be able to help us in matters such as these, instead they are going with the crowd, and crying out for Barabas, instead of Jesus.'[72]

Money's disillusionment with the church became even more profound as the war progressed. While he was serving his second prison sentence in Waikeria, he reported he was among 'stacks' of objectors with a wide range of beliefs. He often felt ashamed of others who professed to be Christian but who had failed to follow their master's teaching, in comparison with many of the 'infidels' in prison who had a noble spirit and high ideals towards the brotherhood of man. The mainstream churches had failed miserably, but that only made it all the more imperative that 'we who are standing for the truth should be faithful'.[73] Although his time in prison was 'miserably wasted', he had spent much time reading and the Bible had been a great book for him.

Money was confident that whatever happened, God would take care of him. Towards the end of his first prison term he wrote: 'After that, God alone knows what I with my other companions will be called upon to undertake … God has called me to bear witness in this manner and I care not what may happen for He is more than all that may be against me.'[74] He added that his time in prison had been a time of bodily rest and spiritual refreshment, because never since his school days had he had so much leisure time. As an evangelist he hoped 'each day to be able to say a word that will help one or another of my companions to put their trust in God'.[75] He enjoyed the times when he was among other Christian objectors – there were differences in their ideas, but they all agreed on one great issue: 'War is the Devil and no Christian can retain the favour of God while meddling with it.'[76]

'Convinced but unaffiliated'

Some of Canterbury's objectors who were classified as religious objectors did not claim to belong to any particular church. But, as noted by historian Geoffrey Troughton, 'Christian ideas, convictions and frames of reference were widely diffused in New Zealand before the Second World War. Christianity's role in shaping moral imaginations and convictions about war and peace could reach beyond the churches.'[77]

Artist and cartoonist Kennaway Henderson, at the age of 39, became one of the older of the Canterbury COs to be imprisoned, and one of the few who were married. From the statement he sent to Allen as minister of defence, which was read at his first court-martial in March 1918, it is clear that he held strong religious convictions, but at the same time he delivered a withering criticism of the church. 'I am endeavouring to show,' he said, 'that the Church has for the sake of power, supported militarism since Constantine, AND THAT MY RELIGIOUS CONVICTIONS ARE BASED UPON THE TEACHING OF

CHRIST AND ALL OF OUR GREATEST THINKERS.'[78] He accused the church of turning its back on the teachings of Christ on the subject of war, and he argued that 'a man need not belong to a church to be a conscientious objector; all that was necessary was that he should be a true follower of Jesus Christ'.[79] There were churchmen who had shares in munition factories, and firms that were said to be helping the empire but were, in reality, making huge profits from the war, he said. At the end of his statement he was applauded by a number of spectators in the court.

Testimony given in court by his friends Leonard Booth and the Christchurch writer Blanche Baughan (who read Henderson's statement to the court 'in her lovely cultured voice'), said that Henderson's

Canterbury Society of Arts class, c. 1912. Standing, left to right: Cecil Kelly, Edwin Bartley, Raymond McIntyre, Alfred Wilson Walsh. Seated: Leonard (Len) Hampden Booth, Andrew Kennaway Henderson, Sydney Lough Thompson, William Menzies Gibb, Charles E. Bickerton. Henderson served two prison sentences as a conscientious objector and was disappointed his friend Len Booth successfully appealed against military service. (Alexander Turnbull Library)

anti-militarism was based primarily on an ethical foundation and that he had adopted Leo Tolstoy's attitudes to war and militarism.[80] Another friend recalled that long before war was declared, Henderson had decided he would be a CO: he had told friends, 'I would go quite mad if I had to kill a man.' He had a 'long-standing conviction of the insanity of war itself and an unshakeable belief that all those who derived prof- its from militarism were the enemies of mankind,' wrote his friend and biographer, Winston Rhodes.[81] A compassionate man, Henderson had contributed to two books of 'Quips and Caricatures' in 1915 to raise funds for the Belgian Relief Fund, the first of which raised 95 pounds. He was reportedly disappointed that his pacifist friends Len Booth and Arthur McIntyre had appealed against their call-up, while he had taken the more defiant path of ignoring it. Booth was granted an exemption because he was the only support for his widowed mother, but McIntyre served most of a two-year sentence.[82]

'I believe War to be wrong'

Robin Page was another religious objector who was not affiliated to any particular faith. His statement at his court-martial has survived, along with a letter from his mother, Sarah, and they give good insight into

Robin Page with his brother Fred and two friends. Left to right: Alf Paterson, Fred Page, Norman Richmond, Robin Page. (Page family)

Page's beliefs and his intellect. Page described himself as a Christian, and told his court-martial at Trentham Military Camp that while he could find nothing in the New Testament that supported war, he found much that was against it. 'As a Christian, I believe War to be wrong and think that our aim in life is Love, and not Hate and Fear.'[83] Sarah, who attended the court-martial, wrote a detailed account of the exchange that took place between Page and the president of the court. War was profitless and calamitous, said Page, and because he regarded war as 'simply organised murder' he was not

Norman Bell (right) with his brother Harold, c. 1909. (Canterbury Museum)

prepared to do any non-combatant work for the military machine. He proceeded to ask the president of the court whether he believed God could protect them, to which the major replied, 'physically most certainly not'. When the president said that Christianity could do nothing for Page in the present time, Page replied, 'That is where we differ.'[84]

Norman Bell was a graduate of Canterbury College with a brilliant academic record; he then went on to Cambridge University in 1909 to do a BA in Classics. Over the next seven years in England and Europe he carried out an extraordinary amount of postgraduate study in the subjects that most interested him – religion, chemistry and education – at London University, the University of Liverpool, St Andrew's University in Fife, and the University of Bern in Switzerland. He graduated with a Bachelor of Divinity and worked in several scientific labs. While in England and Europe he became familiar with the Free Religious Movement, which advocated pacifism, and which featured large in his later life. He returned to New Zealand in October 1916, where he began a short-lived teaching position at Christchurch Boys' High School in March 1917.[85]

Soon after his return, Bell published a 20-page pamphlet, 'A Gospel of Universal Compassion', which set out his theological position, including his pacifist beliefs. Like other religious COs, these were based on the New Testament teachings to love your enemies and do good to those who hate you. This love or compassion left no room for anger, wrote Bell's biographer: 'only unlimited forgiveness is permissible'. Wrongdoers should not be resisted with force, but 'all wrong should be endured without complaint.'[86] When asked to state his religion, Bell described himself as 'a student of religion'.[87] Further evidence of his high moral character was the report that he had 'begged to be sent to the trenches with his brother, just on the grounds that prison was safer and more comfortable, and that it was not danger he wished to avoid; but "sin"'.[88] Because of his very poor eyesight, Bell could have avoided military service by submitting to a medical examination, but he refused; he was court-martialled at Trentham Military Camp and received a two-year prison sentence.[89]

Lancelot Reeves Robinson, another non-affiliated CO, chose not to submit to a medical examination because he was 'not of this world'.[90] When he was interviewed in prison at Kaingaroa he said he 'belonged to the Lord Jesus Christ and had nothing to do with war: he belonged to the One True Church but recognised no sect'.[91] Robinson was classified as a religious objector at the end of the war.

Charles Morgan Williams in 1944.
(Williams family)

'Thou shalt not kill' commandment forgotten by churches

Among Canterbury's COs who were imprisoned were some who were strongly socialist but were clearly influenced by a Christian upbringing. Reg Williams was classified as a socialist and a 'defiant' objector, but he had grown up in a strongly religious family. His older brother Morgan, who was too old to be conscripted, later said they were brought up in a religious atmosphere: their father was a Calvinist Methodist who believed in predestination, and their mother was a Wesleyan Methodist who believed in free will. She was a fundamentalist 'who believed in the literal accuracy of every word in the Bible. In my early teens I went to Church (Wesleyan) at least twice every Sunday and liked it.'[92]

Morgan Williams was shocked by the churches' response to the war, and he resigned from membership of the Ohoka Methodist Church: 'The commandment "Thou shalt not kill" was forgotten and in the Churches of both Germany and the British Empire, both sides were praying to

Charles Warden outside his cottage 'Gaya', a former public works house at Arthur's Pass. (Canterbury Museum)

the same God for victory.'[93] For a time he attended some of the meetings of the Christchurch Quakers, until he got too busy looking after a large herd of cows. Reg also disassociated himself from the 'sects and dogmas' of Christianity, but he believed in Christian ethics. He regarded Christ as a historical character, 'a leader of men whose example was to be admired and followed'.[94]

Charles Warden is a CO who fits no category neatly, though he was classed, probably correctly, as being both religious and a socialist. Employed as a clerk by the Lyttelton Harbour Board and regarded as 'a very useful assistant', his pacifist views became apparent when all employees of the board were required to enrol as reservists in the New Zealand Expeditionary Force.[95] Warden complied, but when he provided evidence of his enrolment to the board, he added the words, 'without however admitting liability under same' – an action that cost him his job.[96] Warden believed the Military Service Act was 'un-Christian and unconstitutional', and he disagreed with the view that conscription would help maintain 'the liberty loved by all Britishers' which had been 'wrested at great cost from both Kings and Parliaments'.[97] Christian concepts are apparent in the letter he wrote to the board following his dismissal:

> When men recognise that Love is stronger than War, and try to do to others as they would that others do to them, then perhaps the greed of gain and the lust of power which make war possible, will die out; the cruelty and misery will cease; and the Kingdom of Heaven may be recognised on Earth. This is the Ideal, which we must ever try to hold before us even though we fail and blunder again and again.[98]

Non-combatant objectors

Objectors who took up non-combatant service were part of the military, and their movements can be traced through their military record. But in the case of several Canterbury objectors, although they were willing to serve in a non-combatant role, because they don't have a personal military record we do not know whether they served or not.[99]

Stretcher bearer Silas Stedman in uniform. (Stedman family)

Silas Stedman is one who did serve in a non-combatant role. His appeal against military service was complicated by the fact that he worked for the Railways Department, which successfully sought an exemption for him because he was doing essential work. When the department later learned he was a CO, however, they attempted to have the appeal for exemption waived, whereupon the chairman of the military service board declared 'the exemption continues unless you give him the sack'.[100] Perhaps he was given the sack, because the following month he appealed as a CO.

Although Silas is believed to have been a member of the Brethren Church by this time, he told the board hearing he was a Christian who did not belong to any particular religious body, and that he was willing to serve in the non-combatant branches. His enlistment and training followed soon after, and in November 1917 he travelled to Britain on the *Willochra*, where he arrived in January 1918. He spent some time in Ewshot, the main training camp for the New Zealand Medical Corps in England, and was then deployed to France with the No. 1 New Zealand Field Ambulance, where he worked as a stretcher bearer. A stretcher bearer's main responsibility was to pick up wounded men from the battlefield. It was dangerous work and Silas was wounded in August 1918, during the Second Battle of Bapaume. He was treated at a casualty clearing station and at a series of field hospitals in France, then was sent back to the No. 2 New Zealand General Hospital at Walton on Thames. After a period of convalescence in England he was discharged as unfit to serve because of his wounds, and he left for New Zealand in June 1919.[101]

Members of the clergy were not exempt from military service, but appeals by the Methodist Church against conscription of their ministers were always successful. Methodist minister Percy Battey, however, appeared before a military service board where he asked to be allowed to serve in a non-combatant role. The military board made a recommendation and three months later Battey entered the medical corps. From there he was seconded for duty with the Young Men's Christian Association (YMCA), and served in France with the New Zealand Field Artillery as a chaplain and YMCA secretary.[102]

On the run?

Roy Bradley was arrested at Big Bay in Fiordland, an extremely remote and rugged part of the South Island, after the military authorities received information that a party of men wanted for military service had gone from Lake Wakatipu to the West Coast. Bradley admitted he had failed to attend a medical examination, and agreed to come out voluntarily. He had tramped to Big Bay with his brother, leaving a day's food in each hut on the way, and as the two-man military search party had run out of food, the Bradley brothers shared their food with them on the way out. Roy Bradley was court-martialled in Dunedin in December 1918 and charged with failing to attend a medical examination in October 1917.

Bradley, who was the son of Quaker and National Peace Council (NPC) stalwart Sarah Bradley, told the court-martial that he was a Quaker and had been exempted from service in the territorials on 29 March 1913. He claimed that he was at sea when his name was drawn in the ballot, and when he came back his papers had been sent to the wrong address. This was clearly not believed: Bradley, who objected to doing non-combatant service, was sentenced to two years' imprisonment as a military defaulter, and although the RAB said he was a Quaker who cited the Ten Commandments, they made no recommendation for his release.[103]

The religious objectors who were imprisoned varied in how they practised and interpreted Christianity. How they responded to conscription also varied, but one thing they all had in common was a knowledge of the Bible, and a desire to live according to Christian teachings. The other thing they had in common was the shared experience of prison life.

CHAPTER 7

THE BEST POSSIBLE CONDITIONS? LIFE IN PRISON 1917–19

The influx of a large number of non-criminal military prisoners into the prison system in 1917 and 1918 presented challenges for the prison service, which was already short-staffed because of the war. Efforts were made to keep the conscientious objectors (COs) separate from civilian prisoners, and to assign them useful outdoor work 'under the best possible conditions'.[1]

While nearly all COs served their longest period in a prison where special provision was made for them, they also often spent some time in a regular civilian prison waiting for a place to become available. Eventually they were usually drafted to one of five prisons: in the North Island they were sent to the Kaingaroa afforestation camp, the Waimarino road-making camp (known as Rotoaira), or the Waikeria reformatory farm near Te Awamutu; and in the South Island, to the newly established Paparua prison farm (Templeton) near Christchurch. Younger men were sent to the Invercargill Borstal. The COs were not necessarily sent to the prison closest to their home: many of the Canterbury COs served their longest sentences in prisons in the North Island, usually at Waikeria or Rotoaira, and a page of 60 signatures of COs who were imprisoned at Paparua shows that more than half of them came from the North Island.[2]

Some COs spent long periods of time in detention at Trentham Military Camp while they waited for their first hearing and sentence. Duncan McCormack, a North Island CO who spent time at Trentham Military Camp, the Alexandra Barracks, Mt Cook and the Terrace prisons, all in Wellington, and Lyttelton and Paparua prisons near Christchurch, said after his two court-martials that 'it was prison to prison, the difficulty being to find enough accommodation for all of us'.[3] Frank Money spent time in all the prisons mentioned by McCormack, as well as nearly two weeks at the Addington women's prison while en route from the Terrace prison in Wellington to Paparua. It appears he served his second sentence at Waikeria.[4]

There were variations in the sentences given for the first period and for the longer prison sentences after court-martial, too. Robin Page, writing from the Alexandra Barracks where he was serving his first 28 days of detention, said that in his group of eight detainees there were sentences of 21, 28, 56 and 112 days – all for the first offence.[5]

In February 1918 the National Peace Council (NPC) passed a resolution expressing horror and indignation at the persecution of some objectors, and protesting about the 'starvation, insults, solitary confinement, stripping, savage assaults, causing bodily pain and injury – savouring of the torments of the Spanish Inquisition'.[6] The resolution was to be sent to Cabinet ministers, bishops and denominational organisations, along with a request for them to endorse the protest. NPC members were well informed about the treatment of COs in prison: their information came mainly from their own members who had visited and spoken with COs at Paparua or Lyttelton prisons, or from the prisoners' families and friends. In 1917 Ida Cooke told them that her husband Fred had lost a stone (6.35 kg) while in Lyttelton prison, and Henry Worrall reported that he had visited both his sons in prison.[7]

The NPC also objected to the conditions in the room at the King Edward Barracks in Cashel Street where COs and military prisoners were held temporarily. The room was smelly, difficult to exit in event of a fire, very cold with no heating, and the noise of horses kicking in the stables next door kept the prisoners awake. All the military prisoners were put there, including those who were drunk and possibly diseased. The blankets were unfit for use, Mackie reported.[8] The following year Blanche Baughan made a similar complaint about the holding room, based on information from Kennaway Henderson's wife and from Charles Murray, who reported that Henderson had been confined in the room for a night with two other objectors and five other men. The small room had only six bunks, was infested with flies and 'in the near neighbourhood of a manure heap'. Two of the soldiers were drunk and 'of

Many of the COs imprisoned at Paparua came from the North Island, but the signatures of some Canterbury men can be seen here, including Kennaway Henderson, Robin Page and William Gray in the left column; George Samms, James Roberts, Frank Robinson, Percy Dodge, Douglas Day and Albert Church in the centre column; and Jim Chapple, John Roberts, Noel Goldsbury, Richard Gadd and Hope Horne in the right column. (Macmillan Brown Library) disgusting language and conduct. The sanitary arrangements were worse than primitive, and very deleterious to health'.[9]

That COs were subject to insults is evident from reports of military service board hearings. In July 1917 the NPC complained of the 'overbearing and discourteous behaviour' of the chairman of the Canterbury Military Service Board, the magistrate Helyar Bishop; later that year Henry Worrall witnessed the court-martial of a religious objector who was told by the president of the court that his trust in God was trust in a 'rotten stick'.[10]

Stripping, solitary confinement and assault

The NPC's accusation of mistreatment of prisoners, including 'solitary confinement, stripping, savage assaults', arose from two incidents that occurred in February 1918, when objectors Ernest Munns and William Worrall refused to wear a uniform.

Mackie later described the case of CO 'E. M.' (Ernest Munns of the Richmond Mission), who was a salesman for the Crown Clothing company. Munns was found unfit for foreign service and was ordered into 'C.1.' camp, but when he refused to go, he was arrested and sent to Featherston Military Camp. His refusal to wear uniform meant he was put in a cell by himself where there was no bed, just boards to sleep on. At night he was given four blankets. From Saturday to Monday he had nothing to wear but his underpants and singlet. He was compelled to eat with his fingers, and drink from a tin. The final indignity, Mackie reported, was Munns had to listen to 'disgusting' language.

Mackie reported a second incident – that of 'W.W.' (William Worrall), who was 'not robust' and was also ordered into 'C.1.' camp. When Worrall refused to put on uniform at Featherston Military Camp, he was forcibly stripped and dressed in uniform by five soldiers: he resisted, but used no violence. He was denied blankets because he refused to sign for them. He went on hunger strike until he was given blankets.[11] Baughan included a more detailed statement about this incident, provided by William's father Henry Worrall and the Richmond Mission, in a submission she sent to every member of both houses of Parliament. In her submission she quoted a member of the mission (presumably

Munns) describing what he had heard through the wall, where Worrall was being forcibly dressed in 'denims': 'The strain was awful. I would sooner be in the Civil gaol five years than put up with much of this, the struggling in the next cell sounded awful. I heard the Sergt. Major say, "Put him on his head", and "I would enjoy more the pleasure of shooting you".'[12]

William Worrall's own statement described how, when he refused to put on the denims, he was frog-marched head down by six men. The sergeant major instructed the men to sit on Worrall: one on his chest, another on his head, and to 'give the b… one under his b… jaw, that will settle him'. The trousers were badly torn in the attempt to get them on – for which Worrall was fined. He was also charged with saying that he refused to go to work, though he couldn't remember having said this.[13]

Complaints about these incidents, made by the NPC, Baughan and others and sent to MPs and church leaders, seem to have had the desired effect. The camp commandant was warned not to allow a repeat of this kind of mistreatment, and several church leaders and church meetings called for 'genuine' objectors to be offered civilian service instead.[14]

Auckland prison (Mt Eden), which at the time was the maximum security prison for the country, was the destination for troublesome COs, in keeping with the policy that any man who refused to work or who agitated and caused discontent among his fellows was to be returned to the main civilian prisons and treated as an ordinary prisoner. Jim Worrall was in Auckland prison at the end of the war – he may have been sent there after an incident at Paparua prison when he was asked by the jailer to do some plumbing but he refused because he knew it wasn't good plumbing practice. The jailer later agreed that Jim's way of doing things was the best.[15] Hard labour at Auckland prison was breaking rocks at the quarry next door, and the diet was porridge, dry bread and black tea in the morning and evening, with a midday meal of coarse beef, potatoes and sometimes a tiny portion of carrot or other vegetable. It was a grim place with terrible food and the possibility of being woken at night and held upside down for an anal search. Jim Worrall was almost certainly there when a religious objector, William White, who had become seriously unwell at Rotoaira prison camp, was transferred to Auckland but was given no medical treatment for six days and died soon after.[16]

The worst cases of brutality and violence used against the COs occurred at the Wanganui Detention Barracks, but the only Canterbury CO who is known to have been sent there – Reg Williams in June 1918 – did not give evidence at the inquiry held into the conduct of Lieutenant Crampton at the barracks, and there is no record of how he was treated. It's probably no accident, however, that Jim Worrall and Reg Williams, both of whom had been leaders in the Passive Resisters Union (PRU) and had served several prison terms before the war, were kept mostly in North Island prisons, well away from their friends and supporters in Christchurch. William Worrall too seems to have been singled out after the incident at Featherston Camp: after his court-martial he spent several months at Point Halswell prison in Wellington, where for most of the time he was the only CO, before he was transferred to Rotoaira.[17]

Predominantly boredom

Most of the COs did not endure a great deal of persecution or brutality, so far as we know: the main privations they suffered were the cold, unheated buildings, a spartan diet, the boredom of doing repetitive hard labour, and the mental stress of being locked in a cell for long periods. But there are few sources of information to draw on, thanks to a combination of censorship of prisoners' letters and the prisoners' own reluctance to complain about their conditions, either during or after the war. The few extant letters written by prisoners tend to be determinedly cheerful – no doubt they were always mindful that however bad a New Zealand prison might be, it did not compare with the horror of trench warfare in Western Europe.

Two Canterbury COs, Frank Money and Robin Page, left detailed accounts of their experiences for at least part of the time they were imprisoned.[18] For both men, their initial experience of being in custody was quite gentle. When Money was arrested at his farm near Matamata on 27 May 1917, the local constable allowed him to stay another night at home before taking him by rail to Paeroa, where he was handed over to the military to spend his first night in the 'cooler'. From there he was taken to Te Aroha for a medical examination, then to Hamilton and Frankton, where he was handed over to the military police. After a long day on the train to Wellington and then to Trentham Military Camp in Upper Hutt, Money spent two nights in 'clink' until a brief hearing before the camp commandant led to a remand to Hut 21, where he found himself with 13 others, mostly religious COs.[19] Money reports a fairly quiet time while living in Hut 21, eating, drinking, sleeping and talking with his companions, whom he found congenial. Most days they were able to take exercise walking about the camp under armed guard, and some days they had to do fatigue work such as unloading coal or scrubbing out their hut. On a wet day when they couldn't go out, they took exercise by dancing over the broom handle. After about a fortnight, Money was taken before the camp commandant again on 15 June 1917, and sentenced to 28 days' detention.

Mt Cook Prison and buildings on Buckle Street, Wellington. The Alexandra Barracks rise above the single-storey buildings in the centre rear of the photo. (Alexander Turnbull Library)

Page, who was arrested in April 1918, apparently travelled across Cook Strait to Wellington on the overnight ferry with his mother, who, he reported on his first day, 'seems able to see me as often as she likes'.[20] On arrival at Wellington they were taken to the barracks (presumably the Alexandra Barracks), and from there Page was taken to Trentham Military Camp, where no one seemed to want him. Finally he was given a tent to sleep in and at about 7pm he went through the process of refusing to accept his kit. The next morning he was put through the same process again, but was otherwise able to wander around the yard and play hockey using a fencepost and an old sock as a ball. This was to be his only day at Trentham, as on the following day he was taken before the camp commandant and, after a 'rather lengthy theological argument', was given 28 days' detention.[21] He was taken back to Wellington with an escort of three, and was met at the station by his mother, who accompanied them on the walk to the Alexandra Barracks.

Not all Canterbury's COs were taken to Trentham Military Camp when they were arrested. Richmond Mission member Douglas Day was sent to Featherston Military Camp after his arrest in July 1918. In stark contrast to Munn's experience, and doubtless because of the publicity given to Munn's case a few months earlier, Day reported being well treated by the military. On condition that he promised not to break camp he was put in a hut with a coke fire, and was allowed to go anywhere within bounds. He later wrote that he had a young fellow from Woodville in the same hut who held the same opinions, and they could talk to each other and read without interruption.[22] Day's court-martial was also held at Featherston.

Robin Page and two friends looking out of a window at the Alexandra Barracks. (Page family)

Detained in military barracks

The Alexandra Barracks, where both Money and Page spent their first 28 days' detention, had been intended as a central prison for New Zealand's worst criminals. It was planned as a building with six wings, but only one was ever built, as the Wellington public had protested against such an ugly building occupying the best site in the city (later the site of the Dominion Museum and, since 2001, part of the Massey University campus). The cells were on the second and third floors of the three-storey building, each one opening on to a gallery. Instead of it becoming a prison, some alterations were made to the narrow windows and it was used instead as a military barracks and home to the Defence Headquarters.[23]

Money's companions in the Alexandra Barracks were a mix of COs and military defaulters.[24] As time went on, light duties such as cleaning the barracks were replaced by outside work demolishing sheds, breaking up bricks for a road, or shifting heavy furniture in Defence Headquarters. The question of whether they were fools or scabs for agreeing to do such heavy work when they were classed as 'detainees' rather than prisoners was the subject of ongoing debate. As an experienced builder, Money found it impossible to work as slowly as his colleagues did. A go-slow policy carried out by some detainees, and a deputation to ask for better food, resulted in some gravy for dinner and a small piece of mutton for tea, Money reported.[25]

The following year Robin Page, serving his first month of detention at the Alexandra Barracks, wrote letters home that make his time there sound almost jolly. A member of a strongly anti-militarist family, he was embarrassed by the number of books and letters they sent him and by their attempts to smuggle food into the prison. He was glad that he was allowed to write just one letter

Frank Money with his wife Ruth (née Read) and their son John, born in 1921. (Money family)

a week, and hoped this might lead to his family writing less often. Two oranges that his mother insisted on leaving with him became the bane of his life: he had to hide them in his mattress and then tear the peel into tiny pieces and scatter it out the window. He pleaded with the family not to put 'BSc' after his name when they sent letters, and asked them to stop asking if he needed or wanted anything. 'When Mother arrives on Wednesday with Weekly Presses, Chessboards, and Esperanto Dictionaries etc etc I shall be strongly tempted to commit murder and I certainly will not accept them', he wrote in April 1918.[26] He didn't get much time for reading, he reported, because someone always wandered in for a yarn. He had a comfortable bed and a compulsory hot bath every night and described some not very arduous duties of keeping his room clean, scrubbing and sweeping. Later, however, when he became the mess orderly, he found the job of laying the table, cutting the bread and butter, carving the meat, dishing out the vegetables for 31 people and then clearing away and doing the washing up with just two helpers, was quite demanding. Every night he ran a mile around the yard. He also reported he was becoming an expert at bridge, which he played 'a good part of the time' with Donald Baxter as his bridge partner.[27]

Yet even while they were being well treated by the staff, some of whom were not the usual kind of prison warden – Page enjoyed long discussions with the 'Bombardier', who was a retired farmer from North Canterbury working without pay for the military police – the COs were always aware of what might lie ahead. In his letters from the Alexandra Barracks, Page reported stories of brutal treatment told to him by COs who had been in the Wanganui Detention Barracks, where Lieutenant J. L. Crampton boasted of being able to prepare the COs for service overseas within a month.[28] Understandably, Page and his family were relieved when he was sent to Paparua prison near Christchurch to serve his two-year sentence, though here, too, he would have heard first-hand information about Wanganui from COs Halkett and Wilson.

The COs were very aware of the government's intention to send COs to the front. The news of the transportation of 'the 14' in July 1917 had spread quickly throughout the community of anti-militarists and COs, and had caused an added layer of concern for the prisoners and their families – as it was intended to do. It was discomforting news for all of them, wrote Money in Hut 21, and the possibility of being transported remained with them, despite a rousing sing-song of hymns.[29] Page, for example, had a roommate whose two brothers had already been 'shang-ied' (shanghaied) – forcibly sent into war – and two days later Page reported that 30 chaps had been 'shangied' that day and 'were very mournful about it'. One of the men, in contrast, was very cheerful: he got one of his friends to shave off all his hair except for a lock in front, which he brushed down over his nose and tied with a red ribbon in a bow. 'You should have seen him trotting down the street under escort, with his hat well back over his head so as to shew the full effect.'[30]

DLC: Disobeying a lawful command

Frank Money was released from the Alexandra Barracks on 12 July 1917, and his brother Edwin from Christchurch, who was also a Christian pacifist, accompanied him on the train to Upper Hutt. At Trentham Military Barracks, Money spent a night in Hut 19 before going through the process of refusing to accept his kit. Edwin was able to visit him with a large quantity of fruit, which Frank ate with relish. That night he and another CO were put into 'clink' where they shared a room with 12 other men, many of whom seemed to him to be 'sexual degenerates'. Others were soaked in beer, and two had been fighting. This was a low point for Money, but the forced association with such men strengthened his resolve not to join the military: 'I thought at the time, if there be no other reason for not wanting to go to the war, to avoid mixing with such a low type of humanity, was one good reason. We are continually being told of one righteous war, but alas, these men, was there ever men whose appearance portrayed such extreme picture of devilishness.'[31]

Money was glad to get out in the fresh air the next morning to be taken before the commandant for his court-martial, where he was accused of the same crime as most of the other COs – 'DLC' (disobeying a lawful command given by his superior officer). With the court-martial behind him he was relieved to be told to return to Hut 21, where he found most of his old friends and where he stayed for the next fortnight.

Henry Worrall, after visiting Trentham, was critical of the length of time men were detained there; and he praised the 'splendid, manly bearing of all the Objectors in Hut 21'.[32] From the army's point of view, however, the men were a nuisance: not only had they refused to work, but they refused to put on uniform and did nothing but 'sleep and eat'. They had to be guarded not only to prevent them escaping, but also to protect them from the soldiers in camp. The example of these 'fat loafers, and rabid anti-militarists living in the lines, doing nothing and priding themselves on their conduct is having a bad effect on the discipline of some men in Camp, especially on raw recruits,' wrote the chief of general staff in August 1917.[33]

Many of the court-martials for Canterbury COs were held at Trentham, making it difficult for their families to attend. Worrall, after he had observed his son Jim's court-martial in November 1917, spoke to the NPC about the difference between court-martials held in Christchurch and those held at Trentham; he said that he felt civilians should be present at all trials. It appears that the Christchurch court-martials were better conducted because they were observed by members of the NPC who made their watchful presence plain – 'sometimes by audible comments', reported Mackie, who made renewed efforts to get more observers to attend court-martials in other centres.[34]

Sarah Page, who attended her son Robin's court-martial at Trentham, had written to Allen the month before to argue that court-martials should be held in the home district of the objector. She was accompanied by Mrs Ballantyne, the mother of Wellingtonian Garth Ballantyne (one of the 14 deported COs), and although they were legally entitled to attend they were refused admission at the gate to the camp. It was only because Sarah Page stood her ground and 'attacked' two staff officers who happened to come along, that they were allowed in.[35]

Sarah's account of the court-martial shows that Robin was well able to stand up to the questioning of the president of the court, Major Talbot, who began his attack by saying that Robin was a child who was incapable of judging for himself and was only quoting what had been 'put into his mouth'.[36] Robin's response was to point out the inconsistency of being called a child by the major who, at the same time, thought him old enough to be sent to fight for older men. To the commonly asked question of what he would do to protect his mother if she were being attacked, Robin replied that his mother's attitude of non-resistance would make them safer than Major Talbot. When the major responded that the Germans hate the COs more than anything, Robin replied that that was because they knew COs were more dangerous to their system than the soldier. When Talbot said that Germans despised men who wouldn't fight for their country, Robin replied that if the major admired the Germans so much he wondered why he wanted to fight them. The major went on to say that of the 14 objectors sent to the firing line, all but one had changed their opinions and taken up the rifle. Robin asked whether reason or force had been used, and he asked for proof of the major's facts. He also asked if the major knew what treatment had driven Archibald Baxter insane. When the major said it was probably not the treatment but natural tendency that had driven Baxter out of his mind, Robin said he was not a specialist on insanity and was quite prepared to yield the palm to the major on inside knowledge on that point. Asked if he were content to live in peace and comfort while others fought for him, Robin replied that he wasn't getting much peace and comfort just now.

Before hearing the next cases the court adjourned for morning tea, during which the major invited Sarah Page and Mrs Ballantyne to sit by the fire with him. 'The old chap certainly enjoyed an argument,' Sarah Page told her family.[37]

Perhaps as a result of Sarah Page's formidable presence in Wellington throughout the seven weeks of her son's incarceration there, Robin Page seems to have been moved to Paparua prison by July 1918.

The reality of prison life

For Frank Money, who was taken to the Terrace prison on 27 July 1917 after being sentenced to 11 months with hard labour, the reality of prison life was a shock. His own clothing and belongings were replaced by a prison suit of flannel drawers and undershirt, cotton top shirt and white moleskin trousers, an old brown coat and vest, moleskin hat, black socks and heavy boots, a strap, handkerchief, towel and bread bag. His hair was shorn off and his fingerprints taken. Locked in his cell with his first meal of porridge and bread, he admitted to weeping as he reflected on what 'standing for truth and righteousness had brought me to, the result of course of a wicked and ungodly Government at the head of affairs …'[38]

Described as a grim, dilapidated place in the early 1900s, there had been improvements to the Terrace by the time COs began to be imprisoned there. If an article in the *Evening Post* is to be believed, it was in 1917 a spotlessly clean place with pure air and no 'gaol smell'.[39] The food was wholesome, there was a library of 1500 books, and prisoners were encouraged in self-education. The main occupations for prisoners at the Terrace were gardening, repairing boots and sewing officers' uniforms and prisoners' clothing.[40]

Money's first impressions of his fellow prisoners were that they were a rough set 'not much reformed by prison life'; 'the language was most

The Terrace prison and gardens, Wellington, c. 1910. (Alexander Turnbull Library)

immoral and degrading', and their features reflected their immoral lives.[41] But after just one day, when he scrubbed cell floors, he was moved to the Mt Cook prison.

Mt Cook Prison, on the same site as the Alexandra Barracks, was a two-storey building containing 16 cells, built in 1844. It housed mainly short-term prisoners who worked at the adjacent brickworks.[42] Money, when he arrived, was put to work shovelling clay; but during most of the two months he spent there he worked as a builder. Most of the prisoners at Mt Cook were military offenders, and Money found just one fellow Christian. But after a few weeks other Christians arrived, until there were seven of them who gained permission to have a bible study group.

Towards the end of 1918, when two Canterbury COs, Warden and Borrows, were detained for six weeks in the 'Alexandra Barrack Prison' (probably the Mt Cook Prison) after they had served their prison sentence and despite the war having ended, they found conditions most unsatisfactory; Warden later spoke of the 'filthy state of the blankets, the want of exercise and light'.[43] They had no bed, chairs or table, meals were eaten sitting on the floor, and they were allowed just one and a half hours of exercise every 24 hours.

'An earthly hell'

Several Canterbury COs spent time at Lyttelton Gaol – a large prison in the centre of the small port town of Lyttelton. From small beginnings in 1857 it had grown to become a dominating, Gothic-style compound, and the main prison for Canterbury. Prison work gangs, who built many of the stone walls and other infrastructure in the town, continued until 1915. Lyttelton was in the process of being replaced by the new prison at Paparua: there were just a few remaining prisoners at Lyttelton by the end of 1918, and all had moved out by the end of 1919. Traditionally the prisoners were employed mainly in the nearby quarry, working for the borough council, but there was also a boot-making department at the prison.[44]

After spending five days in the prison in November 1912, Henry Reynolds condemned the overall system of punishment which offered 'no reward, no hope, no encouragement, no brotherly feeling, no sympathy.' 'Everything it appears is done to dishearten them,' he wrote, referring to the prisoners whose 'indescribably filthy language' gave him 'the feeling of being in an earthly hell'.[45] He described the ill-matching and ill-fitting strong nailed boots that were issued to him: 'that had been a pair once, but which looked now like brother and sisters instead of brothers. They were roomy, so if I could not lift them, I could push them along the ground when walking … I did not need locking in, for I could not have run in them, had I tried.' Reynolds found the meat inedible and the tea undrinkable: it seemed to be 'stewed log-wood or some other concoction'.[46]

Another pre-war prisoner, Reg Williams, complained about the 'alleged tea', and noted that both the porridge and the tea were served without milk. Much of the porridge was not eaten by the prisoners and went instead to the pig bucket: 'the pigs outside, who get a large share of the porridge must be getting nice and fat now'.[47]

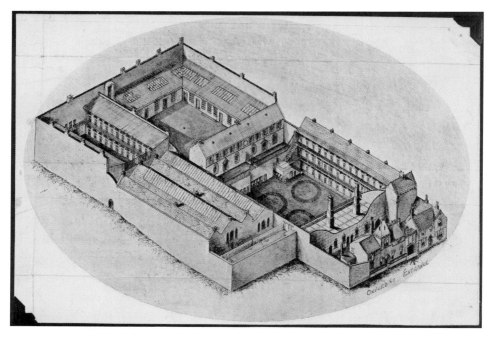

An architect's impression of the Lyttelton Gaol showing the rings where prisoners walked each day, when not out on work parties. (Te Ūaka The Lyttelton Museum)

A visitor to CO Kennaway Henderson in Lyttelton found 'drunken soldiers who were vomiting all over the place; no toilet facilities (only a bucket)'.[48] Reynolds said, more mildly, the sanitary arrangements in the cells were 'very antiquated'. He was critical of the compulsory walking around in circles in the asphalt yards, where three rings were marked out, each 10–12 yards wide. Prisoners who were not in work gangs spent long hours each day walking around in circles, which Reynolds found tiring. It made him giddy, and he thought it would be, 'injurious to the eyesight, bad for nerves and brain. My brain whirled whilst lying in my hammock at night, through the effects of marching round and round.'[49]

The prisoners witnessed some appalling brutality: Williams described the savage punishment given to a 'weak minded' man who had been sentenced to three years of 'reformative treatment'. Because the chief warder had told him never to go outside the gates, the prisoner refused to obey another warder who told him to carry bags of rubbish to the rubbish cart. As a result he was violently manhandled by the warders, who eventually got him into a solitary confinement cell.[50]

For most of the COs, Lyttelton was a place where they waited for a place to become available at Paparua. Some were there at the same time as men serving a sentence for sedition. Albert Church, for example, coincided with Tim Armstrong and Paddy Webb. Church had been in the prison yard for only a few minutes when Armstrong touched him on the shoulder and said, 'You're one of us; you'll get milk in your tea while you're here.'[51] The privilege arose from the fact that Armstrong had known one of the warders in the Waihi strike.

When Douglas Day was moved from the Terrace prison to Lyttelton he missed the fellowship of like-minded Christian COs. In a letter to his mother in October 1918, he explained how difficult it was to apportion his letters when he was allowed to write just one a week. He added that because his sister Margery had visited him while he was in Wellington, that visit had robbed him of a letter. From Lyttelton he wrote that he'd not been well for a week or so, but was clearly anxious not to alarm his family: 'Had an attack of influenza and it left me with a slight turn of dysentery, but feel pretty well today so you need have no worries. Otherwise I am well.'[52]

Hastily built

Conditions were certainly better at the newly opened prison farms, and in line with the more enlightened prison policy of the time the COs were often put to work on their construction. When Frank Money arrived at Paparua prison in December 1917 it was rapidly expanding; from accommodating 24 prisoners in 1915, it grew to house 136 in 1920.

Duncan McCormack, who arrived at Paparua at the same time as Money, was one of a gang of eight, mostly builders, who were immediately put to work adding a second quadrangle about a hundred metres away from the existing quadrangle of two long wooden cellblocks. There was a good relationship between the builder COs and their likeable warder Bill Quinn, himself a carpenter; he sometimes brought them treats of cheese or chocolate. After four or five months spent constructing the cellblocks, the COs moved into them.[53]

It was the prisoners' families and the NPC, rather than the prisoners themselves, who expressed the greatest criticism of Paparua. Robin

Paparua prison farm, Templeton, temporary cellblocks in wood. (Archives New Zealand Te Rua Mahara o te Kāwanatanga)

COs exercising at Paparua prison in 1918. (*The Working Woman*, March 1936)

Page's aunts later described the prison as cold, badly built, badly lit, and the diet as ill-balanced:

> The prison had been hastily built, and the cells in which the prisoners were confined for such long hours were so roughly put together that the rain and even the snow were sometimes blown into them, damping the occupants' bedding and their small stock of clothing … some of the older and less robust prisoners suffered greatly from the cold. This cold, the monotonous ill-balanced diet, and the long confinement in badly lighted cells told heavily on the health and spirits of many of the prisoners.[54]

Mackie, on behalf of the NPC, whose members regularly visited Paparua prison, wrote along similar lines to C. E. Matthews, inspector of prisons, eliciting the response that the prisoners were provided with mattresses and five good blankets each during the winter months; and pointing out the dangers of fire risk if heaters were put into temporary wooden buildings.[55] In a second letter to Matthews, Mackie wrote that while the prisoners at Paparua had not complained of cold, visitors to the prison had experienced 'the extremely bleak situation of the buildings, the draughty state of the premises, and the extremely cold weather. The almost Antarctic weather renders it extremely difficult for those dwelling in comfortable houses to keep moderately warm and we picture with considerable concern the condition of the men in an unprotected building.'[56] Some of the men at Paparua had told him that 'Snow was actually lying in the corridor and the cold was felt intensely … repeated requests were made for extra blankets and … eventually these were supplied.'[57]

A model farm

Waikeria prison, gazetted as a reformatory in 1918, was described as an 'object lesson in useful employment of prison labour' in official reports.[58] Buildings, including a milking shed and dairy, were constructed out of reinforced concrete made on site, as were fencing posts, blocks and pipes. Scrub and swampland was cleared, drained and brought into production for the farm, which featured a dairy herd, a large poultry flock, pigs and bees, as well as a seven-acre orchard and market garden. Miles of fencing was erected and an access road to the main road to Te Awamutu was built with the help of several horses and drays. A visitor to the prison in 1918 described it as a modern building of two storeys without a wall around it. The prisoners were employed on the prison's 1500-acre farm, and grew most of their own food. The same visitor met with a prisoner who was studying for an exam, while another CO had permission to coach him.[59]

Waikeria prison. (Archives New Zealand Te Rua Mahara o te Kāwanatanga)

By September 1918 Reg Williams was at Waikeria and reported that he was content to be working in the open air. He found the gardening work congenial, and he was in good health. He was allowed to write and receive nine letters a month. In his spare time he was studying Spanish and shorthand. By January 1919 he was living in a hut with three others at a 'camp on the farm', probably doing scrub-clearing. He was pleased with the change and with the fact that they could swim in the river on Saturdays and on holidays.[60]

Frank Money wrote no diaries from Waikeria, and in one of his few extant letters said he couldn't say much about their living conditions (no doubt due to the censorship of prisoners' letters), but they were on the whole fairly satisfactory. He reported he was in excellent health and spirits and had never felt so well before. But while he was 'fully persuaded' that plain living was 'in keeping with nature and for the best interests of the human race', he had still found it difficult to make the adjustment. 'I had never in all my experience taken porridge twice in one day, but since coming here, have never failed to take it both morning and evening.'[61]

Farm and reclamation work

Younger objectors up to the age of 25 were sent to the borstal at Invercargill, a newly opened institution which was developing a farm as part of a programme to provide prisoners with productive work.[62] This included the reclamation of a vast area of coastal swampland – achieved by building a large embankment – and an extensive building programme, all of which was carried out by supervised prison labour. Within 10 months the reclaimed land had produced a hay crop, and a dairy farm was being set up. The prisoners were put to work on another large embankment that would result in 300 acres of reclaimed land, intended for a Defence Department rifle range. The borstal had a school room and was planning to introduce other activities for its young inmates.

Christchurch CO Fred Dodge, a builder by trade, was put to work as a carpenter on new buildings. According to Dodge family stories he was generally content with the treatment he received. One story recounts how Fred was locked out: because he didn't have a watch and he became absorbed in his work he often arrived late back to the prison, and had considerable difficulty getting back inside. Another anecdote tells how the warden of the prison owed his rapid promotion to Fred, because he would walk with Fred around the prison farm, seeking his advice on ideas for building and developing the farm. Fred was evidently well regarded by the prison authorities. A rotund man, he liked to wear braces to keep his trousers up, but prisoners were issued with a belt only. When he told the superintendent that he was getting a sore back from having an exposed gap between his shirt and trousers, he was given special permission to wear braces.[63]

Tree planting and road building

Prisoners at the Kaingaroa afforestation camp, situated between Rotorua and the Whirinaki Forest on the Kāingaroa Plains, were put to work extending the exotic forest planting that had been started with prison labour in 1901. By 1918 military prisoners at the camp outnumbered the civilian prisoners. At least two Canterbury COs are known to have served time at Kaingaroa, which also featured a prison vegetable garden, pigs, and oat crops to feed the prison horses.[64] When Defence Minister Allen interviewed eight prisoners at Kaingaroa in November 1917, Lancelot Robinson told him he was quite comfortable, he liked the work and had no grievances; John Ernest Holtham likewise said the work was congenial, except there was little time for study and there was a shortage of light at night-time.[65]

The Rotoaira roadmaking prison camp was another camp in a remote part of the North Island, on the desolate and windy plain at Waimarino (National Park), beneath the three volcanic mountains of Ruapehu, Tongariro and Ngauruhoe. Here the COs worked on building a road between Waimarino and Tokaanu, at the southern end of Lake Taupō. The work included putting in concrete culverts and building wooden bridges from pit-sawn wood cut from the bush. William Worrall described working in a gravel pit and crushing metal for the road. The weather presented a huge challenge to the road builders, with rain or snow often preventing them from working. CO Tim Brosnan, who experienced deep snow during the winter of 1918, called it the Siberia of New Zealand.[66]

Twenty COs who had been held temporarily at Point Halswell prison in Wellington were transferred to Rotoaira in November 1917. At war's end there were eight Canterbury COs at Rotoaira.[67] Norman Bell was one: his only extant letter written from the prison camp is – typically, given his intellectual approach to life – a long dissertation on the need for people to be better educated if wars were to be averted in the future. He was grateful that he was in prison with time to think and write: 'I am afraid prison life which leads to much thinking (I would the whole world were thus in prison!) tends to make one moralise: still that surely is better than murdering or causing pain to anyone. When I think of what I might be doing, then I "rejoice with an exceeding great joy".'[68]

Given his belief in the need for education, it's likely that Bell did some teaching at Rotoaira. William Worrall reported in August 1918 on classes in English, Esperanto, arithmetic, chemistry, bookkeeping, music, art and drama, geography and economics. He noted that there was quite a good library with about a hundred works of fiction by 'some of the best authors', and a personal library that included books brought to him by his father: 'Father's arms must have ached carrying them out here five miles across Waimarino desert.'[69] There seems to have been

Rotoaira Prison Camp No. 2 and Whakapapanui stone bridge. (Archives New Zealand Te Rua Mahara o te Kāwanatanga)

a liberal attitude to the type of reading the COs could enjoy: Worrall reported reading J. W. Graham's *Evolution and Empire*, and he kept up to date with international affairs by reading *The Nation*, a progressive magazine from the United States. The existence of the library and the classes may have been what led detainees to tell Robin Page that the camp on the Waimarino Plains was 'A1'.[70]

Daily routine and work at Paparua

Most of what we know about the daily life of COs at Paparua is thanks to letters from Robin Page to his family. Even taking censorship into account, the letters suggest a relatively peaceful, if tedious, existence. The daily routine, described in some detail in letters and in a doggerel poem sent to his family, can be summarised as follows:

6.30am: Bell rings; prisoners dress, wash faces, fold blankets.

6.45am: Warder unlocks cell door; prisoners are given porridge and meat in a tin can for breakfast; prisoners polish their cutlery and put their folded blankets and pillow on shelf; prisoners sweep cell.

7.30am: Cells are unlocked, prisoners line up in yard and at 8am go off to work. For Page this meant working with 'Charley' [probably Charles Warden] in the prison smithy.

10.30am: Gaoler pays morning call;

12noon: Prisoners line up in yard; are searched (the warders 'very carefully feeling in those parts of one's anatomy where nothing could possibly be concealed') and locked in their cells for dinner of mutton, potatoes and leeks.

1–5pm: Prisoners at work.

5pm: Prisoners are searched and given a tin of porridge and a loaf of bread to take to their cells. After eating there is 'animated discussion' with cell-mate and arguments with other prisoners, presumably through the walls.

9pm: Lights out.

Saturdays: Prisoners receive half a stick of tobacco.

Page's letters to his family were designed to entertain and reassure them, and often contained humorous accounts of prison life. His description of the work he and 'Charley' did at the smithy, for example, would have us believe that they did little apart from fashion flints and steels for their fellow prisoners, used to create a spark for lighting their tobacco: the 'penetrating sound of flint on steel' was heard in the evening when they were locked in their cells.[71]

Unitarian minister James Chapple was a well-respected prisoner at Paparua, sent there for sedition in May 1918. At 52 years old he was less able than the younger men to withstand the cold or the hard work, so the other prisoners would let him rest in the sun, concealed behind piles of concrete blocks.[72] As well as working in the smithy or building the cellblocks, prisoners planted trees or worked on the prison farm. Douglas Day, a farm labourer in civilian life, enjoyed looking after the farm animals, and Kennaway Henderson's skills in draughting were put to use designing new buildings – he used to joke later about the 'hard labour' he had served while lying in the sun doing these drawings, and said he positively enjoyed the times when he was locked in his cell and could read and meditate in peace.[73]

Paparua prison farm, Templeton: the western cellblock, with kitchen, laundry and bathhouse at back. The foundations of the eastern cellblock were already completed but are not visible in the photo. (Archives New Zealand Te Rua Mahara o te Kāwanatanga)

Saturday the 'day of days'

A poem Robin Page wrote as a birthday present for his mother in 1918 provides a detailed picture of the cells at Paparua. The cells were seven by eight foot, with a table on one side fixed to the partition wall. There was a stool, and a little corner shelf where the blankets were stored. On a lower shelf was the prisoner's plate with their mug inverted on top, and a fork and spoon inserted crosswise through the mug handle. Above the shelf was a card with numbers on it that showed how many more days of hard labour were to be served. A hairbrush and a slate hung from the shelf, and a bag for the prisoner's bread. A towel hung behind the door, and a brush for sweeping the cell. Saturday, said Page, was the 'day of days' when they were given their half stick of tobacco, and five times a week they were given a match.[74]

According to Frank Money the food at Paparua was uncommonly plain but always good, and just a little more than they needed. There was little variation in the diet, and so the prisoners were delighted when they were each given a two-pound tin of golden syrup in August 1918: Page said that Jim Chapple celebrated by dancing a Highland fling down the corridor with the tin held high above his head. Many of the prisoners ate the golden syrup in one sitting, leading Page to comment on the folly of this procedure.

Like many of the other prisoners Page caught the flu in November 1918, but in his usual style he presented this in his letters home as a positive experience, because the cell doors of those who were sick

Oh! how can it improve a man
To eat his meals alone
All mixed up in an old tin can
Potatoes leeks and bone
Meat porridge and bread for breakfast
Porridge and bread for tea.
This menu must be clearly classed
As mere monotony.....
You are waked up in the morning
By a beastly bell.
It comes as the day is dawning
Comes like a sound from a well
In theory you at once arise
In practice you do not
For you learn to dearly prize
These moments you have got.
You wash your face and sweep your
room
And all your blankets fold.
A bowl of porridge you condume
And bread and mutton cold.
From eight o'clock you labour sore
Till northwards is the sun,
From one till five you toil once more

Extract from Robin Page's 'Sketch of Gaol Life' as a CO at Paparua prison. The poem was given to his mother as a birthday present in 1918. (Page family)

were left open and they were given a more varied diet that included brown bread twice a week, barley water, hot milk, blackcurrant drink, and occasionally an egg or a piece of bread with butter and lettuce.[75] Other COs were released from their usual duties to look after those who were sick: for Douglas Day this meant more liberty, though he was not allowed visitors.[76] After months of never seeing the night sky, the sick COs whose doors were open were delighted to be able to see stars in the sky.

A sketch of Robin Page drawn by fellow CO prisoner Duncan McCormack in 1919. (Page family)

'Comforts' were provided for the men in Paparua during the epidemic, and at Christmas that year. A food box organised by Sarah Page for each of the 60 COs contained two pieces of cream sponge, sundry pieces of fruitcake, shortbread and Christmas mince pies, two apples, a few cherries, a small bag of sweets, muscatels and a piece of chocolate.[77]

Severe cold

The severe cold and inadequate medical care were the two worst features of prison life for the COs, and their spartan lifestyle had a devastating effect on some. At least two of Canterbury's religious COs died within 10 years of being released from prison. Ernest Munns died in July 1919 at the age of 46 of chronic kidney disease caused, it was believed, by the privations he experienced in prison.[78] Frank Money died in 1929 at the age of 44, and his family believed his early death was a direct result of his prison experience. Both men served their longest sentences in the North Island, far away from the watchful eyes of the NPC. At Paparua, by comparison, there was a 'complete system of visitation and on some occasions as many as 60 persons would visit the gaol. This tended to make the Authorities extremely careful,' Mackie said.[79]

But a remote location may sometimes have been an advantage. In contrast with the numerous classes and the good library that Worrall enjoyed at Rotoaira, the prison authorities at Paparua seemed to take a stricter approach. Despite the NPC's attempts to provide the COs with books and encourage study groups there are no reports of multiple classes taking place, and a jailer censored the books that NPC members left at Paparua: he would allow no socialist literature, had been discarding books of educational value and had prohibited Stead's magazine. Mackie considered the jailer unsuitable as a literary critic, but when he queried the prohibition of Stead's *Review*, justice minister Thomas Wilford replied that it was prohibited because he considered it so depressing.[80]

Money described his time in prison as: 'Eight hours per day go as you please style. 16 hours in the cell' – which meant there was plenty of time in which to write.[81] From his arrest in May 1917 to his arrival at the Terrace prison in April 1918 he kept a diary. His writing paper in the Alexandra Barracks came from an obsolete military book that he was asked to burn. Having got on the 'good side' of a sentry he had been permitted to keep the pages he'd salvaged.[82] Why did he stop keeping a diary when he arrived at the Terrace? Perhaps because it was forbidden. While at the Alexandra Barracks he described an occasion when the Corporal ransacked their 'Dens' looking for 'profane and seditious literature'.[83] He reported losing a letter that was ready to post, some stamped

Watch-guard made of hair from the prison horses' tails by a CO prisoner at Paparua during World War I. (Kaiapoi Historical Society)

envelopes and writing materials, but somehow his writing and diary papers were overlooked. He was, however, reprimanded at one point – it's not clear for what misdemeanour – and threatened with not being allowed to write or receive any further letters.

Some COs filled in time during the long evenings in their cells by engaging in handiwork. A small watch-guard on display at the Kaiapoi Museum is a rare memento:[84] donated to the museum in 1979 by a member of the Clarkville East Eyreton Women's Division of Federated Farmers, it was made of knotted horsehair from the prison horses' tails by a CO at Paparua during World War I. Kennaway Henderson fashioned a small spoon with a handle in the form of a tiki out of a horseshoe nail. 'It must have taken him hours of painstaking work, and sometimes I gaze at it with wonder,' wrote his friend Winston Rhodes, who was given the spoon many years later.[85]

Paparua prison is 21 kilometres from Christchurch, and the closest public transport was either the Riccarton or the Sockburn tram terminus. George Samms' wife Lily walked to the prison from one of these, pushing the pram with baby Margaret in it. It is not known whether a plan by the Women's International League (WIL) to organise transport for family members was put into effect, but members of the Day family, who did not own a car, would try to get a seat in a car with another visitor. Fred Page biked from their home in Papanui every week to see his brother Robin. Visiting day was Saturdays, and one visitor described how, while the warder's back was turned, there was a 'rapid shuffling across under the table of apples, chocolate and tobacco'.[86]

Visiting loved ones in prisons in other parts of the country was difficult. Fred Dodge's wife Maud visited him just once or twice during his year at Invercargill. The Page family were unusual in that three members of the family managed to visit Robin in Wellington: his mother Sarah, his brother Fred, who was reprimanded for taking photos of the Alexandra Barracks, and his aunt Ann Saunders.

Historian Paul Baker concludes that the CO prisoners at Paparua were a 'pretty happy family' who held impromptu concerts. But he also records that prisoners there held a strike to demand better food, and a second strike so that the civilian prisoners would get the same benefit.[87]

Robin Page described some 'trouble' at the prison, starting with letters written by Charley that were 'sarcasm from beginning to end', in the jailer's words.[88] One sentence he particularly objected to was the statement that the prisoners were living in slavery. Charley and the jailer discussed the subject for the greater part of the morning; the jailer said, 'Living in slavery, indeed, when you have got your razors and are going to get treacle. What do you think would happen if the whole lot of you came out one morning armed with your razors?' In another incident, when CO Arthur Borrows said he'd 'eventually' do something he'd been asked to do, the jailer lost his head and started throwing things all over the plumber's shop. They eventually apologised to one another, Page reported.[89] The last letters from prison written by Page and Douglas Day that are still extant were written in December 1918, eight long months before they were released from prison. Perhaps because their families were now able to be in regular contact with them, there was little new to say.

Multiple sentences and rearrests

By May 1918 the NPC had become concerned about the rearrest of COs after their release from prison. They had heard that some were serving a fourth sentence, while others had been left alone after just one. Henry Worrall, back from a visit to Rotoaira prison camp, reported that the COs were 'critically watching' the NPC, and Norman Bell had asked if the NPC could consult Sir John Findlay about the legality of rearrests made after a two-year sentence had expired.[90] As Christchurch woman Grace Wills pointed out in a letter to Allen, the policy of rearresting COs immediately after they had emerged from prison was widely known and discussed as 'the negation of the very principles for which we are said to be fighting'.[91] The COs were being treated worse than criminals, she said.

Censorship prevented the prisoners from writing in detail about their conditions, and the NPC evidently felt that trying to arouse sympathy among the public for the COs would be counterproductive. But they could and did write to government ministers and military officials about the treatment of COs in prison, and more and more frequently they asked when the prisoners would be released.

CHAPTER 8

SUPPORT FOR THE CONSCIENTIOUS OBJECTORS 1917–19

With the imprisonment of seditionists in 1917 and conscientious objectors (COs) in 1918, the peace movement moved its attention to the objectors who were in prison, and the COs who had been deported. Letters sent from Christchurch protesting against the treatment of the imprisoned COs are very apparent in Army Department correspondence files; one historian has noted that more than half of the 'surviving protests against the treatment of C.O.s or the imprisonment of defaulters' came from the city.[1] As the war came to an end, questions about the release of the COs became ever more urgent.

In wartime conditions, the National Peace Council (NPC) carried out most of its work by writing letters. In the first six months of 2017, for example, the organisation raised questions about the sentences received by the labour leaders who were then in prison; protested against the imprisonment of the Auckland Christian pacifist Harry Urquhart; and gathered information about all the men who had been prosecuted under the war regulations. The imprisonment of those who objected to compulsory military training (CMT) was still a concern. In March 1917 the NPC asked for an investigation into the case of a young man who was committed to Rīpapa Island for 28 days without having been fined; later that year the NPC protested against the 1917 amendment to the Defence Act which meant objectors to CMT could be committed to military custody for up to 28 days without the option of a fine. As boys could be imprisoned for each occasion they failed to attend military training, the NPC said, they could conceivably accumulate a long prison sentence in a short time.[2]

The Labour Party, meanwhile, demonstrated that a large number of people were prepared to come out and demonstrate against the cost of living and against conscription. A flashlight image of the 'Combined Labour Demonstration', showing more than 2500 people seated in the

More than 2500 people attended the cost-of-living and anti-conscription demonstration held in the Christchurch Colosseum on 18 March 1917. The site of the Colosseum later became New Regent Street. (Canterbury Museum)

Colosseum on Sunday 18 March 1917, is rare photographic evidence of a mass labour meeting from this period, and has been reproduced many times. The meeting had another purpose: to draw attention to the Labour Party's campaign for the local body elections in April. Speakers, including trade unionists Charles Webber and Ted Howard, condemned rising prices and low wages. MP Paddy Webb claimed that 'the majority of members of Parliament … are growing rich as a result of this war'.[3] Speakers were more circumspect on the topic of conscription, though Webb argued that 'parliament had no right to force conscription on this young

Edwin John (Ted) Howard, c. 1920. (Alexander Turnbull Library)

country' and said that the government should have 'conscribed wealth' when it 'conscribed' men.[4] MP James McCombs drew attention to the issue of soldiers' wages: he said that 'Labour members had always appealed for fair treatment to soldiers', and 'if the Government carried out its duty' (to the soldiers), conscription would not have been mentioned.[5] Webb and McCombs were cheered loudly by the audience. The following month Webb, losing his caution, was arrested and jailed for seditious utterances after speaking in support of Labour candidates in Greymouth. His three-month sentence was served at Lyttelton prison.

Women members of the NPC, Sarah Bradley and Louisa Nuttall, demonstrated solidarity with the striking miners on the West Coast by going with Elizabeth McCombs to a meeting of the Women's National Reserve, where they opposed the proposal that the wives of striking miners be asked to use their influence to get the men back to work.[6]

Māori conscription causes concern

From the outbreak of war, men from the South Island iwi Ngāi Tahu volunteered with enthusiasm both for the Expeditionary Force and later for a Maori Contingent, which had finally been agreed to after representations from Māori MPs. When conscription was introduced the draft bill excluded Māori, but after representations from the Maori Contingent Committee an amendment was made that enabled conscription to be extended to Māori at a later date.[7] This extension took place in June 1917, though it was to be applied only to Māori in the Waikato–Maniapoto district, where the New Zealand Wars and the confiscation of Māori land in the nineteenth century had engendered anger, resentment and a resistance to fighting for the British. A year later the first seven Māori men were arrested and taken to detention at Narrow Neck Military Camp on the North Shore, Auckland. At war's end there were 15 Māori in prison: seven at Mt Eden, the others at Waikeria, Invercargill and one at Kaingaroa.[8]

It was while the Māori objectors were in detention at Narrow Neck that Ada Wells 'spoke feelingly' at an NPC meeting about the issue of Māori conscription, and Mackie wrote a letter of protest to the minister of defence.[9] Concerned at the imprisonment of Māori, the NPC also wrote to the Māori MPs to express its opposition to Māori conscription, for reasons that were well intentioned if perhaps paternalistic:

> the forcing of the Native Races into conflict with Europeans, about whom they can neither know nor care anything, is degrading to their and our manhood, and utterly unworthy of our traditional ideals. We believe that the principle involved in forcing the Maoris into such a conflict as this is extremely serious, especially in face of our past efforts to inculcate the spirit of goodwill amongst them … We have written to the Government to the same effect urging it to refrain from any punitive measures as an act of mercy if for no other reason.[10]

The NPC letter was sincere in its desire to prevent Māori from being imprisoned for a matter of conscience, but it appears to lack understanding of the fundamental reasons why Māori refused to fight for their British oppressors – colonisation, land confiscation, dispossession and impoverishment – or, conversely, why Māori MPs had argued for conscription to be imposed in the first place: Māui Pōmare and Āpirana Ngata wanted it applied to Māori as a matter of self-respect; Māori blood had been spilt overseas, and Māori had a duty to respond.[11]

Women's International League takes action

Members of the Women's International League (WIL) met regularly in 1917 and 1918 and had frequent contact with the NPC through their delegates Ida Cooke and Mrs Ingram. The principles of the Christchurch branch of the WIL, set out in its 1917 Christmas message, bore strong similarities to the Canterbury Women's Institute (CWI)'s manifestos and ended with a quote from Thomas Paine, *The Rights of Man*: 'The world is our country; to do good our religion.' As a women's organisation, they said, they were 'for the cause of Humanity, not on Empire lines, but on a broad International Basis'. They extended deepest sympathy to all women who had lost their loved ones through this 'awful curse of Militarism and War', and they stood for 'the glorious Freedom for Women throughout the world to rear their children in peace and to teach them to love, not hate'.[12]

Perhaps the group's most notable action was promoting the idea of a CO Dependents' Fund for families of the married men in the Second Division who were balloted. In consultation with the NPC, however, it was decided the funds should be for dependents of those being punished for their convictions. The proposal seems to have been absorbed into the fund that was already established when the first seditionists were imprisoned, with Ted Howard as organising secretary. Individuals and groups, including the CWI, donated funds to the Seditious Prisoners and Conscientious Objectors Fund, which collected and dispersed a total of 3680 pounds and five shillings. Howard later wrote a detailed report of how the funds were dispersed.[13]

Non-pacifist women speak out

From January 1917 the protest against the conditions and treatment of COs received help from another cohort of women: those who were not pacifist, but who were concerned with social justice. The case of Thomas Nuttall stirred Blanche Baughan to write to the *Lyttelton Times* and to James Allen on behalf of the COs: she had read of Nuttall's military board hearing with 'horror and with shame' at the injustice of their not allowing the appeal of a man who clearly had a sincere conscientious objection. Sworn testimony as to character and convictions on the part of his neighbours would supply a better test than the present Act did, she suggested to Allen.[14]

Baughan wrote with the confidence of a well-known and respected author whose works were being advertised and reviewed in the newspapers. Her tone to the minister was always that of an equal who was trying to provide the government with a solution to a problem. She repeatedly made clear that she did not agree with the COs, and that if she were a man she would have enlisted long ago. A university graduate from London, Baughan had done social work in the slums and, at the same time, had taught Greek to members of the aristocracy. Her personal experience of the gulf between rich and poor in England was the catalyst for her strong interest in social reform and justice. When she first arrived in New Zealand in 1900 she focused on writing poetry but from 1910 she abandoned poetry for non-fiction.[15]

In a letter to Allen in February 1918 Baughan deplored the fact that 'men of sincerest convictions have been treated as if they had none, because they do not belong to any church or sect'. While she was not

Canterbury poet and writer Blanche Baughan, c. 1926. Baughan sought justice for the COs while not agreeing with them. (Canterbury Museum)

anti-militarist it had become impossible for her to stay silent, 'while New Zealand persecutes honest men, ignores the rights of conscience, and persists in thinking that Might is Right for British military men, although not for Prussian.'[16] In a letter to the editor of the *Press* she discussed the philosophical issue of conscience and included a statement about 'selfishness': she reported that not one single CO had ever 'squealed to me about his fate … their whole attitude is uncomplaining'.[17]

Baughan wrote regularly to the minister of defence and to the local newspapers on three main themes: the need for non-combatant service to be available to COs under civilian authority; the cost of maintaining COs in prison; and the injustice of persecuting genuine COs on the basis of their sincere beliefs, when at the same time the country was fighting for justice and liberty. She also wrote about the deported COs: she asked whether it was true that they had been left naked on the ship when they refused to wear khaki; whether some who had been sent to France were handcuffed; and whether the intention was to deport other COs. The deportation of the 14 men had caused a certain resentment against military rule throughout the community, and anti-militarism was growing daily, she said. In a letter to Robin Page's aunt, Baughan spoke highly of the contribution the COs were making to New Zealand:

> I look on the C.O.s (tho' their opinions are not mine) as the best
> thing the war has given N.Z. little as yet though she knows it.
> My struggle to get them some kind of justice, which continues
> unabated, is *not* for pity for them, but for love of justice & NZ
> … instead of groaning over R [Robin] we ought to be exulting
> over him! I for one feel a glow of gratitude whenever I think of
> him.[18]

Military Service Act not working

Another respected local writer, the journalist and poet Jessie Mackay, did not agree with the stand taken by the COs but had a strong commitment to social justice. A letter sent to every member of both houses of Parliament in March 1918 was signed not just by Mackay and Baughan but also by other women who held the same views: Mary Johnson,

Minnie Hawker and Jessie's sister Georgina. The group began their letter by stating that they had no wish to embarrass the government but had a strong wish to 'facilitate its efforts towards winning the war'.[19] They asked for the Military Service Act to be amended because as it applied to COs it wasn't working. Many responsible citizens saw it as unjust. The churches were uneasy, they said, and 'others, who value liberty of thought as one of the most precious assets of British freedom, view with extreme disfavour the failure of the Act to guarantee this liberty to men who are of no church or sect'.[20] They suggested that the conscience test be replaced with a character test, and that all approved cases be under civil control. Many of the objectors would be willing to do non-combatant work, they said, provided it wasn't under military control.[21]

Such letters may have had more impact on the military authorities than those from recognised peace advocates. A memo written by the adjutant-general Robert Tate (the chief administrative officer in the army), suggesting that the definition of conscientious objection in the Military Service Act was too narrow, had attached to it three letters: one from the secretary of the Congregational Union of New Zealand, one from Blanche Baughan, and the third was a letter written to Jessie Mackay by the minister of defence. Many of the men who went to prison were as worthy of consideration as the few whose cases were approved by the military service boards, wrote Tate.[22] Adding to the pressure on the government was a series of petitions signed by Catholic and Protestant clergy in Auckland, Wellington and other towns in the North Island, protesting against the deportation of conscientious and religious objectors.[23]

Canterbury writer Jessie Mackay was another who wanted changes to the Military Service Act. (Canterbury Museum)

'Twelve men bludgeoned'

In August 1917 the NPC wrote the first of several letters of protest to the government about the deportation and treatment of the 14 COs the previous month. They also took a deputation to the Christchurch Ministers' Association (CMA), and that organisation added its voice to those protesting against the deportations.[24]

News of the ill treatment of the deportees in early 1918 sparked a deluge of protest letters from numerous individuals and organisations, including Sarah Page for the CWI, John Howell for the Christchurch Meeting of the Society of Friends, Annie Gadd and Mary Mathieson for the Christchurch WIL, H. Robinson for the Socialist Party, Hiram Hunter for the United Federation of Labour (UFL), and Morgan Williams. Ethel Mackie wrote to protest against the use of 'Field punishment No. 1' – a particularly vicious form of punishment where a man was tied to a pole out in the open, with his knees and feet bound and his hands tied tightly behind his back.[25]

A strongly worded resolution from the CWI in January 1918 reacted to news that some of the deported COs had been kept in irons in Sling Camp, and that eight men had been sent to France, where they were in danger of being shot 'for refusing to obey orders in the presence of the enemy'.[26] This was published in the *Maoriland Worker* on the same page as a letter from Henry Patton, one of the deported COs, describing brutal treatment he had been subjected to.

Sarah Page, speaking in Victoria Square in February 1918 about the 14 men transported to the European war, questioned Allen's claim that the 14 had eventually 'joined forces with their mates from New Zealand': 'Mind you I am not accepting the report of the men's conversion as necessarily true. Sir James Allen has made – mistakes, shall we call them – before, and this report, unfortunately offers no reliable evidence that our brave lads are not still suffering the tortures of the damned.' She went on to say that if the report were true it would mean that 'Twelve men [had been] bludgeoned into violating their consciences, and you and I and the rest of New Zealand [are] silently acquiescing.'[27]

In response to the general outcry about the ill treatment of the deportees, Allen produced a printed statement that invited the people of New

Zealand to consider the 'clear-cut issue': 'whether defiance of the law is to be permitted and those persons who know no rule but their own inclination are to be practically exempted from military service'.[28] His use of the word 'inclination' instead of 'conscience' seems intended to further denigrate the COs. In a meeting with Allen, Page expressed her

HE CANNOT CHANGE HIS MIND.

New Zealand: Surely, Sir James, you don't really mean to shut out the press and the public from your promised inquiry into the treatment of those conscientious objectors. It would play right into their hands.

Sir James : That's my decree. I can't see my way to alter my opinion. What would become of our glorious Defence Department if people once got the notion that my officers or I ever change our minds ?

'He Cannot Change His Mind' depicts Sir James Allen being questioned by the soldier, representing New Zealand, about his decision not to allow the press or public into the inquiry into the treatment of conscientious objectors. (Edward Brodie Mack, *New Zealand Free Lance*, 4 July 1918, p. 3)

concern for the 14 deported COs. Some were not writing to their families, and she assumed they were in detention and not allowed to write. She told Allen their people were very anxious about them, and Allen promised to make enquiries.

A letter from Archibald Baxter, written in France in March 1918, in which he told his parents that he was being sent to the front the next day, that he was in sound mind, and that whatever happened he would not surrender, arrived in New Zealand some time in late April or early May. His father then received a telegram dated 14 May telling him that Baxter had been admitted to a mental hospital. After Archibald Baxter's letter was read to the NPC in June 1918, it was decided to send a letter to James Allen telling him he was responsible for Baxter's mental illness.

But it was Baughan who succeeded in giving widespread publicity to Baxter's letters. On 11 June a letter signed by Baughan, Mackay and Mary Johnson was sent to every member of Cabinet with a covering note emphasising the obvious conclusion to be drawn from the letter and telegram: that Baxter had been 'driven through repeated punishment as a disobedient soldier, into mental illness'. 'What,' they asked, 'have the Germans done that is worse than gradually torturing into mental instability a fellow countryman – and that for his conscience's sake?'[29] This was followed a few days later by a letter signed by 20 Christchurch women, including Grace Wills, Annie Ensom and Sarah Bradley.[30] On 29 June 1918 *New Zealand Truth* published copies of Baxter's letter and the telegram to his father, along with a covering note from Baughan that said 'pushed too often for refusing to do what his conscience forbade him to do … he has broken down in brain as well

Minister of Defence James Allen. (Alexander Turnbull Library)

as body'.[31] The combined effect of the publication of the letters was a 'storm of protest'.[32]

Millicent Brown, a young Christchurch woman recently returned from university study in England, and who later married Archibald Baxter, has described the impact his letter had on her when she first read it in the winter of 1918. 'My whole life changed. It moved me, right out of my shell into the open; and in the open I have remained, looking into things, questioning them.'[33] She became friendly with Baughan, but because Brown became a pacifist, they often clashed. For the most part Brown kept quiet about her pacifism because of the reaction of people around her: 'There was terrible hostility to any pacifist opinion. I was a coward. Seeing the fierceness of the feelings involved, I simply could not tell people I had changed.'[34]

Surprisingly, Allen was still reported in August 1918 as saying that every one of the 14 objectors who had gone to the front was now 'fighting with his unit'.[35] This prompted a letter from Mackie to the minister of defence, quoting Baxter's letter and calling for an untarnished and concise statement on what had happened to the deportees.[36]

Women sympathisers at court-martials

Because women were not permitted to fight in the armed forces they had more freedom to speak out against militarism. Sarah Page later recalled an occasion when a leading anti-militarist commented to her as they left the platform, 'Well, Mrs Page, they can't jail me without you, for you talked more sedition in five minutes than I in my whole speech.' Sure enough, he was arrested the next day and spent two years in prison, while she went free. [37]

The only woman imprisoned for breaching the war regulations was Ella Elizabeth Price who, with her husband William, was found guilty of hiding their son William, a deserter, in the ceiling of their house at 169 Victoria Street, Christchurch. Both parents were convicted and sentenced to six months in prison, but the jailing of a mother for protecting her son was not popular and Ella's sentence was remitted.[38]

Encouraged by the NPC, a large number of women including, no doubt, members of the CWI and WIL, attended hearings of the military service boards and court-martials when they were held in Christchurch – and they did not remain silent onlookers. They were exploiting the fact that the government was reluctant to jail women and that individual women speaking out in defiance of the war regulations would not be arrested for sedition. There was a 'moderate attendance of the public, women predominating' at the Christchurch court-martials of James Henry Roberts and George Wears Samms in June 1918, and at the court-martials of Noel Goldsbury, James Smyth Walker and Frank Robinson in September.[39] When Roberts told the court that it had married men before it that day and that 'if the members had a spark of manhood left they would spare the wives and children the sorrow of having their husbands and fathers wrenched from them', he won 'the beaming approval of several of the pronounced anti-militarists amongst the women present'. The growing applause 'was quickly checked by the president of the court'.[40]

Several people wrote to the military authorities about Christchurch men being taken to Wellington for their court-martial. Not only did this make it difficult for friends or family to be present but, as Sarah Page pointed out, they seemed to receive different treatment.[41] Baughan wrote to Tate on the subject: she said that she would go herself to Wellington if she could afford it, but 'more than a quarter of my small income already goes to help the war'.[42]

There were so many people, mainly women, who wanted to attend the hearing at the court-martials of COs Charles Warden and Arthur Borrows in the King Edward Barracks that many were shut out. The *Sun* reported that one woman made 'loud-voiced' calls for more chairs for the 'poor old women' who were without seats. Another argued that as the court was open to the public they could not legally be kept out: she was threatened with removal when she continued to argue the point, causing laughter among the women. When the hearing ended a large number of women marched out of the barracks singing 'Keep the Red Flag Flying'.[43] Reports like this, of groups of women who were openly anti-militarist, explain why another report of a group of Christchurch women chasing the members of a 'White Feather League' off the streets is very credible.[44]

'Women were everywhere': the 1918 'riot'

When it became clear in 1917 that Second Division men would need to be conscripted, leagues formed throughout the country to seek better conditions, increased pay, pensions and separation allowances for these married men. In April 1918 when married men with one child were balloted, more than 1600 people attended a large public meeting chaired by the Christchurch mayor, and when two waterside workers, John Flood and Edward Langley, moved that 'No Second Division man shall leave for camp until the demands of the League are acceded to', the audience went wild.

THE SICKENED DIVISION.

'The Sickened Division' depicts Hiram Hunter, John Flood and Edward Langley, briefly imprisoned for their role in a meeting that resolved that no Second Division men should leave for camp until the demands of the Second Division League were met. (William Blomfield, *New Zealand Observer*, 18 May 1918, p. 1)

After a slight amendment the motion was passed with just four dissenting.[45] When the first of the Second Division men gathered at the King Edward Barracks the following day, a huge crowd of 5000 gathered, aiming to prevent the men leaving. According to one report the crowd comprised mainly women:

> Women were everywhere. In fact, the whole of the crowd seemed to consist of women – women with babies in arms, women with children by the hand, women in pairs, in threes, in fours and in groups, women with go-carts and women with dogs. The city was ALIVE WITH CHATTERING WOMEN … In that array of five thousand women were all the elements of a raging storm.[46]

Another report said many of the women were in a very ugly mood – they 'hooted and jeered and urged on the men to defy the military'.[47] Military officers made repeated attempts to rope off part of the barracks for a roll call, but the crowd prevented them from doing so. In the end the volunteers were told to leave the barracks singly and make their own way to the railway station. Once the willing men had left by the Montreal Street entrance, a mêlée broke out at the Cashel Street entrance, mainly centred on police attempts to arrest a man. When a policeman tried to grab an 'obstreperous' youth in knickerbockers, he was attacked by a woman with an umbrella.[48] The crowd succeeded in preventing a good proportion of the men from being processed, though nearly all were processed in the days following.

Flood and Langley and Hiram Hunter, who had seconded the motion at the meeting on 28 April, were all arrested and sentenced to imprisonment for sedition – six months for Flood and Langley, and three months for Hunter – under the war regulations. Less than three weeks later the government remitted their sentences, much to the indignation of those who had been calling for harsh measures to be taken against the protesters.[49] A press report attributed the disturbance to extremists who had been making themselves obnoxious lately, and said that a number of women, mainly young women, had been most obnoxious of all. The report also quoted Mayor Henry Holland as saying that if the government had announced its increase in the allowance to married men earlier, there would have been no disturbance.[50]

At least one woman made an individual protest on the inadequacy of military pay. In April 1917 Bridget Cremin appealed to the military service board on the grounds that her husband's military pay and the government's separation allowance were insufficient to support her and her children. Her husband John Cremin had enlisted without consulting her. As a result of her appeal he was granted indefinite leave without pay.[51]

Working with Labour

Sarah Page and Ada Wells, meanwhile, had thrown in their lot with the Labour Party. Ada Wells spoke about conscription on behalf of women at the party's 1917 conference; and as part of a Labour Party deputation to government minister William Herries she described conscription as the curse of Europe which had been planted in New

Zealand: 'It was astounding that they had arrived at a time when men who stood up for freedom and the boasted right of their civilisation were put into prison cells … Imperialism was costing the New Zealand people too much.'[52]

Before the April 1917 local body elections Page worked on the Labour Representation Committee (LRC), and Ada Wells stood as a candidate. Labour Party candidates in Christchurch had made the repeal of the Military Service Act the main plank of their campaign, against the advice of more moderate leaders Howard, McCullough and McCombs. The greatly reduced vote that Labour received – 29 per cent, down from 42 per cent in 1915 – was widely seen as a general endorsement of conscription in the community.[53] Another way of looking at the election results, however, was to see it as a victory – that 'five New Zealand Labour Party (NZLP) candidates … elected while running on an anti-war, anti-conscriptionist and anti-exploitation

The 1917 board of the Christchurch Technical College included well-known anti-militarists Ada Wells nd Henry Worrall. The Quaker John Howell, director of the college, is seated fourth from the right. (Ara Institute of Canterbury)

ticket' was just one less than in the previous election.[54] It was also a victory for Ada Wells, who became the first woman to serve on the Christchurch City Council. Admittedly Wells was probably elected despite her 'exuberant and pacifist' campaign, not because of it: she was already well known for her long history of community service for women and children.[55]

'Wonderful things in the name of "LIBERTY"'

At war's end Mackie still felt that people had gone 'completely off their heads'. By this time he was feeling even more despondent and cynical about the impact the government's wartime actions had had on democracy.

> War madness overtook us as rapidly and as effectually as in other countries and sent the people completely off their heads. They gave themselves up to a perfect saturnalia of war lust and hatred and in its onward rush the storm swept away parliament, Church, law, and everything else that we had been foolish enough in brighter days to imagine were stable institutions of the State. We have had no elections since 1914. We have eliminated 'parties' since then, we have suspended many of our laws, and we have in truth done wonderful things in the name of 'LIBERTY'.[56]

The NPC and CWI had protested throughout the war at the loss of democratic decision-making and the 'tyrannical powers vested in ministers by Section 29 of the Expeditionary Forces Act 1915'. By redefining the term 'time of war' the government had given itself the ability to place the country under martial law and to call out the militia at any time during the war.[57] Likewise the CWI called on New Zealand voters to 'demand the abolition of the system of governing the people by regulations framed in secret at the instance of military authorities, and not submitted to Parliament'.[58]

In an effort to provide the government with some grassroots opinion, the NPC convened a meeting in April 1918 to consider the visit of the premier, Massey, and his deputy Joseph Ward to an imperial conference in London where the terms of peace would likely be discussed. Forty-three delegates from labour and other progressive organisations attended the meeting: the CWI, WIL, the Socialist Party, the Social Democratic Party (SDP), several unions, the UFL, the Trades and Labour Council – and the NPC itself which, in addition to four delegates, had 10 members in attendance. Resolutions passed by the meeting objected to Massey and Ward going to London; endorsed Labour's policy for the abolition of war; repudiated any proposal for the retention of Sāmoa; supported the idea of a League of Nations; and called for a general election before the New Zealand representatives departed for England, or before the Expeditionary Force was increased. The resolutions were sent to unions for endorsement, and to MPs.[59]

Peace Treaty a 'breach of that international morality'

When the terms of the Peace Treaty with Germany became known in August 1919 the peace movement was deeply disappointed. The treaty constituted an 'indefensible breach of that international morality whose vindication it was the declared aim of the Allied and Associated Governments to ensure', said the CWI.[60] This resolution prompted derision from a *Star* editorial, which not only criticised the resolution for shedding copious tears over the plight of 'poor unfortunate Germany' but also belittled the work of the CWI, surmising that it was neither large nor representative. The same editorial took a swipe at the COs in Paparua:

> We do not know exactly who or what the Canterbury Women's Institute is, but we suspect that it is composed of ladies of peace-at-any-price and anti-militarist brands. We have never heard that it performed any patriotic service during the war, or that it did anything for the soldiers in or out of New Zealand. We strongly suspect that it reserved its admiration and energies for the benefit of the peculiar gentry whose war labours were confined to the Paparua front. We believe also that the Canterbury Women's Institute, in spite of its pretentious title, has a very short membership roll, and that it is by no means representative

of the women of Canterbury. The 'resolution' was forwarded to us by Mrs Sarah S. Page, honorary secretary of the C.W.I., but beyond the information that it was passed at a general meeting on Friday last it does not explain anything. Was this lengthy production passed at a meeting of a dozen very estimable but too-confiding ladies, or was that a full house and an attendance of hundreds?[61]

The newspaper's guess of 'a dozen ladies' at a meeting may have been accurate. The membership in 1919 was about twenty, including Ada Wells, Rose Atkinson, Sarah Bradley, Annie Ensom, Louisa Nuttall, Ida Cooke and Naomi Macfarlane, all of whom were also members of the NPC; Mrs Gadd, Mrs F. Robinson and Mrs Henderson, whose husbands were COs; and Florence Chapple, whose husband had been imprisoned for sedition.[62]

This was the last year that the CWI held regular meetings, and even in the preceding year reports of meetings had fallen away after March 1918, when Page spent three months in Wellington while her son Robin was in the Alexandra Barracks. Possibly Page and Wells' anti-militarist and socialist views and their espousal of party politics – which was a major shift from the CWI's stance when it began in the 1890s – had alienated some members, or perhaps the two leaders felt that with the release of the COs their job was done and they could afford to take a well-earned rest. They were also unsuccessful in their bid to be elected to the Christchurch City Council in 1919, after campaigning along-side James Chapple for municipal ownership of housing and land, municipal baths, creches, kitchens, laundries and playgrounds.[63] The Christchurch WIL also seems to have lapsed by the early 1920s, possibly because its members decided their greater loyalties were with the labour movement.[64]

When will they be released?

As the war neared its end, the peace movement focused on the treatment of COs who were still in prison, and the all-important question of when they would be released.

In March 1919 a deputation of Christchurch anti-militarists met with George Russell, minister for internal affairs and public health, who was facing a commission of inquiry into the handling of the recent influenza pandemic. The three matters on the agenda of this meeting were the proposal to increase territorial training to four months; the ongoing detention of COs; and the Wanganui Detention Barracks. The deputation, which was headed by William Ensom and included Hiram Hunter, secretary of the National Federation of Labour, unionists Tim Armstrong and Fred Cooke (who was also president of the LRC), and NPC stalwarts Harry Atkinson and Charles Mackie, claimed to represent a large body of the workers of the dominion. Sarah Page and Ada Wells from the CWI also spoke at the meeting, which featured a certain amount of heckling and revealed deep division between those present and the minister. On the matter of the COs the minister said 'he would not move one hand to obtain the release of the men who were now serving terms of imprisonment in connection with offences against the law'.[65]

The deputation received widespread coverage in the nation's newspapers, but most gave prominence to a 'violent outburst' from S. Smith, president of the Christchurch branch of the New Zealand Socialist Party (NZSP), and the heckling that ensued after he spoke.[66] As a result, most press reports had headlines that focused on 'Kindly words for the Germans', the 'Wild talk' and 'Pro-German sentiments' rather than the statements made by the deputation about military training or the need to release the COs.[67]

Numerous individuals and organisations in Christchurch, including the CWI and the Socialist Party, were still writing to the minister of defence urging the release of all COs. Others called for the release of a particular group of COs: Baughan, for example, wrote in June 1919 to press for the release of the religious COs. Others wrote about individual cases, including Jessie MacKay writing about Kennaway Henderson and Robin Page in July 1919.[68] Sarah Page wrote in May asking for a personal interview with Allen when he was next in Christchurch as she wanted to convince him of the injustice of the treatment of COs, which, she said, was so utterly opposed to the spirit of the British

Constitution as expressed in the Magna Carta: 'To no one will we sell, to no one will we deny or delay right or justice.' She wrote again the following week to ask why deeply religious and honest men such as Henderson were being held in prison to complete second sentences of two years, while other sincere COs were being released after serving a first sentence of one year or less. In June, she wrote to beg for the release of all military prisoners, and in July 1919, as secretary of the CWI, she congratulated the government on the release of Māori COs and expressed the hope that all COs, military defaulters and military prisoners would now be released.[69] The government's response was to say that COs should not be released until all soldiers had returned to New Zealand – a position that was probably wise, according to Paul Baker, given public sentiment and a barrage of letters being sent to the government from the Returned Servicemen's Association.[70]

Other letters were concerned about the acquittal by a court-martial of Lieutenant J. L. Crampton, commandant of the Wanganui Detention Barracks, despite the evidence given against him during the magisterial inquiry conducted by J. G. Hewitt. The Christchurch WIL protested emphatically against the verdict, and the CMA expressed its 'detestation of the ferocity and brutality exhibited by those in charge of the Wanganui Detention Barracks, in their treatment of conscientious objectors'.[71]

The government was continuing to court-martial deserters and objectors. Two men court-martialled and sent to Paparua in July 1919 were released just a few weeks later. Mackie found this mystifying and unfair: why, he asked, were men like Kennaway Henderson still in prison? The answer the NPC received from the prime minister was that they would continue to prosecute defaulters until all the men under sentence were released.[72]

Meanwhile the issue of the proposed loss of civil rights for military defaulters had become a matter of concern.

Religious advisory board

The Expeditionary Forces Amendment Bill, introduced into Parliament in December 1918, provided for the loss of civil rights for

10 years for all military defaulters and objectors except for 'bona fide' religious objectors. In order to identify which objectors were genuinely religious, a religious objectors' advisory board (RAB) was set up to interview and report on all the COs still in prison. The members of the board were C. E. Matthews, the inspector of prisons; Rev J. R. Burgin, a chaplain to the forces; Rev J. G. Chapman, a Methodist minister from Wellington; and, representing labour, though many in the labour movement would have said he was not a true labourite, M. J. (Joe) Mack, the general secretary of the Amalgamated Society of Railway Servants.[73] Starting in Wellington on 30 January 1919, the RAB proceeded to visit Paparua, Invercargill and Rotoaira prisons in February, and Kaingaroa, Waikeria and Auckland prisons in March 1919; in all they interviewed 273 men.

For many of the religious prisoners, especially the Quakers, this desire to identify the 'genuine' religious objectors smacked of preferential treatment. During the war years Quakers had consistently tried to win the same privileges as they had for other COs; now they once again protested to the minister of defence.[74] Probably because of the influence of Quaker prisoners, many of the COs at Waikeria tried to make a similar protest and decided to declare themselves 'defiant' objectors before the board 'in order that they will not be liberated before *all* are freed'.[75] Not everyone thought this was a wise move: Reg Williams reported that about two thirds of his fellow prisoners at Waikeria had refused to see the board – an action that he thought they might later regret. He also thought it was hardly fair of the Quakers to influence others in this regard, as they were unlikely to go on the military defaulters list, whether or not they saw the board – though he hastened to add it was the Quakers' *actions* he thought were wrong, not their absolute sincerity or good intentions.

Williams wrote in some detail about his own interview with the RAB, which, he reported, was pleasant throughout and they parted good friends. He found the board members amiable, particularly Burgin. He was asked about the 'class of literature' he read, and about the length of time he had held the opinions he expressed.[76] Most of the lengthy interview, he reported, was taken up with a debate with

Joe Mack, whose line of questioning included 'Would you be prepared to work on the wharf with a chinaman?' This somewhat surprising approach was apparently aimed at trying to expose fallacies or inconsistencies in Williams' beliefs. Having established that Williams saw compulsory unionism as a 'necessary evil', Mack drew a comparison between Williams' beliefs and those of a man who had conscientious objections to joining a union, and he queried whether Williams was showing a humane or international spirit when he said that such a man 'would have to go elsewhere'. Williams explained there was a vast difference between the two situations: 'All the experience of the past and the present goes to show that war in all its effects is injurious to mankind, while all such experience in connection with unionism shows that its effects have been manifestly beneficial to the industrially organised.' Mack: 'But don't you see old man where I am trying to get you to?' Williams: 'Quite clearly thank you.'[77]

Williams dealt equally competently with Mack's question about the so-called 'yellow peril' – the fear of 'invasion' by Asian populations. Would Williams fight if a capitalist syndicate introduced 10,000 Japanese workers to exploit New Zealand? 'The enemy in that case would not be the Japanese but the capitalists,' said Williams. 'So far as the Japanese were concerned it would be better to educate them than to kill them'.[78] When Burgin asked Williams how he regarded Christianity, Williams said he agreed with Thomas Paine: 'The World is my Country, Mankind my Brethren, and to do Good my Religion.' Chapman approved of this: 'Those are splendid sentiments.'[79]

Williams seemed cheered by his meeting with the RAB and was still writing optimistically in April 1919 when he reported they were all looking forward to the results of the board's visitation, and particularly the military defaulters list. To some, particularly school teachers, he said, it was of the utmost importance. 'We are all in good health and quite cheerful. The weather is getting cooler, the sandflies and mosquitoes scarcer and the day of release is nearer so why worry.' But he hinted at the underlying frustration of still being in prison, so many months after the war had ended, when he wrote, 'It looks as if some of us are going to die in gaol.'[80] A month later he was rejoicing in the fact that his sentence was past the halfway mark. 'Correspondents still seem hopeful of our "early" release, but we who are inside are becoming more and more sceptical.'[81] By late May, he said that while some remained hopeful of being released in early June, he thought he was more likely to be released on about 1 February 1920.[82]

The report of the RAB named 113 men as genuine religious objectors, and their names were not included on the list of defaulters, published in June 1919. Those who were on the list lost their voting rights and the eligibility to stand for local or national government for 10 years. In addition, they could not be employed by any government agency or local body. This was a severe blow to many of the COs.

The publication of the list had an unsettling effect on some of the CO prisoners in Paparua named on the list, who refused to work in protest at one of their fellow prisoners being locked in his cell after he refused to take part in a fire practice because he didn't believe in saving government property. Twelve military prisoners 'of the red fed persuasion' were locked in their cells as punishment. The jailer reported that the religious objectors had not joined in.[83]

The NPC described the military defaulters list as foolish and brutal, and urged people to vote only for candidates who pledged to repeal the measure in the upcoming parliamentary elections. Imposing additional and as yet indeterminate punishment was constitutionally unsound and 'inimical to the maintenance of stable government'.[84] It was also haphazard in its impact: some COs would be prevented from working at the only occupation they knew, while others would be free to return to their former occupation. And the fact that those on the list would not be able to stand for election meant the citizens of New Zealand were being deprived of the free choice of candidates. Finally, the NPC argued that the military defaulters were not criminals, and had won the esteem and respect of all who had dealt with them.[85]

Williams, clearly deeply disappointed at being named a defaulter, considered appealing, but doubted that he would receive an impartial hearing when he learnt that his case would probably be heard by the visiting magistrate to Waikeria – a former soldier who had sat on military court-martials held at Featherston Military Camp.[86]

There are no further extant letters from Williams to Mackie in the latter months of 1919, perhaps because there was little to write about. Life at Waikeria had become a matter of just waiting for release. Williams proved to have made a fairly accurate prediction about the date of his own release, which came on 1 January 1920.

Release of the conscientious objectors

In July 1919 a meeting of 2000 people in the Christchurch Opera House heard Harry Holland, MP and former editor of the *Maoriland Worker*, speak on 'Peace and the conscientious objector'. Ann Saunders, who was in the audience, later wrote that she had tears in her eyes as Holland read accounts written by deported COs Mark Briggs and Archibald Baxter.[87] At the conclusion of the meeting Sarah Page and Ada Wells moved and seconded a motion urging the release of all imprisoned COs, military defaulters and other military prisoners, and pledging support for the Labour Party's move to secure the restoration of civil rights to the COs. The resolution was carried unanimously with enthusiasm.[88]

The largest release of CO prisoners occurred just a few weeks later, after the government decided to release all 56 of the 'bona fide' religious objectors still in prison at the end of August, along with another 14 who were serving their second terms of imprisonment.[89] By this time, 23 of Canterbury's COs had already gained their freedom, and another 23 were released under this provision – 12 from Paparua on 30 August, and 11 on 1 September 1919 from Waikeria, Rotoaira and Invercargill prisons.[90] Another three

Harry Holland, trade unionist and socialist activist, had edited the *Maoriland Worker* and written a critique of the conscription policy and practices during the war, titled 'Armageddon or Calvary', before he became leader of the Labour Party in 1919. (Alexander Turnbull Library)

were released early in September, and William Hill in November. The last of the Canterbury objectors to be released was William Michael Ryan who, unusually, served almost the full two years of his sentence before his release in July 1920.[91]

CHAPTER 9

SOWING THAT OTHERS MAY REAP: THE LEGACY OF THE WORLD WAR I PEACE MOVEMENT

Soon after the war began, a friend told Mackie it was now clear that they couldn't expect their peace work to bring results in their life-time: they could only be the sowers, others must reap.[1] Mackie was clearly disappointed by the number of supporters who abandoned the peace cause during the war: 'so many of our peace friends have found themselves drawn into the whirlpool'.[2] Seven years later he still felt deeply disillusioned at how little the peace movement had been able to achieve during the war, when they had been crippled financially and under severe censorship.

There were other, more tangible legacies of the war for the peace movement and the conscientious objectors (COs), too. Many of the COs, after their release, were forced to change their occupation, and the stigma against them could be long-lasting. But for many the same idealism that had spurred them to become objectors is evident in their commitment to working for a better world, through a variety of political and community organisations.

For Mackie, the ongoing censorship of his correspondence was an annoying reminder of wartime conditions. A request he made in October 1919 to have the mail that had been detained under the war regulations sent to him was refused: in fact, most of the literature sent to him had been destroyed and Mackie remained a marked man, singled out for 'special attention'.[3] Censorship of the National Peace Council (NPC)'s mail seems to have continued until July 1920.[4]

John Howell, who in 1917 had been appointed official visitor to Quakers imprisoned as COs, also paid a price. Despite being highly successful in his role as director of the Christchurch Technical College, he came in for harsh criticism for continuing to include a prayer for the enemy in the college's daily assembly; for not giving the college a holiday when Bulgaria surrendered; and for not flying the flag on that same day. In addition he was accused of being responsible for CO Noel Goldsbury's actions. Howell, in turn, criticised a board decision that had asked him to prepare a list of the children of alien enemies attending the college: 'The spirit that can desire to pillory innocent children will be, I hope, for ever far removed from any who are called upon to take part in the administration of education.'[5] Ada Wells, who sat on the technical college board as a representative of the city council, also came under attack for her support of Goldsbury. Even before the war Reginald Ford, who moved to Whanganui in 1913 to set himself up as an architect, told Mackie that he had to keep mum because Whanganui was a very conservative military centre.

Impact of the military defaulters list

There were added challenges for the 24 Cantabrian COs on the military defaulters list, especially for those who had been in the public service. The impact on Norman Bell, released on 12 April 1919, was particularly harsh.

Bell had taken a principled stand of not appearing before the religious advisory board (RAB) and, probably because of this, was placed on the military defaulters list – a major blow for a school teacher in the public service. A letter to Allen pleading for Bell's name to be removed from the list, written by an acquaintance of his, had no effect. Bell had refused to have a medical examination because he wanted to demonstrate to his high-school students that moral convictions were important; to punish him further was cruel and unjustifiable, the letter said. 'No one who knows Mr Bell can do other than esteem him for his simple and manly character.'[6] Allen's reply reflects the gulf between the views of the COs and the government of the day. He said he could not understand how a conscience could be created 'which permits a man to escape his duty to his country, thereby possibly saving his life: whilst others give themselves for their country's safety'.[7]

Bell instead became a private tutor in languages, including Hebrew, Māori and Esperanto; and in science and mathematics; and as a tutor at the Canterbury WEA from 1919 he taught sociology, international relations and Esperanto. He devoted his life to several good causes, including the peace movement, and was elected a member of the NPC in June 1919. Understandably, he seems to have chosen to work among groups who would be sympathetic to his ideals.[8]

The NPC highlighted the iniquities of the military defaulters list by nominating Bell as a Labour candidate for the Christchurch North parliamentary seat. The party's Christchurch North Branch, knowing he was ineligible, decided not to nominate another candidate and instead passed a resolution, moved by Ada Wells, that described the military defaulters list as: 'peculiarly arbitrary, vindictive and unjust, as by depriving men of their political and civil rights the Government is also depriving them of their means of livelihood. We believe this penalisation of men who have followed their convictions is not only a personal but a national calamity.'[9]

John Roberts, who had resigned from the Woolston Borough Council while in prison, was also on the defaulters' list. With his lifelong commitment to the labour and peace movements, he would almost certainly have stood for public office after the war if he had been eligible. By the late 1930s he was 'one of the most indefatigable workers for the Labour Movement in the Dominion'.[10] As well as president of the Canterbury District Trades Council, he was serving on the national executive of the Labour Party, and as president of the North Canterbury Labour Representation Committee (LRC). A 1938 profile of Roberts attributed the success of Labour candidates in the recent municipal elections to his organising ability.

George Samms is another Canterbury CO who would probably have stood for office after his release if he had not been on the military defaulters list. Before his imprisonment he had stood for election to the Woolston Borough Council, and he later served as secretary of the Woolston branch of the Labour Party for 21 years.[11] His friend and fellow defaulter Frank Robinson had also played a leading part in the labour movement before his imprisonment – as president of the Woolston Branch of the Labour Party, president of the Christchurch Iron and Brass Moulders Union and of the New Zealand Moulders Federation. Six years before his death in 1948 he was elected to the Christchurch Drainage Board.[12]

Working for a better world

The careers of those COs who were not named on the list of defaulters were also often affected by their time in prison. Kennaway Henderson had emerged from the experience embittered – not by his treatment in prison, but by the actions of those in authority who, he believed, had deliberately and self-righteously 'besmirched and trodden underfoot the principles of human justice and ethical behaviour'.[13] His punishment had been particularly harsh because, after serving nine months' imprisonment with hard labour, he appeared before another court-martial in November 1918, just days before the armistice, on a second charge of failing to parade for a medical examination. The following day he was sentenced to two years' imprisonment with hard labour, even though fighting had already ceased and the war was about to end.

On his release from Paparua prison Henderson's one desire was to move to a piece of land where he and his wife Pauline could practise a self-sufficient way of life. In Henderson Valley, near Auckland, living on six acres of land, half of it in native bush, they were 'happy and hopeful' in 1921.[14] However, despite hard work and kind and helpful neighbours, Henderson later left Auckland and found work as a caricaturist in

Sydney. In 1931 the Hendersons returned to Christchurch, where he pursued his dream of founding a radical independent journal. With the support of two members of the academic staff at Canterbury College, he proceeded to produce the journal *Tomorrow*, which ran from July 1934 until April 1935, and from July 1935 until 1940. The editorial policy of the paper was against war and fascism, and in favour of socialism and cooperation. Many of New Zealand's most promising young writers became regular contributors, and according to Denis Glover, 'When you knocked at Kennaway's door you entered into another world … It was a world where the nicest, quietest, kindliest man in the country was preparing to demolish the System.'[15] During World War II *Tomorrow* was forced to cease publication in 1940 when its printers were threatened with prosecution for sedition.

After the war, Thomas Nuttall and his wife Maud moved to Taihape, where Thomas became a commercial traveller. They were keen to get away from the stigma of Thomas being a CO – the white feathers and the 'nasty letters'. They later moved back to Christchurch, where he served on the Linwood Avenue and Christchurch West school committees, the School Committees Association, and the board of governors of

Thomas Nuttall with his wife and children. From left to right: Betty, Thomas, Thomas Burson, wife Maud and Ron. (Nuttall family)

Christchurch Technical College. Like many other COs he wanted to work for the betterment of society. He was active in the Labour Party and in the trade union movements. In 1938 he was appointed secretary of the Canterbury Clerks, Cashiers and Office Employees Union, was elected to the Christchurch City Council, and became a council representative on the North Canterbury Hospital Board.[16]

Charles Edward (Charlie) Warden was another CO who lost his employment as a direct result of his refusal to serve. He went to live at Arthur's Pass where Grace Adams, who frequently visited Arthur's Pass as a child, saw him as having a 'hint of mystery', as he had 'done almost no regular work for years and had buried himself at Arthur's Pass without ever once budging … It was said he'd been a conscientious objector … and, going by his current reading, was now a socialist – perhaps even more left than that!'[17] In 1929 Warden was appointed to a part-time position as the first resident park ranger for the Arthur's Pass National Park Board.[18]

The post-war life stories of Kennaway Henderson, Thomas Nuttall, Charles Warden and Reg Williams, all highly intelligent and articulate men, show a desire, at least initially, to 'hide' – which is understandable, given the hostility that their stand had aroused in many communities and workplaces. Williams initially remained in touch with the NPC after his release: he sought their support for a plan to travel around the country in a horse-drawn van from which he would make his living by selling publications such as the Union of Democratic Control (UDC)'s *Foreign Affairs* and the *Beacon* (a

Reg Williams as the trapeze artist Delgado in the 1930s. His act, called the 'Slide of Death', was a highlight of the Hippodrome Vaudeville Company's show. (*Ellesmere Guardian*, 26 March 1935, p. 3)

short-lived magazine published and partly funded by William Ensom), while also holding meetings, delivering addresses and talking to people.[19] He had held successful meetings in other parts of the country before the war, and he now felt the 'growing need to reach the country districts for the purpose of educating the people on the great issues of the day'. Some in the labour movement supported the scheme, but Williams didn't want to become a mouthpiece for the Labour Party because, although he loyally supported its ideals, he would find it difficult to explain 'why one Labour MP is

Robin Page. (Page family)

wasting his time crying out for war memorials or another asking for a "Navy" as New Zealand's first line of "defence"'.[20] By one account he became a 'rather idiosyncratic figure touring the country preaching peace from a small gypsy caravan'.[21] Later he worked as a circus acrobat, and he developed an aquarium. This rather eclectic progression of jobs seems at variance with the natural abilities he had displayed as an articulate organiser, writer and orator as a young man.

Old and new careers

Ernest Munns, another CO and a leading member of the Richmond Mission, started his own business, a men's clothing shop, after the war because he found it impossible to find work.[22] Noel Goldsbury, who had to resign from his position at the technical college, went to work for Ivory Brothers, distributors of orchard supplies, and later became a successful apple grower at Loburn.[23]

Robin Page never expressed any regrets or bitterness about his wartime experiences but nonetheless he seems to have made an unexpected career move post-war. His brilliant academic record as a student would normally have been followed by overseas study and an academic career, but although he was permitted to return to Canterbury College after the war, and completed his MSc, he then took a job as industrial chemist at the Woolston Tanneries, where he became general manager at the age of 28. He eventually gained his DSc in 1934. He was well respected by his peers, and enjoyed his work, friends and sport.[24]

Self-employed tradesmen such as Jim Worrall were possibly among the least affected by the restrictions imposed on them as COs. A plumber before the war, Worrall was described as a building contractor afterwards. Henry Reynolds returned to his trade as bootmaker and continued to play an active part in the anti-militarist movement in the 1920s and 30s. During World War II he faced further charges of publishing subversive material when he placed posters and pictures in his shop window. The charges were withdrawn after he agreed to stop displaying such material, but he declared that his commitment to peace work would continue.[25] Douglas Day returned to similar work in the agricultural sector post-war, and remained a committed member of the Richmond Mission.

Conscientious objectors who had spent time in prison were determined to work towards improving conditions for prisoners after the war. They formed a Returned Objectors' Association, but it was short-lived and seems to have petered out by 1921.[26] Individuals carried on the prison reform work – such as Florence Smith, co-founder of the Richmond Mission, who became a prison visitor. The mission continued to help recently released prisoners for many years after the war. By 1921 Blanche Baughan and Norman Bell were organising lectures and concerts at 'our various prisons', including Paparua.[27] In 1924 Baughan founded the Howard League for Penal Reform, after reading about the English league in the *Spectator*. Charles Mackie and Lincoln Efford became committed and long-serving members.[28]

Labour Party and National Peace Council part company

The escalating cost of living under the coalition government during the war was a contributing factor to the development of the Labour Party. In the 1919 general election, three out of six Christchurch electorates returned Labour Party members of Parliament. The renowned pacifist and anti-conscriptionist Ted Howard defeated the retired Christchurch mayor, Henry Holland, for the Christchurch South seat; and in the Avon electorate Dan Sullivan defeated Cabinet minister George W. Russell. With the election of Tim Armstrong in Christchurch East in 1922, and with McCombs still holding the Lyttelton seat, Labour now had four Christchurch MPs. But the experience of working alongside anti-militarists and prohibitionists against conscription, and the divisiveness caused by such issues, had taught the Labour Party that such pressure groups could not be allowed to take control of party policy. In the words of labour historian Elizabeth Plumridge, 'Anti-militarism and prohibition were at heart extraneous issues. Both had to be laid aside.'[29]

This did not happen overnight. The NPC had spent considerable time in 1918 discussing the party's position on war and peace, and it sent remits to the Labour Party conference, along with a new recommended platform on defence, called 'Internationalism and Peace'.

The following year Norman Bell, who represented the NPC on the Christchurch LRC, was supported by Fred Cooke, Tim Armstrong and Walter Nash in a bid to have the party declare its unequivocal opposition to militarism in all its forms. The move was narrowly defeated, but in 1920 the party's conference showed an anti-militarist determination in passing resolutions that demanded immediate international disarmament, and the requirement that workers respond to the declaration of war by a general strike.

The NPC sent delegates to this 1920 Labour Conference, but by 1925 it had severed all links with the party.[30] Bell later explained that it had withdrawn because of the requirement that members agree to abide by all present and future decisions of the party. For Bell it was a matter of conscience, but given the Labour Party's move towards a stronger perception of itself as a party of the working class with its own political message, it seems that the NPC would not have been able to remain affiliated to the party, even if it had wanted to.[31]

New groups, new workers

Some of the COs came out of prison wanting to establish a new and more proactive pacifist organisation. There was talk of calling a meeting of representatives from local organisations to discuss the formation of a Total Disarmament Society, which Mackie suggested could be formed along the lines of the old Anti-Militarist League (AML). A few months later there was discussion about changing the constitution, with a view to having a 'World Peace' organisation. The status quo prevailed, however, and Mackie continued to maintain relationships with individuals and peace groups locally and internationally, while working on national issues such as CMT, which was still in place. By 1922 there had been 22,000 prosecutions under the Defence Act. In 1927, when theological student Alun Richards refused to drill he had to pay a fine, and lost his civil rights for 10 years. The publicity surrounding this prosecution gave rise to a petition and deputation to the prime minister, with the result that CMT was finally ended in 1930.[32]

According to David Grant, by the late 1920s pacifist groups in New Zealand were in a precarious state – although Mackie would probably have disagreed with Grant's assessment of the NPC as being 'barely alive'.[33]

The League of Nations Union, established in Britain in October 1918, had failed to live up to its idealistic beginnings. In New Zealand the first branch of the union was established in Wellington in 1922, with Presbyterian minister James Gibb as chairman.[34] A Christchurch branch was active by 1925, with William T. Airey as president and members and supporters of the NPC among its members: Mackie and Harry Atkinson were on the council, and Robert Laing and Elizabeth Taylor were vice-presidents. (Taylor, as president of the New Zealand Women's Christian Temperance Union (WCTU) from 1926 to 1935, also consistently promoted world peace through that organisation.)[35] But just as the League of Nations failed to maintain world peace, the League of Nations Union became ineffective: it suffered from internal disagreements between those who were pacifist and those who believed the League of Nations needed to act with force at times.[36] The challenge of establishing pacifist organisations in the post-war years fell to another generation of peace workers who, in Christchurch at least, had strong connections to the 'old guard' who had been active before and during World War I. Fred Page was one: his mother Sarah had set an inspirational example, and he had been so deeply affected by seeing his elder brother imprisoned for his beliefs that he had written to the minister of defence to say that, as he shared his brother's views, he would like to have the privilege of sharing his imprisonment.[37]

After the war Fred dedicated himself to the cause of world peace, speaking and writing about the dangers and futility of war. 'Surely it is time we realised that there is nothing that will lead to more certain disaster than a continuance of war,' he wrote in July 1919. His pacifism was based firmly on his Christian belief in an all-powerful God of love; he argued that: 'The only salvation is faith in the power of Love – a realisation that Christianity will work even where everything else has failed – that the teaching of the New Testament is not true because Christ said it, but that Christ said it because it is true.'[38] Two years later he warned that fear was driving the build-up of arms and military capacity, and was leading the world closer to 'the brink of the precipice of destruction … We shall gain real security only when we cast aside fear and have courage to hope that our neighbours will feel kindly disposed towards us as long as we are kindly disposed towards them.'[39]

The conflict between the supremacy of individual conscience and the state or other authorities was to be a theme of Fred Page's life. A short-lived career as a teacher at Christchurch Boys' High School came to an end after he protested against an amendment to the Education Act which empowered

Fred Page. (Page family)

school committees to refuse admission to any child who refused to salute the flag and sing the national anthem. His request that a conscience clause be added to the customary oath of allegiance for all teachers led not just to his dismissal, but he was also banned from the teaching profession.[40] For Fred this meant more time for peace advocacy work, while he taught privately as a university coach. He also held classes for workers at the Woolston tanneries, and gave weekly lectures at Paparua prison.[41]

'Morality, Honesty and Brotherhood'

Several of the new generation of peace workers attributed their commitment to world peace to the influence of the Socialist Sunday School. The school began in 1918 under the leadership of the Rev Jim Chapple, who the previous year had officiated at a dedication of children into the socialist movement. The meeting was opened by singing the Red Flag, followed by a short address to the parents: 'All the children were lined up at once in front of the stage, and the New Zealand Socialist Party's banner was held over them while the Rev Chapple dedicated them to the Socialist movement.'[42]

In January 1918 the Socialist Party organised a special tram and motorboats to take a crowd of children to the camping ground at Pleasant Point on the Avon estuary where the Woolston Social Democratic Party (SDP) hosted a day of picnicking, games and races, ending with entertainment in a big shed. Parents were urged to send their children to be taught 'Morality, Honesty and Brotherhood' at the Socialist Sunday School, which began meeting in February on Sunday afternoons.[43]

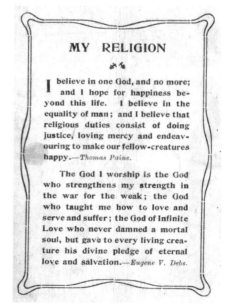

MY RELIGION

I believe in one God, and no more; and I hope for happiness beyond this life. I believe in the equality of man; and I believe that religious duties consist of doing justice, loving mercy and endeavouring to make our fellow-creatures happy.—*Thomas Paine.*

The God I worship is the God who strengthens my strength in the war for the weak; the God who taught me how to love and serve and suffer; the God of Infinite Love who never damned a mortal soul, but gave to every living creature his divine pledge of eternal love and salvation.—*Eugene V. Debs.*

Lincoln Efford's 'My Religion' card from the Socialist Sunday School, 1920s. (Efford family)

Fred Page was a teacher at the school, as were his aunt Ann Saunders, Norman Bell, Charlie Warden and Andrew Kydd. Between 50 and 120 children attended the school in the 1920s, and they formed lifelong friendships there. The name of the school was problematic for some; the words Sunday School suggested a Christian organisation, but could it be both Christian and socialist? Leonard Isitt, former Methodist minister and current Liberal MP for Christchurch North, accused the socialist Sunday School of opposing and undermining the teaching of the Christian church. In response Ann Saunders challenged him to visit the school where she said their mottos were: 'Abandon hate all ye who enter here', and 'All for each and each for all'. Their book of 'Golden Sayings', she argued, contained many of the words of Jesus, and the Christian faith and teaching were precious to many of their members.[44] The Sunday School's membership card stated: 'We desire to be just and loving to all men and women; to work together as brothers and sisters; to be kind to every living creature, and to help to form a new society with justice as its foundation and love as its law.'[45]

The first Canterbury Workers' Educational Association Summer School, held at Oxford in 1920. Members of the Page, Ockenden, Struthers and Johnson families were among the participants. Anti-militarists Ted Howard, Clyde Carr and Robert Laing are also in this group. (Canterbury WEA)

Families such as the Pages, the Ockendens and the Joneses were all involved. Muriel Morrison (née Ockenden), who later attended the Sunday School for four or five years, said it had made a big impression on her and was the basis for her religious life.[46] She recalled Chapple as: 'a tall dignified figure dressed in a long black overcoat with a red rose in his buttonhole, leading the children in the School's own set of hymns of justice and peace which merged socialism and pacifism; the debates, sometimes forceful, on the perils of capitalism and militarism; and above all, the close feeling of family as the faithful harmonised to create a new society'.[47] The school's parting saying was: 'We have met in love, we now part in love. May nothing of ours that is unworthy spoil the sweetness or stain the purity of this good day.'[48] In the words of Eugene Debs:

> While there is a lower class I am in it. While there is a soul in prison, I am not free … We were taught about the evils of the capitalist system, about the causes of war, about the injustices that resulted from man's greed, about those who suffered for righteousness sake. All this was entirely without bitterness or rancour. Our teachers were people of outstanding quality and integrity … They built better than they knew.[49]

Norman Bell and James Chapple – a former CO and an imprisoned seditionist – were among the eight editors listed in the first issue of *The International Sunbeam*, published by the Socialist Sunday School from 1923 to 1930. By the fourth issue just two editors, Bell and Fred Page, were named.[50] At some point, probably around 1930, the Sunday School seems to have faltered, before it was reformed in 1932 as the Socialist Guild of Youth – but students from the old school still met as a lively socialist discussion group every Sunday night. Connie Jones (later Summers), who was a member of the Socialist Guild of Youth in the 1930s, was greatly influenced by Charles Cole, one of the teachers. She later joined the Christian Pacifist Society (CPS), and in 1941 she became the only woman to be imprisoned during World War II for anti-war activity.[51]

The No More War Movement and War Resisters' International

The influence of the Socialist Sunday School can be seen in the New Zealand No More War Movement (NMWM), founded by Fred Page at a meeting in Christchurch in February 1928. Page, the organising secretary, described the group as the New Zealand section of the War Resisters' International and said they aimed to set up branches in other centres. Former COs were well to the fore in the organisation: Norman Bell was president and George Samms, F. Robinson (presumably Samms' friend Frank) and William Worrall were all on the committee, along with Lincoln Efford.[52]

The main difference between this group and earlier anti-militarist and peace organisations in New Zealand was the pacifist pledge that members signed on joining, which read:

> War is a crime against humanity. I am therefore determined (a) not to support or take part in any war, international or civil; (b) to work for total disarmament, the removal of all causes of war, and the establishment of a new social and international order based on the pacifist principle of co-operation for the common good.[53]

It was important to Bell that the pledge was a declaration of 'present attitude', not a binding pledge for future action.

Fred Page was killed in 1930 by a faulty gas waterheater in the home where he was staying in Paris, where he had gone for a meeting of War Resisters' International. Tributes written after his death described his complete and

Lincoln Efford as a young man in 1928. (Efford family)

The No More War committee in 1929. Fred Page is standing second from left; Ada Wells is standing second from right. Sarah Page is seated in the centre of the middle row; her sister Ann is seated at the right end of the front row. Charles Mackie is sitting second from left in the front row. (Page family)

selfless dedication to the cause, which many saw as Christ-like. Bell, for example, wrote:

> He left behind him an example of honesty and straightforward-
> ness, an example of genuine love of his brother man and kindliness
> towards all men and women; an example of readiness to help in
> some way all those genuinely in need; an example of fearless cham-
> pionship of what he thought right and for the benefit of mankind.[54]

The inscription on his grave in the Wiltshire village of Lavington is a fitting one, from Matthew 5:9: 'Blessed are the peacemakers: for they shall be called the children of God.'

Charles Cole, who had been secretary of the NMWM since at least April 1929, resigned from his position as pastor of the St Albans Baptist church to become secretary of the NMWM, and Sarah Page was assistant secretary.

The Christchurch peace movement lost other older members in the 1920s, too. William Ensom died in London in May 1923; and his wife Annie Ensom, who died six years later at the age of 89, left generous bequests to numerous organisations that were dear to her heart. The largest, of £1000 to the WEA, was to go towards educational work that would promote international understanding and peace; half of the bequest was to be used to teach the international language Esperanto. The Labour Party received £500. A £250 gift to Canterbury College, to be used annually as a prize for the best essay advocating 'a constructive policy for the promotion and preservation of international peace and goodwill and the discontinuance of armaments, etc', caused some unease among members of the college board because of the conditions attached.[55] Ten local charitable organisations received gifts of £50 or £100, including the Howard League. A Sarah Ann Ensom Bequest fund was established, and Charles Mackie became one of the trustees for the fund – and, on occasion, an applicant for funds.[56]

In December 1930 a photograph of Fred Page was unveiled at a meeting of the National Peace Council, to hang in the Peace Council rooms. Norman Bell, seated centre, is holding the photo of Page, who had died in Paris in July 1930. Sarah Page is sitting on Bell's left. Charles Mackie is standing second from the right, with Lincoln Efford at the far right. (Efford family)

When Ada Wells was not well enough to attend the 1933 annual meeting of the NPC, Mackie wrote to express their sympathy and said he trusted they would see her again soon. Wells replied with a poignant note written shortly before her death – a personal farewell to her colleagues, as well as a wish for world peace:

> Good-bye Mr Mackie and the good workers of the Peace Council. You have heartened me up many a time by your faithfulness. Now 'I pass but do not die'. May the Peace that passeth all understanding soon dawn on this troubled world. Farewell! I shall meet you all again.[57]

A new, united peace organisation?

In 1932 Sarah Page, as assistant secretary of the NMWM, wrote to Mackie to say that the NMWM felt there should be a joint peace association, which would be convened by the NPC. She took the initiative in organising a 'Round Table Conference' in September 1932, but nothing seems to have eventuated.[58] 'Original' NPC members Mackie and Atkinson, by now fighting a rearguard action to keep their organisation alive, sent out a circular letter in 1934 responding to moves that were being made to form 'an effective unity' of 'all those bodies which are definitely opposed to War'. Such a unifying body already existed, they pointed out, with representatives from 10 societies as members: 'We would, therefore, respectfully suggest that this organisation, now operating, with its valuable assets of knowledge gained by long experience and extensive correspondence, with its material and other equipment, built up during more than twenty years, should not be lightly set aside.'[59]

The six constitutional aims of the NPC, printed in the margin of this letter, show how the NPC had grown in scope since its original constitution 20 years earlier: it now aimed 'to strive for the establishment of permanent peace by the organisation of social relations on a basis of justice'. Other objectives included 'the establishment of an economic "League of Peoples" as a basis of a World Federation', and 'The definite repudiation of militarism and all its instruments, with immediate

disarmament within New Zealand'. The NPC, they said, was working in 'active co-operation with the Union of Democratic Control …
to secure the conduct of International Policy on a purely democratic
basis', and the 'creation and education of public opinion in the direction
of these objects'. The NPC aimed to keep in touch 'by correspondence and otherwise with all organisations and persons willing to assist
in the promotion of these aims'. Membership of the council had not
changed: it comprised delegates from organisations that were in sympathy with the NPC's aims, and individuals who were nominated and
elected by the council members. But the impossibly wide scope of its
aims had become a weakness. The NPC had been at its most effective
in the pre-war period when it had an immediate challenge, as expressed
in the second object of its original constitution: 'To unite those who are
opposed to Compulsory Military Training and to work for the repeal of
the Compulsory Clauses of the Defence Act.'[60]

Mackie and Atkinson ended their letter by inviting organisations that
were in sympathy with the objects of the NPC to join them. Instead,
however, several more sharply focused groups were established in the
1930s.

Fellowship of Pacifist Ministers, Peace Pledge Union and Christian Pacifist Society

John Russell Hervey, who is remembered now as a poet rather than as a
peace activist, was an Anglican vicar who retired from active ministry
in 1934 at the age of 35 because of ill health.[61] In September 1935 he
was one of 25 clergy from Canterbury and Westland who formed the
Fellowship of Pacifist Ministers in Christchurch. Their aim was 'to work
for the establishment of enduring peace in the spirit and by the methods
of the Lord Jesus Christ'.[62]

This was the first of three pacifist organisations to be established in
the city over the next few years. The Christchurch branch of the Peace
Pledge Union (PPU) was formed at a meeting attended by nine people
in June 1938, four years after the PPU had been founded in England by
the Rev H. R. L. (Dick) Sheppard. B. Godward became secretary and
John Hervey was assistant. The union pledge was brief: 'I renounce war

and I will never support or sanction another.' At the time, there were 44 members in New Zealand and more than 100,000 in England.[63]

When a branch of the PPU was formed at Rangiora in 1939, Noel Goldsbury became chairman. At a meeting of about twenty-five members in August 1939 a resolution to 'urge the Government to institute a Department of Peace' was carried unanimously.[64] That same month Goldsbury wrote to the local *Gazette* in defence of a statement the Rev Roger Taylor had made at a PPU talk in Rangiora, when Taylor referred to the 'same wretched bugles … calling the same stupid tunes of hatred and calling men to the slaughter-house that they may murder their fellowmen'.[65] Goldsbury drew attention to the failure and casualties of war:

> Ten million soldiers and thirteen million civilians, including some of the finest women and children in the world were slaughtered, and much of the world's wealth of culture destroyed in the war of 1914–1918, and the aftermath of pain and suffering is beyond estimate.
>
> The war failed to bring the end of war or to make the world safe for democracy or bring about any of the benefits hoped for. Is it any wonder that men everywhere are condemning the war-mongers and the 'wretched bugles' for calling the young men to face another similar catastrophe in the same stupid way?[66]

The CPS, formed in Wellington in 1936, went on to become the most significant pacifist group during World War II. The Christchurch branch was established in 1938, with Ron Scarlett as secretary and Russell Thurlow Thompson as chairman.

With three Christian-based pacifist organisations now meeting in the city, there was a strong reaction when an Anglican clergyman, A. H. Norris, proposed a toast to the 'Army, Navy, and Air Force' at a farewell function in May 1938, and stated that 'The day of the convinced pacifist is over.' Mackie, Efford and Hervey were all stirred to dispute his claim. Mackie said that 'the "convinced pacifist" is still here in just as large numbers as ever, and that his rank and file are growing fast'.[67]

Efford wrote that they would miss Canon Norris because he had long been the outstanding example of the Christian minister who was ready to 'support and make propaganda for the fighting forces past, present, and future', and he went on to state the pacifist position: 'The pacifist believes that the only strong defence of everything worthwhile is non-violent resistance … there is no defence by military methods against the destructive forces that can be loosed against the civilian populations. Both sides are doomed to suffer enormous losses if not total annihila-tion.'[68] Hervey argued that all the evidence indicated a 'sturdy advance of the principles of pacifism, especially of Christian pacifism'.[69] Both Hervey and Mackie referred in their letters to an International Union of Anti-militarist Clergymen and Ministers, established in 1928.

The CPS does not seem to have figured much in news reports until 1939 when it was issued with permits to hold open-air meetings in the city, something that was denied to other pacifist organisations. For reli-gious pacifists to receive favourable attention ahead of other equally sincere non-religious groups was reminiscent of their preferential treat-ment during World War I, and prompted several letters to the editor. They deplored the fact that the CPS had received privileged treatment, and Mackie once again found himself defending the right of freedom of speech: 'The City Council may think it has the privilege of vetoing free speech, but, after all, it is the people who must decide. Had we a more perfect form of democracy embodied in the "initiative, referendum, and recall", I am convinced there would be no curtailment of free speech, much less the unjust discrimination between organisations.'[70]

By this time Britain and Germany were at war and the government had ignored an appeal from the New Zealand NMWM, chaired by Norman Bell, and the PPU, represented by Russell Thurlow Thompson, to remain neutral in any conflict in Europe that might develop over the Polish question. In November 1939 the PPU and CPS combined to call a meeting in the Choral Hall, where about 350 people heard the Rev Ormond Burton speak – a Wellington Methodist minister who had been a decorated hero in World War I but was now a leader in the Christian Pacifist movement. Mackie was among the line-up of pacifist leaders on the platform.[71]

Labour and conscription

In the 1930s the Labour Party came into its own as a political party. Christchurch became the first city to have a Labour mayor and city council: the Baptist Rev John K. Archer was elected mayor in 1925, and the first Labour-controlled city council was elected in 1927. Another Labour council member, Dan Sullivan, replaced Archer as mayor in 1931, making Christchurch the only New Zealand city to have a Labour-led council during the country's worst recession of the 1930s.[72]

In 1935 the country elected its first Labour government, with Michael Savage as prime minister. Four men who had formerly been imprisoned for their anti-militarist or anti-conscription views were in Cabinet: Fraser, Semple, Webb, and Tim Armstrong from Christchurch. Ted Howard and Morgan Williams (newly elected to the Kaiapoi seat), Clyde Carr (first elected Labour MP for Timaru in 1928), and Jim Thorn in Thames were now among the long-standing anti-militarists in the government. Jack McCullough, meanwhile, was appointed to the Legislative Council, where he served from 1936 to 1947; he remained a strong socialist and pacifist to the end. Sadly James McCombs, who died suddenly in 1933, did not live to see the Labour success he had worked for. His wife Elizabeth, who was elected to his seat in Parliament six weeks later, died just two years after James, and was succeeded by their son Terence McCombs.

The Labour government's decision to introduce conscription during World War II was a difficult issue for those Canterbury Labour MPs and activists with long-standing pacifist or anti-militarist ideals. For Thomas Nuttall's son, Thomas Burson Nuttall, however, it was straightforward: he followed his father's example, and told an armed forces appeal board he would do civil ambulance work but not military: 'I feel that the methods used by any army are out of bounds for me as a Christian.' Thomas senior attended the board hearing and submitted a statement in support of his son: he confirmed to the presiding magistrate that his son had been brought up to regard war, or any participation in it, as wrong.[73] One can only guess at the depth of disappointment he felt at the Labour government's introduction of conscription at this time.

Morgan Williams, as a Labour MP, was still resolutely against conscription. Tim Armstrong, who became minister of labour and immigration in 1935, eventually supported the government's approach, on condition that there were guaranteed economic controls to ensure the working class had a buffer in terms of the cost of living.[74] Ted Howard, the oldest member of the Labour caucus, was disappointed not be appointed to Cabinet: he died in 1939.

George Samms, who was secretary of the Woolston Branch of the Labour Party from 1917 to 1938, received high praise for his work for the party when he retired. He was elected president of the North Canterbury LRC in 1939, but resigned later the same year over the Labour government's decision to introduce conscription. Instead he proudly addressed a meeting of the Anti-Conscription Campaign, attended by about 800 people: 'I am going to say exactly what I think. I am anti-conscription and I am anti-war. In 1914 New Zealand entered the war, and then the war slogans began. The first one was that the war was to make the world safe for democracy. What a lie that was.'[75] Labour leader John Roberts eventually resigned from the presidency of the North Canterbury LRC in 1949 over his 'uneasiness over the conduct of the military service referendum and the submerging of many planks of Labour's original platform'.[76]

For Mackie, too, the Labour government's decision to introduce conscription was a heavy blow. In the 1943 general election he refused to vote for Labour, an action that has been described as his last political gesture: 'Church and party, in the end, had betrayed him on war and conscription.'[77] John Cookson has depicted Mackie as disappointed and

George and Lily Samms on a visit to England in 1951. (Patricia Smith)

ineffectual in the interwar period. He argues that the revival of pacifism after the war owed more to Fred Page, and to the CPS of New Zealand led by Ormond Burton and Archibald Barrington:

> In spite of Mackie's best efforts … the NPC never regained its place as the central body in a coalition of like-minded organisations. The new generation of pacifists in the inter-war period regarded the NPC as a spent force. The gentlemanly Mackie, whose bearded elegance earned him the ironical sobriquet of 'Royal Navy' Mackie, was regarded with friendly tolerance.[78]

Mackie resigned as secretary of the NPC in February 1943 due to ill health, just a few months before his death. The NPC paid tribute to his 30 years of service as secretary, noting that it was: 'rare to find a man … willing to devote his time systematically to a purely humanitarian and unpopular movement, from which its leaders can expect no material compensation or reward other than such as may arise from the betterment of Society'.[79]

A new leader takes up the challenge

Lincoln Efford, appointed secretary of the NPC in March 1943, remained committed to the peace movement all his life; he was the most noteworthy leader of the peace movement to emerge in Christchurch between the wars. His family background included strong connections with the previous generation of peace workers: his grandfather John Ash Efford, a socialist trade unionist and Baptist temperance campaigner, worked at the Addington Railway Workshops and was part of a 'close kin network' that included Jack McCullough and Harry Atkinson.[80] Lincoln's father William Harris Efford also worked at the Addington Railway Workshops and was a pacifist who left the Baptist Church in disgust at the church's support for World War I. As a 13-year-old, Lincoln Efford attended the first summer school of the Canterbury WEA in 1920 under the guardianship of McCullough, 'socialist and pacifist mentor and life-long friend'.[81] Jim Chapple, whom Efford would have come to know at the Socialist Sunday School, was another mentor.

Efford campaigned for the abolition of CMT in the early 1920s, and in April 1922 he was exempted from training on religious grounds. His involvement with the NMWM, which began in 1928, continued throughout his life. In 1930–31 he headed Christchurch's World Disarmament petition committee, which collected signatures for a Women's International League for Peace and Freedom (WILPF) disarmament petition: nearly 42,000 signatures were gathered nationwide.[82]

His pamphlet 'You, the Atomic Bomb and World Peace' is undated, but seems to have been published soon after the war ended. On 5 September 1945 he convened and was one of three speakers at an anti-nuclear protest meeting in the Radiant Hall in Christchurch.[83] In June 1946 he organised a national peace conference, and when the PPU and the NPC merged to form the Peace Union, he became secretary. The union's first Hiroshima Day march was held in Christchurch in 1947, though a lack of enthusiasm for the new organisation led to his resignation in 1953.[84]

A similar sense of disappointment was apparent in a letter he wrote to Blanche Baughan about the work of the Howard League for Penal Reform. Agreeing that it might seem that the Howard League had not accomplished much, Efford said he often felt the same about the peace movement: he offered the same biblical consolation as was given to Mackie at the beginning of the war:

> When I think of the great hopes of the pioneers, and the seeming successes, and then, it seems that all the work that has been done has had no effect at all. The only consolation is that it must have always been the same. People have sown and have never reaped, or seen any results of their labours. There must be more in it than that and when the time is ripe the seed does sprout.[85]

Efford didn't give up: one of the last photographs of him was taken on Hiroshima Day 1961, just eight months before his death: he is pictured with the Rev Alan Brash, general secretary of the New Zealand Council of Churches, leading the Hiroshima Day march in Christchurch. Women peace activists Elsie Locke and Mary Woodward are close behind.[86]

Thirty years later, in 1991, Elsie Locke's *Peace People* was published – a ground-breaking history of 'peace activities in New Zealand'. It brought the history of the peace movement up to 1975, when New Zealand's leadership of a Pacific-wide anti-nuclear movement had been dealt a blow by a change of government. The story of New Zealand's later anti-nuclear peace movement, which ultimately led to New Zealand becoming a nuclear-free nation in 1985, was continued by her daughter Maire Leadbeater in *Peace, Power and Politics: How New Zealand became nuclear free*.[87]

A clear line of descent is evident from the first faltering peace society and the women's and socialist groups of the 1890s, to the establishment of the National Peace and Anti-Militarist Council in 1911 by Christians and members of the women's and labour movements, to the new pacifist organisations of the 1930s who carried the peace movement into the nuclear era.

* * *

While this study has focused on the Canterbury region, it has arrived at the same message as the conclusion of Elsie Locke's *Peace People*, where she commented on the 'whole forest of peace activity' that had grown 'from seeds planted long ago … A knowledge of the genetic strain, and of the dedication and methods by which the seedlings have been nurtured and mature trees cherished, will, I hope, serve as a garden guide for today's and tomorrow's peace people.'[88]

NOTES

ABBREVIATIONS

AJHR	Appendices to the Journals of the House of Representatives
ANZ	Archives New Zealand Te Rua Mahara o te Kāwanatanga, Wellington
ANZC	Archives New Zealand Te Rua Mahara o te Kāwanatanga, Christchurch
ATL	Alexander Turnbull Library, Wellington
CM	Canterbury Museum
DNZB	Dictionary of New Zealand Biography
MBL	Macmillan Brown Library, University of Canterbury, Christchurch
MCH	Ministry for Culture and Heritage
NZJH	*New Zealand Journal of History*

INTRODUCTION

1   Len Richardson and Shelley Richardson, *Anthony Wilding: A sporting life*, Canterbury University Press, Christchurch, 2005, pp. 353–54; Doreen Lange, writing about her father Gerald Connor's decision to go into hiding in the West Coast bush during the war, made a similar comment: 'The courage to refuse to go must have been greater than the courage to go to war in his day', in Doreen Lange, *Cricklewood*, Doreen Lange, Invercargill, 1982, p. 25. See ch. 5 for more about Gerald Connor's decision.

2   Sarah Page to Ormond Burton, 7 September 1939, MS-Papers-0438-037, Burton Papers, ATL.

3   Voices Against War (http://voicesagainstwar.nz/home) was launched at the University of Canterbury in May 2016.

4   Geoffrey Troughton and Philip Fountain, 'Pursuing peace in Godzone', in Geoffrey Troughton and Philip Fountain (eds), *Pursuing Peace in Godzone: Christianity and the peace tradition in New Zealand*, Victoria University Press, Wellington, 2018, p. 23.

5   John Armstrong, 'Review: *Gallipoli: The scale of our war*, Museum of New Zealand Te Papa Tongarewa. April 2015–April 2019', *New Zealand Journal of Public History*, vol. 5, no. 1, 2017, p. 62.

6   H. E. Holland, *Armageddon or Calvary: The conscientious objectors of New Zealand and 'the process of their conversion'*, H. E. Holland, Wellington, 1919.

7   Archibald Baxter, *We Will Not Cease,* Cape Catley, Auckland, 2003; David Grant, *Field Punishment No. 1*, Steele Roberts, Wellington, 2008.

8   Heather Devere, Kelli Te Maihāroa, Maui Solomon and Maata Wharehoka, 'Regeneration of indigenous peace traditions in Aotearoa New Zealand', in Heather Devere, Kelli Te Maihāroa, Maui Solomon and Maata Wharehoka (eds), *Peacebuilding and the Rights of Indigenous Peoples*, The Anthropocene: Politik—Economics—Society—Science, vol. 9, Springer, Cham, 2017, pp. 58–59.

9   Ministry for Culture and Heritage, 'Invasion of pacifist settlement at Parihaka', 2021, https://nzhistory.govt.nz/occupation-pacifist-settlement-at-parihaka

10 Tim Shoebridge, 'Imprisoned conscientious objectors', https://nzhistory.govt.nz/war/the-military-objectors-list

11 'Alleged defaulters', *Evening Post*, 13 December 1918, p. 4; 'Military defaulters sentenced', *Lake Country Press*, 19 December 1918, p. 5.

12 The conference was organised by the Stout Research Centre for New Zealand Studies and the Labour History Project, in association with the Ministry for Culture and Heritage and the Archives and Records Association of New Zealand.

13 Jared Davidson, 'Dissent during the First World War: By the numbers', 2016, https://blog.tepapa.govt.nz/2016/06/28/dissent-during-the-first-world-war-by-the-numbers/

14 Paul Baker, *King and Country Call: New Zealanders, conscription and the Great War*, Auckland University Press, Auckland, 1988, pp. 204, 208.

15 Graham Hucker, 'The great wave of enthusiasm: New Zealand reactions to the First World War in August 1914 – a reassessment', *NZJH*, vol. 43, no. 1, 2009, p. 62.

16 Baker, *King and Country Call*, p. 18.

17 Jock Phillips, 'War and national identity', in David Novitz and Bill Willmott (eds), *Culture and Identity in New Zealand*, GP Books, Wellington, 1990, pp. 91–110; Megan Hutching, '"Turn back this tide of barbarism": New Zealand women who were opposed to war 1869–1919', MA thesis, University of Auckland, 1990.

18 Hucker, 'The great wave of enthusiasm', p. 64.

19 Stevan Eldred-Grigg, *The Great Wrong War: New Zealand society in WWI*, Random House, Auckland, 2010, pp. 93–95.

20 Hucker, 'The great wave of enthusiasm', pp. 60, 64.

21 Cyril Pearce, *Comrades in Conscience: The story of an English community's opposition to the Great War*, Francis Boutle Publishers, London, revised edn, 2014, p. 20.

22 Gwen Parsons, 'Challenging enduring Home Front myths: Jingoistic civilians and neglected soldiers', in David Monger, Sarah Murray and Katie Pickles (eds), *Endurance and the First World War: Experiences and legacies in New Zealand and Australia*, Cambridge Scholars Publishing, Newcastle upon Tyne, 2014, p. 71.

23 Parsons, 'Challenging enduring Home Front myths', p. 68.

24 Gwen Parsons, 'Debating the war: The discourse of war in the Christchurch community', in John Crawford and Ian McGibbon (eds), *New Zealand's Great War: New Zealand, the Allies and the First World War*, Exisle Publishing, Auckland, 2007, pp. 550–68.

25 Papers Past, National Library of New Zealand Te Puna Mātauranga o Aotearoa, https://paperspast.natlib.govt.nz/

26 Elsie Locke, *Peace People: A history of peace activities in New Zealand*, Hazard Press, Christchurch, 1992; Elizabeth Plumridge, 'Labour in Christchurch: Community and consciousness 1914–1919', MA thesis, University of Canterbury, 1979.

27 Steven Loveridge and James Watson, *The Home Front: New Zealand society and the war effort, 1914–1919*, Massey University Press, Auckland, 2019.

28 Jared Davidson, *Dead Letters: Censorship and subversion in New Zealand 1914–1920*, Otago University Press, Dunedin, 2019.

1 THE PROGRESSIVE NETWORK OF RADICAL CHRISTCHURCH 1880s–1910

1 Jim McAloon, 'Radical Christchurch', in John Cookson and Graeme Dunstall (eds), *Southern Capital Christchurch: Towards a city biography 1850–2000*, Canterbury University Press, Christchurch, 2000, p. 162.

2 Margaret Lovell-Smith, *Easily the Best: The life of Helen Connon 1857–1903*, Canterbury University Press, Christchurch, 2004, p. 71. In 1893 there were more women enrolled as arts students than men in the whole college.

3 Meeting 11 December 1889, 2008.144.19, Women's Christian Temperance Union (WCTU) Minute Book, Christchurch Branch 1889–1892, CM; The WCTU had begun in America but joined with the British Women's Temperance Association in 1884 to become an international organisation.

4 'Dr Kate C. Bushnell and Mrs Andrew, M.A.', *Prohibitionist*, 5 November 1892, p. 3.

5 'The Peace Society', *Lyttelton Times*, 20 February 1889, p. 4; 'Women's work', *Press*, 21 February 1889, p. 5; 'Can we get rid of war?', *Press*, 19 February 1889, p. 5.

6 Margaret Lovell-Smith, 'Canterbury Women's Institute', in Anne Else (ed.), *Women Together*, Historical Branch Department of Internal Affairs and Daphne Brassell Associates, Wellington, 1993, p. 76, https://nzhistory.govt.nz/women-together/canterbury-women%E2%80%99s-institute. Several CWI members, including Sheppard, Wells, Lucy Smith and Sarah Saunders Page, were also members of the WCTU.

7 'Canterbury Women's Institute', *Star*, 20 July 1896, p. 4.

8 'Canterbury Women's Institute', *Star*, 17 August 1896, p. 4. The CWI's reasons for opposing intervention were spelled out in five points prepared by its president and secretary, Bain and Wells.

9 'Armenia', *White Ribbon*, 15 September 1896, p. 6.

10 'Christian Ethical Society', *Press*, 14 June 1890, p. 6.

11 James E. Taylor, '"To me, socialism is not a set of dogmas but a living principle": Harry Atkinson and the Christchurch Socialist Church, 1890–1905', MA thesis, Victoria University of Wellington, 2010, p. 87.

12 Ibid., p. 85.

13 Ibid., pp. 82, 87–88; Roberta Nicholls, 'Cunnington, Eveline Willett', DNZB, 1996, https://teara.govt.nz/mi/biographies/3c44/cunnington-eveline-willett. The Fabian Society had about forty members; it met regularly in 1896–97 and was still sending delegates to other meetings in 1898.

14 Taylor, '"To me, socialism is not a set of dogmas"', pp. 83, 148–49.

15 Ibid., p. 53.

16 Herbert Roth, 'In memoriam: Harry Albert Atkinson', *Here & Now*, June 1956, p. 19.

17 Taylor, '"To me, socialism is not a set of dogmas"', p. 158.

18 Socialist Church Monthly leaflet, no. 1, February 1897, Item 51, Harry A. Atkinson Papers, CM.

19 Roth, 'In Memoriam: Harry Albert Atkinson', p. 19.

20 Herbert Roth, 'The Labour Churches and New Zealand', *International Review of Social History*, vol. 4, no. 3, 1959, p. 364. Six issues of *The Socialist* were published.

21 Margaret Lovell-Smith, 'Rose Atkinson: A long-standing commitment to peace', 2016, http://voicesagainstwar.nz/exhibits/show/women-peacemakers/rose-atkinson--a-long-standing

22 Taylor, '"To me, socialism is not a set of dogmas"', p. 157. Taylor (p. 148) concluded the 'cross-over between these groups, or mixed

membership was a striking aspect of "Radical Christchurch" of the late 1890s onwards'.

23 Edith Searle Grossmann, 'In Cathedral Square', *Otago Witness*, 14 June 1900, p. 64.

24 Dorothy Page, *The National Council of Women: A centennial history*, Auckland University Press with Bridget Williams Books, Auckland, 1996, p. 36.

25 'Women and war', *Lyttelton Times*, 3 April 1897, p. 4.

26 'Lay down your arms', *White Ribbon*, September 1898, p. 7.

27 Ibid.

28 Ibid. Children were sacrificed as burnt offerings to Moloch, a Canaanite God referred to in the Old Testament: the term is used to describe a costly sacrifice.

29 'Peace on Earth', *White Ribbon*, December 1898, pp. 6–7.

30 Betty Holt, *Women in Council: A history of the National Council of Women of New Zealand 1896–1979*, National Council of Women of NZ, 1980, p. 30.

31 'Ladies' gossip', *Lyttelton Times*, 26 June 1899, p. 6 (reprinted from the *Canterbury Times*).

32 Ibid.

33 Michael King, *The Penguin History of New Zealand*, Penguin Books, Auckland, 2003, pp. 282–83. Mounted troops departed from Lyttelton in 1899 and 1900.

34 Taylor, '"To me, socialism is not a set of dogmas"', p. 119.

35 Untitled report of meeting of the Socialist Church, *Star*, 12 October 1899, p. 1.

36 Untitled report of meeting of the Socialist Church, *Star*, 17 October 1899, p. 4.

37 'Perverse socialists', *Lyttelton Times*, 18 October 1899, p. 3.

38 'The Addington Workshops demonstration', *Star*, 22 May 1900, p. 1.

39 Nellie G. H. MacLeod, *The Fighting Man: A study of the life and times of T. E. Taylor*, Dunbar and Summers, Christchurch, 1964, pp. 55–56.

40 'Passing notes', *Otago Daily Times*, 21 October 1899, p. 2.

41 'And there shall be peace', *White Ribbon*, December 1899, p. 7.

42 'President's address', *White Ribbon*, May 1900, p. 3.

43 Megan Hutching, '"Turn back this tide of barbarism": New Zealand women who were opposed to war 1869–1919', MA thesis, University of Auckland, 1990, p. 40. Bain's address to the 1900 conference was reported in the *Otago Daily Times,* 11 May 1900, p. 2.

44 'The Women's National Council and the war', *Otago Daily Times*, 12 May 1900, p. 8.

45 Ibid.

46 'Soldiers preaching peace', *Lyttelton Times*, 27 January 1900, p. 4.

47 Megan Hutching, '"Mothers of the World": Women, peace and arbitration in early twentieth-century New Zealand, *NZJH*, vol. 27, no. 2, 1993, p. 175.

48 'The Boer War', *Otago Daily Times*, 14 May 1900, p. 2.

49 'President's address', *White Ribbon*, June 1901, p. 1.

50 'Our real foes', *White Ribbon*, June 1902, pp. 5–6.

51 'National Council of Women', *Taranaki Daily News*, 14 September 1903, p. 4.

52 'International Council of Women', *White Ribbon*, September 1904, p. 9; Megan Hutching, 'Bain, Wilhelmina Sherriff', DNZB, 1996, https://teara.govt.nz/en/biographies/3b3/bain-wilhelmina-sherriff

53 'Peace resolutions', *White Ribbon*, 1 January 1902, p. 9.

54 'Peace and arbitration: Report of New Zealand delegate', *White Ribbon*, March 1905, p. 4.

55 'The Boston Peace Congress', *White Ribbon*, 15 December 1904, p. 1; 'Remarks of Miss Wilhelmina Sherriff Bain', from her address to the thirteenth Universal Peace Congress 1904, MS-Papers-7202-258, Locke Papers.

56 McAloon, 'Radical Christchurch', p. 177.

57 William Ranstead, 'New Zealand notes', *Clarion*, 14 April 1900, p. 117.

58 'The N.Z. Socialist Party', *Evening Post,* 29 July 1901, p. 6; Dan Bartlett, 'Fred and Harry Cooke: The father and son who stood up for socialism', 2016, http://voicesagainstwar.nz/exhibits/show/the-response-of-the-labour-mov/fred-and-harry-cooke--father-a

59 James Thorn, *The Formation and Development of Trades Unionism in Canterbury*, Standard Press, Wellington, 1950, p. 8; McAloon, 'Radical Christchurch', p. 168.

60 Melanie Nolan, 'McCullough, John Alexander', DNZB, 1996, https://teara.govt.nz/en/biographies/3m4/mccullough-john-alexander

61 'News of the Day', *Press*, 28 April 1903, p. 4. A further example of such a meeting occurred in 1908 when delegates from the CWI, WCTU, Trades and Labour Council, the School Committees' Association and the Socialist Party met to consider a report of the commission set up to enquire into the Te Oranga Home. 'Te Oranga Home', *Southland Times*, 14 May 1908, p. 3.

62 Mark Dunick, 'Making rebels: The New Zealand Socialist Party, 1901–1913', MA thesis, Victoria University of Wellington, 2016, p. 79.

63 'The naval crisis', *Lyttelton Times*, 23 March 1909, p. 7.

64 Ibid.

65 'HMS New Zealand: "A grim and formidable fighting machine"', https://collections.tepapa.govt.nz/topic/1049

66 'The Trades and Labour Council', *Star*, 23 March 1909, p. 3.

67 Roth, 'In Memoriam: Harry Albert Atkinson', p. 19.

68 Letter to the editor, *Lyttelton Times*, 24 March 1909, p. 8.

69 Jim McAloon, 'Thorn, James', DNZB, 1998, https://teara.govt.nz/en/biographies/4t15/thorn-james

70 'The dreadnought offer', *Lyttelton Times*, 7 April 1909, p. 7; 'A statement by Mr Taylor', *Lyttelton Times*, 23 March 1909, p. 7.

71 Ibid.

72 C. R. N. Mackie, 'The Christian's attitude to war', *New Zealand Baptist*, June 1909, p. 347.

73 'A pioneer anti-militarist: Chat with Mr L. P. Christie', *Maoriland Worker*, 24 November 1911, p. 17.

2 'RAISE OUR VOICES FOR PEACE': THE PRE-WAR PEACE MOVEMENT 1911–12

1   Paul Baker, *King and Country Call: New Zealanders, conscription and the Great War*, Auckland University Press, Auckland, 1988, p. 11.

2   Eight hundred former students fought in World War I, in what the headmaster Brown declared was a 'divine mission'; 147 of them lost their lives there. Bruce Harding, '"To serve them all his days": Rewi Alley's schooling for war, and the birth of a people's warrior', unpublished paper, 2018, pp. 17, 30–33; Jim Gardner, 'Tradition and conscience: Canterbury College and R. O. Page, Conscientious Objector, 1918–1919', in *History Now*, vol. 9, no. 2, May 2003, p. 6.

3   'New Defence scheme', *Timaru Herald*, 5 April 1911, p. 6.

4   Monty Soutar, *Whitiki! Whiti! Whiti! E! Māori in the First World War*, David Bateman, Auckland, 2019, pp. 36–37.

5   R. L. Weitzel, 'Pacifists and anti-militarists 1909–1914', *NZJH*, vol. 7, no. 2, 1973, pp. 129–34.

6   See for example, Mackie's letter to the Methodist Conference, 4 February 1913, 2017.38.3777, Mackie Papers, CM.

7   'Report on the Work of the National Peace Council (NPC) from its Inception', 1915, pp. 2–3, 2017.38.1429, Mackie Papers, CM.

8   Ibid.

9   'A disorderly meeting', *Lyttelton Times*, 27 May 1911, p. 10.

10 'Christchurch and militarism', *Maoriland Worker*, 9 June 1911, p. 11.

11 Letter from Robert Milligan, 3 September 1912; Charles R. N. Mackie to Milligan, 6 September 1912, 2017.38.2969 and 2017.38.2970, Mackie Papers, CM.

12 'Compulsory training', *Maoriland Worker*, 11 August 1911, p. 11.

13 'Christchurch Anti-Militarist League Constitution', undated, 2017.38.1219; 'Constitution of the National Peace Council of New Zealand', undated, 2017.38.1216. The minute books of both groups record initial meetings on the same date, 18 August 1911.

14 'A pioneer anti-militarist', *Maoriland Worker*, 24 November 1911, p. 17

15 Meetings 13 February 1912, 25 April 1912, 1 May 1912, 28 May 1912. Minute Book of the National Peace Council 1911–1913, MB524, Ref59695, Richard Thompson Papers, MBL; Report of the Work of the NPC from its Inception, pp. 7–8, 2017.38.1429, Mackie Papers.

16 *The Anti-Militarist*, Items 1–4, Mackie Papers Pamphlets, CM.

17 Weitzel, 'Pacifists and anti-militarists', pp. 129–30.

18 Charles R. N. Mackie to M. H. Hudson, 4 January 1913, 2017.38.3699, Mackie Papers, CM.

19 Margaret Lovell-Smith, 'Charles Mackie and the National Peace Council (NPC)', 2019, http://voicesagainstwar.nz/exhibits/show/pre-war-anti-militarism-and-th/charles-mackie-and-the-nationa

20 J. E. Cookson, 'Mackie, Charles Robert Norris', DNZB, 1996, https://teara.govt.nz/en/biographies/3m20/mackie-charles-robert-norris; 'Lavington' was in Rolleston Street, Linwood, later re-named England Street.

21 'Secretarial notes', Supplement to the *New Zealand Baptist*, December 1906, p. 1.

22 C. R. N. Mackie, 'The World Missionary Convention', *New Zealand Baptist*, October 1910, p. 183. In India he visited the New Zealand Baptist Church's Mission stations and attended the World's Christian Endeavour Conference in Agra. He also attended a world Sunday School convention at Washington DC, and a world missionary convention at Edinburgh.

23 Mackie to Mr Forbes, 30 July 1912, 2017.38.2300; Mackie to A. Macrae, 9 August 1912, 2017.38.2818, Mackie Papers, CM.

24 List of leaflets either published or received, 15 October 1915, 2017.38.1466, Mackie Papers, CM. This five-page list was evidently produced as a supplement to the first (1915) NPC report.

25 Robert M. Laing, Prefatory note and table of contents, in *Shall War and Militarism Prevail?* L. M. Isitt, Christchurch, 1911.

26   Mackie to the Trustees of the English Society of Friends, 23 August 1912, 2017.38.507, Mackie Papers, CM; Peter Lowe, 'Ford, Charles Reginald', DNZB, 1998, https://teara.govt.nz/en/biographies/4f19/ford-charles-reginald

27   Morgan Williams, *The Great White Elephant*, Repeal Printery, Christchurch, 1914; Margaret Lovell-Smith, 'Charles Morgan Williams: The anti-war Kaiapoi farmer who became a Labour MP', 2018, http://voicesagainstwar.nz/exhibits/show/pre-war-anti-militarism-and-th/charles-morgan-williams--the-a

28   Titles of articles included 'Military training and equivalent service', 2017.38.3524; and 'The truth about Japan', 2017.38.3525 and 3526, Mackie Papers, CM.

29   'Report on the Work of the NPC from its Inception', p. 5, 2017.38.1429, Mackie Papers.

30   Weitzel, 'Pacifists and anti-militarists', p. 131.

31   Mackie to J. A. Farrer, 21 November 1912, 2017.38.2886, Mackie Papers, CM.

32   Report of organising trip R. F. N. Mackie and W. Ensom, undated, 2017.38.1462; Mackie to Atkinson, 8 July 1912, 2017.38.1642, Mackie Papers, CM.

33   'Obituary: Mrs S. A. Ensom', *Press*, 19 June 1929, p. 2; Robyn Gosset, *The History of Mrs Pope Ltd*, Mrs Pope Ltd, Christchurch, 1981, pp. 14–17.

34   Williams to the NPC, 22 July 1912, 2017.38.2170, Mackie Papers, CM.

35   Mackie to Clifford, 29 August 1912, 2017.38.2562, Mackie Papers, CM.

36   Murray to Mackie, 19 October 1915, 2017.38.3364, Mackie Papers, CM; Elizabeth Plumridge, 'Labour in Christchurch: Community and consciousness 1914–1919', MA thesis, University of Canterbury, 1979, p. 19.

37   'Report on the Work of the NPC from its Inception', pp. 3, 8–9, 2017.38.1429, Mackie Papers.

38   'Christchurch 1912' – a report of the Fourth Conference and First Annual Meeting of the Society of Friends in New Zealand, held at Christchurch 11–16 May 1912. Society of Friends Christchurch Minutes 1913–1938, MB 147, MBL; Margaret Lovell-Smith,

'Ellen and John Howell: Active members of the National Peace Council', 2016, http://voicesagainstwar.nz/exhibits/show/women-peacemakers/ellen-and-john-howell--active-; Martin Crick, 'John Percy Fletcher, the Society of Friends and the campaign against compulsory military training in New Zealand 1909–1914', 2020, http://voicesagainstwar.nz/exhibits/show/pre-war-anti-militarism-and-th/john-percy-fletcher--the-socie

39   Items 316–328, Mackie Papers Pamphlets, CM; Margaret Lovell-Smith, 'Help from abroad: T. C. Gregory and the Advice to Emigrants Campaign', 2020, http://voicesagainstwar.nz/exhibits/show/pre-war-anti-militarism-and-th/help-from-abroad--t--c--gregor

40   'Boy heroes for conscience sake in New Zealand', 2017.38.2428, Mackie Papers, CM. Elizabeth Josephine Peckover was the niece of Priscilla Peckover of the Wisbech Peace Society.

41   'New Zealand Labour Party', Hiram Hunter letter to the editor, *Lyttelton Times*, 18 July 1911, p. 3; 'Anti-militarism', *Lyttelton Times*, 24 July 1911, p. 8.

42   'Wanted to be martyrs', *New Zealand Herald*, 19 July 1911, p. 7; 'Compulsory registration', *Lyttelton Times*, 19 July 1911, p. 7.

43   'Compulsory registration', *Lyttelton Times*, 19 July 1911, p. 7.

44   'News of the Day', *Press*, 7 July 1911, p. 6.

45   Weitzel, 'Pacifists and anti-militarists' p. 134.

46   'Jailed anti-conscripts', *Maoriland Worker*, 20 September 1912, p. 5.

47   'Harry Cooke's "Welcome home"', *Maoriland Worker*, 15 September 1911, p. 13.

48   'Night of disorder', *Lyttelton Times*, 22 August 1911, p. 7.

49   'Fighting Conscription – F. R. Cooke writes', *Maoriland Worker*, 1 September 1911, p. 14.

50   'Ibid.

51   'The morning after', *Star*, 22 August 1911, p. 3.

52   Ryan Bodman, '"Don't be a conscript, be a man!": A history of the Passive Resisters' Union, 1912–1914', BA (Hons) dissertation, University of Auckland, 2010, p. 11.

53   'The Passive Resisters: Why we will not obey the Defence Act', Item 620, Mackie Papers Pamphlets, CM.

54 'News of the Day', *Press*, 9 February 1912, p. 6.

55 'Things we ought to know', *Maoriland Worker*, 8 March 1912, p. 6.

56 D. [David] McNicoll to Mackie, 31 July 1913, 2017.38.3843, Mackie Papers, CM; this case was well made by Ryan Bodman in '"Don't be a conscript, be a man!"'.

57 'Failing to register', *Press*, 21 February 1912, p. 3.

58 Margaret Lovell-Smith, 'Worrall family showed united front against militarism', 2017, http://voicesagainstwar.nz/exhibits/show/pre-war-anti-militarism-and-th/worrall-family-showed-united

59 'The Defence Act', *Lyttelton Times*, 5 March 1912, p. 7.

60 'Compulsory service', *Oamaru Mail*, 7 March 1912, p. 6.

61 Ibid.

62 Ibid.

63 'The Territorials', *Taranaki Daily News*, 11 March 1912, p. 8.

64 'The anti-militarists', *Star*, 11 March 1912, p. 1.

65 'Compulsory training', *NZ Truth*, 16 March 1912, p. 1.

66 'The anti-militarists', *Star*, 11 March 1912, p. 1.

67 Peter Franks and Jim McAloon, *Labour: The New Zealand Labour Party 1916–2016*, Victoria University Press, Wellington, 2016, pp. 58–59.

68 The Housewives Union aimed to provide women engaged in housework with a union equivalent to a trade union, which could both educate and take political action. The Christchurch branch was formed in February 1912: 'News of the Day', *Press*, 9 February 1912, p. 6; Elizabeth Taylor was national president, and Elizabeth McCombs general secretary. They announced their resignations from the short-lived organisation in May 1912. 'Labour column', *Lyttelton Times*, 27 January 1912, p. 12; 'Town and Country', *Lyttelton Times*, 7 May 1912, p. 6.

69 Mackie, Atkinson, Ford and Ellen Howell had all urged him to attend. Melanie Nolan (ed.), *War and Class: The diary of Jack McCullough*, Dunmore Press, Wellington, 2009, p. 208.

70 Nolan (ed.), *War and Class*, p. 208.

71 'Defence Act: A batch of prosecutions', *Press*, 24 August 1912, p. 3. A similar number were charged on 21 September: 'Magisterial', *Lyttelton Times*, 21 September 1912, p. 4.

72 The NPC responded to each stage of the process, with two memos, and a final leaflet on the Defence Amendment Act. Items 459-61, Mackie Papers Pamphlets, CM.

73 'Passive Resisters' protest to Parliament', *Maoriland Worker*, 20 September 1912, p. 6.

74 Territorial Force – Religious objectors return of 1914, AD1 724 10/22/14, ANZ. Similar numbers were granted in Auckland and Wellington.

75 Nolan (ed.), *War and Class,* pp. 18, 244–45.

76 Mackie to Mr Isitt, 30 August 1912, 2017.38.2137, Mackie Papers, CM.

77 'Jailed anti-conscripts', *Maoriland Worker*, 20 September 1912, p. 5.

78 'Military training', Ada Wells, letter to the editor, *Lyttelton Times*, 7 April 1913, p. 10.

79 Mackie to E. Stevenson, 1 October 1912, 2017.38.560, Mackie Papers, CM; Margaret Lovell-Smith, 'Henry William Reynolds: Bootmaker pays the penalty for promoting peace', 2017, http://voicesagainstwar.nz/exhibits/show/the-response-of-the-labour-mov/henry-william-reynolds--boot-m

80 'Life in Lyttelton Jail', *Maoriland Worker,* 17 January 1913, p. 8.

81 Ibid.

82 Sarah Page, 'Wartime reminiscences', *The Working Woman*, March 1936, p. 6.

83 'Family ruined by conscription', *Daily News and Leader*, 5 May 1913, reprinted in Item 326, Mackie Papers Pamphlets, CM.

84 'Extending the "Thin red line"', *Maoriland Worker*, 28 July 1911, p. 9.

85 At the 1914 annual meeting of the CWI, for example Ada Wells and Sarah Page were elected president and secretary respectively, with Eveline Cunnington, Ellen Howell, Rose Atkinson and Sarah Ann Ensom among the vice-presidents. 'Canterbury Women's Institute', *Sun*, 16 February 1914, p. 4.

86 'Fair play for the conscientious objector', *Press*, 4 April 1914, p. 12.

87 Rose Atkinson to James Allen, 16 July 1912, 2017.38.935, Mackie Papers, CM. She also raised the wider issue of the arms race.

88 'Military training', Ellen Vickers Howell letter to the editor, *Lyttelton Times*, 22 March 1912, p. 8. She was also critical of the 'increasing burden of expenditure' which had been 'imposed upon a young country'.

89 Eveline Willett Cunnington, *The Lectures and Letters of E. W. Cunnington*, printed by Lyttelton Times, Christchurch, 1918, letter dated February 1910, p. 120.

90 Ibid., letter dated October 1911, pp. 129–30.

91 Ibid., letter dated October 1912, p. 134.

92 Margaret Lovell-Smith, 'Sarah Saunders Page: A courageous advocate for peace', 2016, http://voicesagainstwar.nz/exhibits/show/women-peacemakers/sarah-saunders-page--a-courage

93 Sarah Page, 'Wartime reminiscences', *The Working Woman*, March 1936, p. 6.

94 'Peace propaganda rejected by Ashburton people', *Lyttelton Times*, 10 October 1913, p. 8.

95 'Cadet camps', *Lyttelton Times*, 28 February 1910, p. 5.

96 National Peace Council 'To the Women of New Zealand', Item 493, Mackie Papers Pamphlets, CM. Page and Wells may also have been behind an unsigned flyer printed in Auckland in 1913 under the names of the AML and the NPC. Headed 'The hand that rocks the cradle, rules the world', the flyer posed a series of questions, and concluded with an exhortation to women: 'We women, whose mission is Peace and Love, must speak out. We must protest in the name of humanity. Turn back this tide of barbarism! You can help by making these things known, and by your vote at the polling booth': 'The hand that rocks the cradle, rules the world', Item 204, Mackie Papers Pamphlets, CM.

97 Lucy Smith's paper was later published in the *White Ribbon*, August 1912, pp. 1–2.

98 The Defence Act WCTU [1912] Item 763, Mackie Papers Pamphlets, CM.

99 Margaret Lovell-Smith, 'Ada Wells: First woman councillor outspoken in the peace cause', 2016, http://voicesagainstwar.nz/exhibits/show/women-peacemakers/ada-wells--first-woman-council

100 'The Defence System', *Star*, 10 August 1912, p. 6.

101 'Holy City', *Maoriland Worker*', 13 December 1916, p. 2.

102 'A stormy interview', *Star*, 10 May 1912, p. 3.

103 Ibid.; 'The Defence Act', *Southland Times*, 11 May 1912, p. 6.

104 'The women's deputation', *Evening Post*, 20 May, 1912, p. 3.

105 Mackie to Miss L [Lucy] Bell, 21 September 1912, 2017.38.2271, Mackie Papers, CM.

3 'A GOOD KICK WILL FINISH THE BUSINESS': THE PEACE MOVEMENT AND THE PASSIVE RESISTERS 1913–14

1 Mackie to T. C. Gregory, 26 September 1913, 2017.38.2417, Mackie Papers, CM; Fletcher who originally went to Australia under his own volition, had now come to Christchurch under the authority of the Society of Friends London Yearly Meeting: Martin Crick, 'John Percy Fletcher, the Society of Friends and the campaign against compulsory military training in New Zealand 1909–1914', 2020, http://voicesagainstwar.nz/exhibits/show/pre-war-anti-militarism-and-th/john-percy-fletcher--the-socie

2 The Vag [Ted Howard], 'Christchurch fightable', *Maoriland Worker*, 7 March 1913, p. 7.

3 Mackie to Alexander, 17 February 1913, 2017.38.2753, Mackie Papers, CM.

4 'Women and defence', *Lyttelton Times*, 21 February 1913, p. 9.

5 'Town and Country', *Lyttelton Times*, 21 February 1913, p. 6.

6 John Percy Fletcher and John Francis Hills, *Conscription under Camouflage*, John Francis Hills, Adelaide, 1919, p. 106.

7 'Confusion at Christchurch', *NZ Truth*, 5 April 1913, p. 6; Margaret Lovell-Smith, 'Reg Williams: A passionate opponent of militarism', 2017, http://voicesagainstwar.nz/exhibits/show/the-response-of-the-labour-mov/reg-williams--a-passionate-opp

8 The Vag, 'Free speech fight', *Maoriland Worker*, 2 May 1913, p. 6.

9 Melanie Nolan (ed.), *War and Class: The diary of Jack McCullough*, Dunmore Press, Wellington, 2009, p. 258.

10 'Unity Congress', *Dominion*, 10 July 1913, p. 9.

11 'Social Democratic Party', *Lyttelton Times*, 1 October 1913, p. 7.

12 'Studious Jimmy', *NZ Truth*, 30 June 1927, p. 4.

13 Jim McAloon, 'Working class politics in Christchurch 1905–1914', MA thesis, University of Canterbury, 1986, p. 181.

14 'Women and defence', *Lyttelton Times*, 21 February 1913, p. 9.

15 Eveline Willett Cunnington, *The Lectures and Letters of E. W. Cunnington*, Lyttelton Times, Christchurch, 1918, letter dated October 1913, p. 139.

16 Ibid.

17 Elizabeth Plumridge, 'Labour in Christchurch: Community and consciousness 1914–1919', MA thesis, University of Canterbury, 1979, p. 224.

18 Reg Williams, 'The truth about Lyttelton Gaol', *Repeal*, no. 2. May 1913, p. 10.

19 Ibid., p. 12.

20 'The cost of the defence', *Nelson Evening Mail*, 9 April 1913, p. 6; 'The garnishee', *Repeal*, 10 July 1913, p. 4.

21 Mackie to Corder, 19 June 1913, 2017.38.3274, Mackie Papers, CM.

22 Nolan (ed.), *War and Class,* p. 258.

23 R. L. Weitzel, 'Pacifists and anti-militarists 1909–1914', *NZJH*, vol. 7, no. 2, 1973, p. 138.

24 'Military detention', *Lyttelton Times*, 13 June 1913, p. 9. They were later joined by six West Coasters: Thomas Nuttall to Mackie, 6 July 1913, 2017.38.4269, Mackie Papers, CM.

25 Louisa Nuttall, letter to editor, *Lyttelton Times*, 12 June 1913, p. 5.

26 Susan Worrall letter to editor, *Lyttelton Times*, 13 June 1913, p. 9.

27 'Anti-militarism', *Lyttelton Times*, 16 June 1913, p. 2.

28 'Defence Act offences', *Hawera & Normanby Star*, 17 June 1913, p. 4.

29 'Military detention', *Greymouth Evening Star*, 19 June 1913, p. 5.

30 Reg Williams, 'The Ripa Island farce', *Repeal*, 10 August 1913, pp. 9–12.

31 *Maoriland Worker*, 18 July 1913, p. 2.

32 R. L. Weitzel, 'Pacifists and anti-militarists', pp. 145–46.

33 'Massey's victims', *Maoriland Worker*, 25 July 1913, p. 8.

34 S. V. Bracher, 'Ripa Island: A lesson for conscriptionists', Peace Committee of the Society of Friends, London, 1913, p. 1.

35 Ibid., pp. 4, 13.

36 'Ripa Island', *Lyttelton Times*, 5 July 1913, p. 10.

37 Henry Worrall to James Allen, 25 September 1913, Supplement to the NPC Monthly Circular, Item 88, Mackie Papers Pamphlets, CM.

38 Henry Worrall to James Allen, 8 October 1913, Supplement to the NPC Monthly Circular, Item 88, Mackie Papers Pamphlets.

39 Ibid.

40 'Ripa Island', *Maoriland Worker*, 26 September 1913, p. 5.

41 Mackie to Ford, 23 September 1913, 2017.38.3461, Mackie Papers, CM.

42 'An amazing document', *Repeal*, January 1914, pp. 12–13.

43 The mayor initially gave permission for the women to use the council chamber for a meeting but later said no to this too: 'The mayor and his word', 30 January 1913, 2017.38.1663, Mackie Papers, CM.

44 Mackie to Mr McNicoll, 19 May 1913, 2017.38.3840, Mackie Papers.

45 'Miss Ida Bradley: Tragic death of a prominent peace worker', *Maoriland Worker*, 15 August 1913, p. 6.

46 Driver to Mackie, 20 June 1913, 2017.38.2422, Mackie Papers, CM.

47 Circular letter from Mackie, 5 May 1913, 2017.38.1491, Mackie Papers, CM.

48 Mackie to George Ogle, 14 October 1912, 2017.38.2961, Mackie Papers, CM.

49 Alexander to Mackie, 1 July 1913, 2017.38.2743, Mackie Papers, CM.

50 Alexander to Mackie, 11 July 1913, 2017.38.2747, Mackie Papers. Urging Alexander to take a deputation to meet with James Allen in June 1913, Mackie said it would be a good opportunity to show Allen that 'not all the agitation is in Christchurch'. A Freedom League had also been established in Nelson in August 1913, though it seems to have been short-lived: Mackie to Alexander, 2 June 1913, 2017.38.2731, and Mackie to Wilson, 15 August 1913, 2017.38.4431, Mackie Papers, CM.

51   McNicoll to Mackie, 19 June 1913, 2017.38.3842, Mackie Papers, CM.

52   'Ashburton', *Otago Daily Times*, 10 October 1913, p. 5.

53   'Peace propaganda rejected by Ashburton people', *Lyttelton Times,* 10 October 1913, p. 8.

54   'Topics of the Day', *Evening Post*, 10 October 1913, p. 6.

55   'Anti-militarists: Stormy meeting at Ashburton', *Auckland Star*, 10 October 1913, p. 8.

56   Several other Christchurch organisations, including the CWI, supported the NPC's stance.

57   'Friday, "Crucifixion Day"', *Repeal,* March 1914, pp. 18–19.

58   'Conscripts! Take notice', *Repeal*, no. 12, March 1914, p. 8.

59   'The Court of Whispers', *Star*, 17 April 1914, p. 6.

60   'Clogging the wheels', *Sun*, 3 July 1914, p. 5.

61   Rose Atkinson Notebook, MS-Papers-82-213-06, Roth Papers, ATL.

62   'Correspondence', *Lyttelton Times*, 25 February 1914, p. 10.

63   *Repeal*, no. 12, March 1914, p. 5.

64   Nolan (ed.), *War and Class,* p. 273.

65   'Our defence system', *Otago Daily Times*, 9 June 1914, p. 6.

66   'Objectors unfit' *Star*, 8 May 1914, p. 1.

67   'Anti-militarist fiction', letters to editor from Percy Fletcher, *Press*, 24 June 1914, p. 10 and 26 June 1914, p. 4.

68   'Some questions to be answered', *Press*, 24 June 1914, p. 8.

69   'The anti-militarists', *Lyttelton Times*, 6 May 1914, p. 6.

70   'The Defence Act', *Press*, 8 June 1914, p. 10.

71   'Defence scheme', *Lyttelton Times*, 8 June 1914, p. 3.

72   'Territorial discontent', *Manawatu Evening Standard*, 4 May 1914, p. 4.

73   'The anti-militarists', *Lyttelton Times*, 6 May 1914, p. 6.

74   'Governor's proclamation', *Dominion*, 6 August 1914, p. 6.

4 THE 'CONSCIENCE OF SOCIETY': THE PEACE MOVEMENT 1914–16

1   Elsie Locke, *Peace People: A history of peace activities in New Zealand*, Hazard Press, Christchurch, 1992, p. 62.

2   Meeting 11 August 1914, Christchurch Anti Militarist League Minute Book, MS 0445-67, Efford Papers, ATL.

3   'Anti-militarists and the war', *Lyttelton Times*, 14 August 1914, p. 2.

4   The Constitution of the National Peace Council of New Zealand, undated, 2017.38.1216, Mackie Papers, CM.

5   Mackie to the Methodist Conference, 22 February 1915, 2017.38.3779, Mackie Papers, CM.

6   Ibid.

7   Forbes to Mackie, 23 August 1914, 2017.38.2858, Mackie Papers, CM.

8   Mackie to Ridland, 13 August 1919, 2017.38.3438, Mackie Papers, CM.

9   Mackie to McNicoll, 25 March 1922, 2017.38.3844, Mackie Papers, CM.

10   'General notes: Passive resisters volunteer', *Lyttelton Times*, 12 August 1914, p. 9.

11   Mackie to Brown, 29 November 1913, 2017.38.3335, Mackie Papers, CM.

12   Herbert Roth, 'Hell, no, we won't go', *Monthly Review*, October 1970, pp. 21–22.

13   'The Westland Contingent', *Press*, 31 May 1915, p. 9.

14   'Progress of the war', *Press*, 31 May 1915, p. 6.

15   'Editorial notes', *Star*, 31 May 1915, p. 4; 'Personal and political', *Maoriland Worker,* 9 June 1915, p. 4.

16   Denton, Harold Ernest – WWI – 23/121 – Army, Personnel file, ANZ.

17   Thackwell, Harold William – WWI – 25/365 – Army, Personnel file, ANZ.

18   Discussed by Jared Davidson in *Dead Letters: Censorship and subversion in New Zealand 1914–1920*, Otago University Press, Dunedin, 2019, pp. 104–06.

19   'National Register', *Ashburton Guardian*, 12 November 1915, p. 3; 'American News', *Lyttelton Times*, 4 December 1915, p. 11.

20   Melanie Nolan (ed.), *War and Class: The diary of Jack McCullough*, Dunmore Press,

Wellington, 2009, pp. 15–16; Charles R. N. Mackie to Mr Ensom, 4 November 1915, 2017.38.4125, Mackie Papers, CM.

21 Ford to Mackie, 28 March 1918, 2017.38.3483, Mackie Papers, CM.

22 Paul Baker, *King and Country Call: New Zealanders, conscription and the Great War*, Auckland University Press, Auckland, 1988, p. 65

23 Jim McAloon, 'Hunter, Hiram', DNZB, 1996, https://teara.govt.nz/en/biographies/3h46/hunter-hiram; Jim McAloon, 'Howard, Edwin John', DNZB, 1996, https://teara.govt.nz/en/biographies/3h37/howard-edwin-john

24 P. S. O'Connor, 'Barmy Christchurch: A melodrama in three parts', *Comment*, June 1968, no. 35, pp. 21–28.

25 Sarah Murray, *A Cartoon War: The cartoons of the* New Zealand Freelance *and* New Zealand Observer *as historical sources August 1914–November 1918*, New Zealand Cartoon Archives Monograph Series No. 1, ed. Ian F. Grant, Wellington 2012, p. 41.

26 Ibid.

27 Archibald Baxter, *We Will Not Cease,* Cape Catley, Auckland, 2003, p. 20.

28 Nolan (ed.), *War and Class*, p. 348.

29 Mackie to Ensom, 21 October 1914, 2017.38.4113, Mackie Papers, CM.

30 Meeting 4 August 1914, NPC Minute Book, MS 0445-F/1, Efford Papers.

31 'Work of the Peace Council for the past twelve months', December 1917, 2017.38.1431; Mackie to Ford, 21 April 1913, 2017.38.3451, Mackie Papers, CM.

32 Ian Dougherty, *The People's University: A centennial history of the Canterbury Workers' Educational Association 1915–2015*, Canterbury University Press, Christchurch, 2015, pp. 15–21, 32–33.

33 Items 743, 744, 745, Mackie Papers Pamphlets, CM.

34 Mackie to Brown, 30 June 1914, 2017.38.3341, Mackie Papers, CM.

35 Meeting 5 August 1915, NPC Minute Book, MS 0445-F/1, Efford Papers, ATL.

36 Mackie to Alexander, 25 January 1915, 2017.38.2781, Mackie Papers, CM.

37 Mackie to the *Ashburton Guardian*, 12 August 1913, 2017.38.3946, Mackie Papers, CM.

38 Thorn to Mackie, 16 September 1915, 2017.38.4769, Mackie Papers, CM.

39 Invoices Independent Labour Party to Mackie, 26 June and 30 July 1915, 2017.38.4738 and 2017.38.4739, Mackie Papers CM.

40 Advice from the Solicitor-General, 17 December 1915, AD10 11 19/33, ANZ; Charles Mackie to Canterbury Women's Institute, Socialist Party et al., 3 December 1915, 2017.38.1532, Mackie Papers, CM. See also Davidson, *Dead Letters*, pp. 36, 39, 182–83.

41 Tanner to Gibbon, 4 March and 12 May 1916 with advice from the Solicitor-General dated 22 May 1916, AD10 11 19/33, ANZ.

42 Mackie to Allen 22 December 1915; Mackie to the Chief Military Censor, 22 February 1916, AD10 11 19/33, ANZ.

43 Report of the Work of the NPC December 1917, 2017.38.1431, Mackie Papers, CM.

44 Report of the Work of the NPC August 1918, 2017.38.1436, Mackie Papers, CM.

45 Rutter to Mackie, 30 January 1916, 2017.38.4081, Mackie Papers, CM.

46 Meeting 27 January 1916, NPC Minute Book, MS 0445-F/1, Efford Papers.

47 'Report of Sub-committee appointed to enquire into the financial position of the Council', 29 June 1916, 2017.38.1430, Mackie Papers, CM. One of the regular donors was NPC member George Wells, who gave £24 per year; it caused a financial crisis for the NPC when he stopped his donation in 1924. Mackie to Mrs Ensom, 28 July 1924, 2017.38.4191, Mackie Papers, CM.

48 Rutter to Mackie, 27 March 1915 and 26 April 1915, 2017.38.4071 and 2017.38.4073, Mackie Papers, CM; 'Christianity and War', by Dr Alfred Salter, printed in Wellington 1915, Item 715, Mackie Papers Pamphlets, CM.

49 Mackie to Mrs Page, 27 November 1916, Series 523, Mackie Papers, CM; Meetings July 1916 to September 1917, NPC Minute Book, MS 0445-F/1, Efford Papers

50 Page to Mackie, 3 September 1915, 2017.38.3371, Mackie Papers, CM.

51 *White Ribbon*, 18 March 1914, p. 2.

52 'Criminal nations', *White Ribbon*, 18 March 1915, p. 1.

53 'Thirty-third Annual Convention of the N.Z. W.C.T.U.', *White Ribbon*, 18 April 1918, p. 2; Megan Hutching, '"Turn back this tide of barbarism": New Zealand women who were opposed to war 1869–1919', MA thesis, University of Auckland, 1990, pp. 146–50.

54 'An appreciation by a fellow worker', *White Ribbon*, 18 October 1928, p. 12.

55 'The C.W.I.', *Maoriland Worker*, 31 March 1915, p. 5.

56 'Canterbury Women's Institute', *Sun*, 10 August 1914, p. 9.

57 Annika Wilmers, 'Feminist pacifism', online International Encyclopedia of the First World War, 2015, https://encyclopedia.1914-1918-online.net/article/feminist_pacifism

58 Ibid.

59 Canterbury Women's Institute', *Star*, 12 July 1915, p. 8; Ada Wells also read the congress resolutions to an NPC meeting. Meeting 3 June 1915, NPC Minute Book, MS 0445-F/1, Efford Papers.

60 'Canterbury Women's Institute', *Star*, 13 October 1915, p. 1.

61 'Prevention of war', *Evening Post*, 25 August 1916, p. 9; three English Quakers known to the Christchurch peace movement – Charlotte Bracher, Margaret Lloyd and Elizabeth Rutter – were asked to represent the CWI at the conference.

62 Baker, *King and Country Call*; P. S. O'Connor, 'The awkward ones: Dealing with conscience 1916–18', *NZJH*, vol. 8, no. 2, 1974, pp. 118–36.

63 'Canterbury Women's Institute', *Maoriland Worker*, 15 September 1915, p. 4.

64 'The labor movement', *Evening Star*, 13 September 1915, p. 2.

65 Ibid.; another newspaper editorial about the NPC circular referred to the Peace Society emerging from its 'patriotic obscurity' to express its alarm and consternation: 'From obscurity', *Sun*, 3 September 1915, p. 5.

66 'After the war: Peace manifesto', *Maoriland Worker*, 22 December 1915, p. 11.

67 'Canterbury Women's Institute', *Maoriland Worker*, 22 December 1915, p. 11.

68 'Peace manifestos', *Lyttelton Times*, 18 November 1916, p. 7.

69 'Social Democratic Party Peace Manifesto', Item 721, Mackie Papers Pamphlets, CM.

70 Elizabeth Plumridge, 'Labour in Christchurch: Community and consciousness 1914–1919', MA thesis, University of Canterbury, 1979, pp. 43–44; 'The S.D.P. in Christchurch', *Maoriland Worker*, 22 December 1915, p. 4.

71 '"The price of glory" to Henry William Reynolds', *NZ Truth*, 29 January 1916, p. 7. Reynold's claim that 34,000 men would not kill or help to kill their fellow men came from the government survey of November 1915. All eligible men were required to register and state their willingness to volunteer for overseas service, or for civil service in New Zealand; 34,386 men said they would not volunteer in either capacity. Baker, *King and Country Call*, pp. 58–59. The cartoon on p. 165 refers to the same 'war register'.

72 Ibid.

73 'An indomitable pacifist', *NZ Bulletin*, February 1935, MS–6164-0-3, Roth Biographical Notes, MS-Copy-Micro-0714-20, ATL. Most of the article, apart from a prologue and conclusion, is a first-hand account by H. W. Reynolds.

74 'Three months hard labour for attempting to evade the censor', *Ashburton Guardian*, 12 September 1916, p. 4; *New Zealand Police Gazette*, 10 January 1917, p. 17.

75 Ensom to Morel, via Arthur Ponsonby, 17 October 1917; 'Secret' [report], 19 March 1918, AD10 11/19/35, ANZ.

76 'The Military Service Bill: A protest from the National Peace Council', 6 June 1916, 2017.38.1166, Mackie Papers, CM.

77 'Women's societies', *Maoriland Worker*, 26 April 1916, p. 3.

78 'The latest Christchurch cranks', *Marlborough Express*, 4 May 1916, p. 4.

79 'Untitled', *Sun*, 22 May 1916, p. 6.

80 'Reply to the Prime Minister', *Maoriland Worker*, 17 May 1916, p. 3.

81 Baker, *King and Country Call*, pp. 71–72; Jim McAloon, 'Radical Christchurch', in John

Cookson and Graeme Dunstall (eds), *Southern Capital Christchurch: Towards a city biography 1850–2000*, Canterbury University Press, Christchurch, 2000, p. 180.

82 'Adela Pankhurst', *Maoriland Worker*, 21 June 1916, p. 3.

83 'Notes of a tour', *Maoriland Worker*, 19 July 1916, p. 3.

84 'Amusements', *Press*, 7 June 1916, p. 5.

85 WILPF Series III, Folders 11–13, 1915–25, Archives and Special Collections, University of Colorado, Boulder. They also wrote to Canterbury doctor Jessie Scott, not realising she was in Europe.

86 'Canterbury Women's Institute', *Maoriland Worker*, 22 March 1916, p. 3.

87 Margaret Lovell-Smith, 'The Women's International League for Peace and Freedom (WILPF): The oldest women's peace organisation in the world meets in Christchurch', 2016, http://voicesagainstwar.nz/exhibits/show/the-legacy-of-the-world-war-i-/the-women-s-international-leag

88 'Anti-conscriptionists', 'Britisher', letter to the editor, *Lyttelton Times*, 13 June 1918, p. 8.

89 'Anti-conscription', *Lyttelton Times*, 15 June 1916, p. 6; 'Peter Scott Ramsay', *Maoriland Worker*, 13 December 1916, p. 4.

90 'War regulations', *Lyttelton Times*, 21 September 1916, p. 7.

91 'Conscription Repeal League', *Lyttelton Times*, 28 November 1916, p. 8.

92 'Lively scenes', *Lyttelton Times*, 8 December 1916, p. 8.

93 H. Moreton to Mackie, 31 January 1917; and Letter from Mackie, 14 February 1917, Series 609, Mackie Papers, CM.

94 Baker, *King and Country Call*, p. 67.

95 Ibid.

96 Peter Franks and Jim McAloon, *Labour: The New Zealand Labour Party 1916–2016*, Victoria University Press, Wellington, 2016, p. 70.

97 Baker, *King and Country Call*, p. 156.

98 Ibid., pp. 156–57; 159–61.

99 Meeting, 14 December 1916, NPC Minute Book, MS 0445-F/1, Efford Papers.

5 'THE ONLY PLACE FOR A DECENT SOCIALIST ... WAS GAOL': SEDITIONISTS AND OBJECTORS 1917–19

1 Mark Dunick, 'Making rebels: The New Zealand Socialist Party, 1901–1913', MA thesis, Victoria University of Wellington, 2016, p. 79.

2 Ibid., p. 105.

3 'Manifesto of the N.Z. Socialist Party', *Maoriland Worker*, 28 February 1913, p. 3.

4 'Unity Congress Committee', *Maoriland Worker*, 28 February 1913, p. 7; 'Socialists and the Hardie-Vaillant resolution', *Maoriland Worker*, 28 February 1913, p. 7. The amendment read: 'Among the means to be used in order to prevent and hinder war, the Congress considers as particularly efficacious the general strike, especially in the industries that supply war with implements (arms and ammunition, transport etc.), as well as its propaganda and popular action in their most effective forms.' The New Zealand FOL supported the Hardie–Vaillant amendment.

5 Jim McAloon, 'Cooke, Frederick Riley', DNZB, 1996, https://teara.govt.nz/en/biographies/3c29/cooke-frederick-riley

6 There were, however, some objectors described as socialist who did not produce clear statements of belief, and allowances were made for those who were clearly not fit for military service or for prison life. Another socialist objector, Frank Rogerson, agreed to serve in the medical corps, although an accident to his finger and a dose of flu may have prevented any effective service.

7 'Labour men arrested and jailed', *Maoriland Worker*, 3 January 1917, p. 4; Dan Bartlett, 'Bob Semple: Miner, unionist and Labour politician', 2016, http://voicesagainstwar.nz/exhibits/show/the-response-of-the-labour-mov/bob-semple

8 'Mr. Fred. R. Cooke', *Maoriland Worker*, 3 January 1917, p. 5.

9 Ibid.

10 Elizabeth Plumridge, 'Labour in Christchurch: Community and consciousness 1914–1919', MA thesis, University of Canterbury, 1979, p. 113.

11 'Mr James Thorn: J.P. says he could be hung',

Maoriland Worker, 3 January 1917, pp. 5–6.

12 'Those conscientious objectors', *Manawatu Standard*, 19 November 1920, p. 5.

13 Dan Bartlett, 'Tim Armstrong: "A very seditious character"', 2016, http://voicesagainstwar.nz/exhibits/show/the-response-of-the-labour-mov/tim-armstrong

14 'Mr. T. H. Armstrong', *Maoriland Worker*, 24 January 1917, p. 4.

15 Ibid.

16 'A seditious tendency', *NZ Truth*, 27 January 1917, p. 5.

17 'Good-bye, Dad', *Maoriland Worker*, 31 January 1917, p. 4.

18 'Mr. Reg. Williams', *Maoriland Worker*, 31 January 1917, p. 4.

19 Margaret Lovell-Smith, 'Reg Williams: a passionate opponent of militarism', 2016, updated 2017, http://voicesagainstwar.nz/exhibits/show/the-response-of-the-labour-mov/reg-williams--a-passionate-opp; Williams, Edward Reginald – WWI 84172 – Army, ANZ.

20 Margaret Lovell-Smith, 'Peter Scott Ramsay: Long-standing member of the peace and labour movements defies conscription', 2016, http://voicesagainstwar.nz/exhibits/show/the-response-of-the-labour-mov/peter-scott-ramsay--long-stand

21 'Holy City', *Maoriland Worker*, 13 December 1916, p. 2.

22 '"Free speech"', *NZ Truth*, 10 February 1917, p. 5.

23 Ibid.

24 'Seditious tendency', *Maoriland Worker*, 7 February 1917, p. 5.

25 Ibid.

26 'Sedition: P.S. Ramsay sentenced', *Press*, 3 February 1917, p. 3.

27 Ibid.

28 Ibid.

29 'News in brief', *Sun*, 11 May 1918, p. 12.

30 *Rangitikei Advocate and Manawatu Argus*, 2 November 1918, p. 4; 'Court martial at Dunedin', *Press*, 11 December 1918, p. 4. Ongoing references to a Socialist Party in Christchurch show a group continued to meet despite the Christchurch branch having transferred its allegiance to the Social Democratic Party.

31 'Military defaulters sentenced', *Lake Country Press*, 19 December 1918, p. 5.

32 'Sent to gaol', *Lyttelton Times*, 3 March 1916, p. 7. Brown served two months in prison.

33 'Court-martialled: H. W. Reynolds on trial', *Sun*, 2 June 1917, p. 2.

34 Ibid.

35 'Foolish Reynolds', *NZ Truth*, 9 June 1917, p. 4; Reynolds was released on 12 September 1917. Tim Shoebridge, 'Imprisoned conscientious objectors 1916–1920', https://nzhistory.govt.nz/war/the-military-objectors-list

36 Reynolds and family to Mackie, 10 October 1917, 2017.38.4210, Mackie Papers, CM.

37 'An indomitable pacifist', MS–6164-0-3, Roth Biographical Notes, MS-Copy-Micro-0714-20, ATL.

38 'Seditious notices', *Press*, 4 May 1918, p. 6.

39 Meeting 22 November 1917, NPC Minute Book, MS 0445-F/1, Efford Papers, ATL.

40 'Failure to report', *Star*, 20 September 1917, p. 1; Military Prisoners, 23 November 1917, AD1 733 10/407 Part 1, ANZ; Shoebridge, 'Imprisoned conscientious objectors 1916–1920', https://nzhistory.govt.nz/war/the-military-objectors-list

41 Letters from William Worrall to his family, 1918, William Worrall Letters, Worrall family collection; Margaret Lovell-Smith, 'Worrall family showed united front against militarism', 2017, http://voicesagainstwar.nz/exhibits/show/pre-war-anti-militarism-and-th/worrall-family-showed-united

42 William Worrall to Annie Worrall, 15 February 1918, William Worrall Letters.

43 W. W. to the Superintendent and Teachers of the Richmond Methodist Sunday School, 15 February 1913, William Worrall Letters; like many other COs he was sentenced to two years' imprisonment with hard labour.

44 'Court martial', *Lyttelton Times*, 1 September 1917, p. 2.

45 'Court martialled', *Sun*, 31 August 1917, p. 10.

46 Shoebridge, 'Imprisoned conscientious objectors 1916–1920', https://nzhistory.govt.nz/war/the-military-objectors-list; HANNAM,

Edward – WWI-81971-Army, ANZ; Religious Advisory Board report. AD1 734 10/407/15 ANZ; confusingly his name is often spelt Hannan in written reports. He was placed on the Military Defaulters List and was finally released from prison on 1 September 1919.

47   The initials SDP by his name may have been a clerical error.

48   Libby (Elizabeth) Plumridge, 'The necessary but not sufficient condition: Christchurch labour and working-class culture', *NZJH*, vol. 19, no. 2, 1985, p. 139.

49   'The S.D.P. in Christchurch', *Maoriland Worker*, 22 December 1915, p. 4.

50   Ibid.

51   Dan Richardson, 'John and James Roberts: Socialist brothers against conscription', 2019, http://voicesagainstwar.nz/exhibits/show/the-response-of-the-labour-mov/john-and-james-roberts---socia

52   Kath Clark, 'John William Roberts', DNZB, 1998; https://teara.govt.nz/en/biographies/4r20/roberts-john-william

53   'Conscientious objectors', *Press*, 8 March 1918, p. 4.

54   'Court martial', *Lyttelton Times*, 8 March 1918, p. 8.

55   'John Roberts has rich memories of early socialists', *New Zealand Building Worker*, August 1954, p. 6.

56   'Courts-martial', *Sun*, 1 July 1918, p. 9.

57   Lincoln Efford's Socialist Ten Commandments card from the Socialist Sunday School, 1920s, Efford family.

58   'Courts-martial', *Sun*, 1 July 1918, p. 9.

59   'Court martial, *Star*, 1 July 1918, p. 5.

60   'General News', *Press*, 3 July 1918, p. 6.

61   Dan Bartlett, 'George Wears Samms: A socialist and a pacifist', 2016, http://voicesagainstwar.nz/exhibits/show/the-response-of-the-labour-mov/george-wears-samms--a-socialis

62   'Court martial', *Lyttelton Times*, 7 September 1918, p. 7.

63   'Courts-martial', *Sun*, 6 September 1918, p. 9.

64   'Court martial', *Lyttelton Times*, 7 September 1918, p. 7.

65   'Courts-martial', *Sun*, 6 September 1918, p. 9.

66   'Reservists sentenced', *Otago Witness*, 11 September 1918, p. 26.

67   'Trials deferred', *Sun*, 19 January 1918, p. 8.

68   'Court-martialled', *Sun*, 22 January 1918, p. 5.

69   'Short shrift for socialist "C.O."', *Sun*, 26 July 1918, p. 4.

70   Ibid.

71   Quartermain, George Ernest, WWI 92889 – Army, ANZ.

72   Margaret Lovell-Smith, 'James Chapple: The socialist preacher who was jailed for sedition', 2016, http://voicesagainstwar.nz/exhibits/show/the-response-of-the-labour-mov/james-chapple--the-socialist-p; Chapple's eldest son Leonard, who did not agree with his father's pacifism, had enlisted.

73   'A New Zealander in exile', *Maoriland Worker*, 26 April 1916, p. 2.

74   Geoff Chapple, 'Chapple, James Henry George', DNZB, 1996, https://teara.govt.nz/en/biographies/3c12/chapple-james-henry-george

75   'Rev Chapple convicted', *Ashburton Guardian*, 18 May 1918, p. 5.

76   Ibid.

77   Ibid.

78   Years after his death, Chapple became the inspiration for the main character in the award-winning *Plumb* trilogy written by his grandson, Maurice Gee.

79   'Horne's case', *NZ Truth*, 7 December 1918, p. 5.

80   Editorial, *Star*, 30 November 1918, p. 8.

81   'A "learned decision"', *Sun*, 11 September 1918, p. 8.

82   'Court-martial', *Lyttelton Times*, 7 November 1918, p. 8; Religious Advisory Board report, AD1 734 10-407-15, ANZ.

83   Discussed in Seán Brosnahan, '"Shaming the Shoneens": The Green Ray and the Maoriland Irish Society in Dunedin, 1916–1922', in Lyndon Fraser (ed.), *A Distant Shore: Irish migration and New Zealand settlemen*t, Otago University Press, Dunedin, 2000, pp. 117–34; see also Jared Davidson in *Dead Letters: Censorship and subversion in New Zealand 1914–1920*, Otago University Press, Dunedin, 2019, pp. 104–07; and Paul Baker, *King and Country Call: New Zealanders, conscription*

and the Great War, Auckland University Press, Auckland, 1988, pp. 203–04.

84 Doreen Lange, *Cricklewood*, published by Doreen Lange, Invercargill, 1982, p. 44.

85 Ibid., p. 45.

86 Ibid.

87 Ibid., p. 25.

88 Letter to editor from Ellen Vickers Howell, *Press*, 16 March 1918, p. 7; 'Conscientious objectors', *Press*, 8 March 1918, p. 4.

6 'LOVE YOUR ENEMIES': RELIGIOUS OBJECTORS 1917–19

1 Geoffrey Troughton, 'Christianity, peace and opposition to war', in Geoffrey Troughton (ed.), *Saints and Stirrers*, Victoria University Press, Wellington, 2017, pp. 12–13, 20–21. Two of Canterbury's imprisoned objectors, Edward Murrane and William Ryan, identified as being in the Catholic Church, but they objected on the grounds that they were Irish and were therefore classified as political rather than religious objectors.

2 Chris Marshall, 'Remembering Jesus on Anzac Day: Just war or just another war?', in Geoffrey Troughton and Philip Fountain (eds), *Pursuing Peace in Godzone: Christianity and the peace tradition in New Zealand*, Victoria University Press, Wellington, 2018, p. 218.

3 Peter Lineham, 'First World War religion', in John Crawford and Ian McGibbon (eds), *New Zealand's Great War: New Zealand, the Allies and the First World War*, Exisle Publishing, Auckland, 2007, p. 478.

4 Ross Anderson, 'New Zealand Methodism and World War I: Crisis in a liberal church', MA thesis, University of Canterbury, 1983, p. 1. Anderson argues that the elderly Rev W. J. Williams remained editor of the *New Zealand Methodist Times* during the war because he reflected the views of both the Methodist clergy and the laity.

5 'The way to peace', *Sun*, 14 October 1915, p. 9.

6 Murray to Mackie, 19 October 1915, 2017.38.3364, Mackie Papers, CM.

7 Lineham, 'First World War religion', p. 469.

8 Exodus 20:13. All the biblical quotes in this chapter come from the King James version of the Bible, which was in use at the time of World War I.

9 Isaiah 2:4; the vision is repeated in the book of Micah 4:3.

10 Matthew 5:9–11.

11 'Richmond Mission', Douglas H. Day, letter to the editor, *Sun*, 14 June 1918, p. 4.

12 'Opposed to war', *Sun*, 11 January 1917, p.10. The New Testament verse cited is Matthew 10:34.

13 Peter Lineham, 'The rising price of rendering to Caesar: The churches in World War One', in Steven Loveridge (ed) *New Zealand Society at War, 1914–1918*, Victoria University Press, Wellington, 2016, p. 198.

14 Peter Lineham, 'Sects and war in New Zealand', in Geoffrey Troughton (ed), *Saints and Stirrers*, Victoria University Press, Wellington, 2017, p. 166.

15 Paul Baker, *King and Country Call: New Zealanders, conscription and the Great War*, Auckland University Press, Auckland, 1988, pp. 173–74; see also Kevin Ross Adams, 'The growth and development of the Society of Friends in New Zealand 1840–1920', MA thesis, University of Canterbury, 1986, ch. 5.

16 David Littlewood, *Military Service Tribunals and Boards in the Great War: Determining the fate of Britain's and New Zealand's conscripts*, Routledge, Oxford, 2018, p. 137, 139.

17 Baker, *King and Country Call*, pp. 87, 108. Using section 35 proved to be unexpectedly complicated, and while 689 men were eventually conscripted in this way (24 per cent of those investigated), the practice was discontinued in March 1917.

18 'Converted too late: Six religious objectors', *Sun*, 8 February 1917, p. 8; Tim Shoebridge, 'Imprisoned conscientious objectors 1916–1920', https://nzhistory.govt.nz/war/the-military-objectors-list

19 'Military Service Board', *Dominion*, 26 July 1917, p. 9; Lineham, 'Sects and war in New Zealand', p. 173.

20 The 13 Canterbury members of the Testimony of Jesus imprisoned during World War I were:

Isaac Samuel Aicken, Thomas Edward Fowler, David Robert Gray, John Gray, William George Gray, John Ernest Holtham, Albert Edwin Joyce, Arthur Charles Neville McIntyre, John Henry Nixon, Robert Clayton Patton, Robert Stockdill, James Vallance and Bertie Wilfred Morgan.

21 Margaret Lovell-Smith, 'David Gray: Transported to Europe in error', 2016, http://voicesagainstwar.nz/exhibits/show/conscription--and-those-who-ob/david-gray--transported-to-eur. Robert was David Gray's second name, and there was apparently confusion with another Robert Gray. In May 1917 Ernest Holtham complained to James Allen about the inconsistent treatment of the two brothers: Robert (David) was in a civil prison, while John was doing civil work at camp: James Allen to the Commandant, 19 May 1917. AD1 734 10/407 Part 2 1917, ANZ; David Gray's first sentence dated from 27 April 1917. Shoebridge, 'Imprisoned conscientious objectors 1916–1920', https://nzhistory.govt.nz/war/the-military-objectors-list

22 David Grant, *Field Punishment No. 1*, Steele Roberts, Wellington, 2008, pp. 39–40, 45.

23 Archibald Baxter, *We Will Not Cease,* Cape Catley, Auckland, 2003, p. 92.

24 Memo for Base Records Branch, New Zealand Military Forces, Wellington, 10 June 1919. AD1 734 10/407/3 Part 2, ANZ.

25 Isaac was sentenced to an initial 28 days' detention in August 1917, and a two-year sentence in September the same year. He was released in April 1919. 'Military service boards', *Press*, 8 February 1917, p. 9; Shoebridge, 'Imprisoned conscientious objectors 1916–1920', https://nzhistory.govt.nz/war/the-military-objectors-list

26 'Short shrift for religious objector', *Ashburton Guardian*, 4 January 1917, p. 2.

27 'Testimony of Jesus', *Star*, 4 January 1917, p. 5.

28 'Military Service Board', *Dominion*, 26 July 1917, p. 9; 'A little-known sect', *Sun*, 4 January 1917, p. 9; Patton was released from prison on 17 April 1919.

29 Hilary Jack, 'Early days in Oxford', private

collection. Vallance continued to work as a missionary for 30 years.

30 'Unordained "minister"', *NZ Herald*, 16 May 1918, p. 4; 'Conscientious objector', *Auckland Star*, 15 May 1918, p. 4; 'Appeals of reservists', *Auckland Star*, 30 May 1918, p. 6. Vallance was sentenced to 28 days' imprisonment in June 1918, and two years in August 1918, of which he served just over a year before his release from Paparua prison on 30 August 1919. Morgan received similar sentences to Vallance and was released from Invercargill Borstal in September 1919.

31 Notes of interview between Hon. Sir James Allen, Minister of Defence and 8 Conscientious Objectors undergoing imprisonment at Kaingaroa, 15 November 1917, AD1 733 10/407 Part 1, ANZ.

32 McIntyre, Arthur Charles Neville, WWI 64796 – Army, ANZ.

33 The nine members of the Richmond Mission imprisoned were Keith Hamilton Broughton, Albert Edwin John Church, Frederick Church, Douglas Henry Day, Percy Clarence Dodge, Ernest Edward Munns, Thomas Brown Struthers, John Stubberfield and William James Young. In addition to the nine imprisoned members, Harry Bernard Loomes was detained at Featherston Military Camp for several months; Charles Wilfred Forest Dodge had his appeal dismissed but does not seem to have been arrested; and Theodore Gibbs agreed to do non-combatant work.

34 David Smith to Colonel R. W. Tate, 22 June 1917, AD1 734 10/407 Part 2 1917, ANZ.

35 Colonel R. W. Tate to the Solicitor-General, 16 May 1917, AD1 734 10/407 Part 2 1917, ANZ; P. S. O'Connor, 'The awkward ones: Dealing with conscience 1916–18', *NZJH*, vol. 8, no. 2, 1974, pp. 126–30.

36 'Military service', *Star*, 14 July 1917, p. 9. The two members concerned were Percy Clarence Dodge and Harry Bernard Loomes.

37 A paraphrase of Matthew 20:21; 'Treasures on Earth', *Sun*, 17 March 1917, p. 14.

38 'Treasures on Earth', *Sun*, 17 March 1917, p. 14. Albert's second sentence of 11 months was given on 20 August 1917, and his third

sentence of two years dates from 7 May 1918; 'Military service boards', *Press*, 11 August 1917, p. 4; 'Military service', *Star*, 10 August 1917, p. 6.

39   'Military service', *Sun*, 16 May 1917, p. 10.

40   'Military service boards', *Press*, 14 March 1917, p. 2; 'Military service', *Sun*, 13 March 1917, p. 8; Shoebridge, 'Imprisoned conscientious objectors 1916–1920', https://nzhistory.govt.nz/war/the-military-objectors-list. The case of another Dodge brother, Fred, a member of the Exclusive Brethren, is discussed later in the chapter.

41   'The conscientious objector', *Ohinemuri Gazette*, 16 September 1918, p. 3.

42   Munns' appeal was dismissed in December 1917 and he was sentenced to one year and 11 months' hard labour. 'Military service', *Sun*, 6 December 1917, p. 9.

43   'Richmond Mission', Douglas H. Day, letter to the editor, *Sun*, 14 June 1918, p. 4; Margaret Lovell-Smith, 'Douglas Day: Christian conscientious objector who identified with Christ's suffering', 2016, http://voicesagainstwar.nz/exhibits/show/conscription--and-those-who-ob/douglas-henry-day--christian-c

44   'Richmond Mission', Douglas H. Day, letter to the editor, *Sun*, 14 June 1918, p. 4.

45   Douglas to his mother Ruth Day, written from H.M. Prison Lyttelton, 13 October 1918, author's collection.

46   Douglas Day to his mother Ruth Day, written from H.M. Prison Templeton, 20 December 1918, author's collection.

47   Mary Petersen, *To the Glory of the Lord who called them to serve: The history of the Richmond Mission Christchurch, 1911–1984*, North Avon Baptist Church, Christchurch, 1995, pp. 29–30.

48   Lineham, 'Sects and war in New Zealand', p. 171.

49   Noel Hendery, 'Seven generations in New Zealand: The history of the Hendery family', private collection, 2018, p. 10.

50   Margaret Lovell-Smith, 'The case of Noel Goldsbury: A Quaker whose "leave of absence" caused a furore', 2016, http://voicesagainstwar.

nz/exhibits/show/conscription--and-those-who-ob/the-case-of-noel-goldsbury--a-

51   'Peace message from the Society of Friends (New Zealand)', General Meeting, 10–14 July 1915, Item 701, Mackie Papers Pamphlets, CM.

52   'A determined "C.O."', *Sun*, 22 July 1918, p. 9.

53   'Courts-martial', *Sun*, 6 September 1918, p. 9; 'Court-martial', *Sun*, 7 September 1918, p. 2; 'Eleven months', *Sun*, 10 September 1918, p. 4.

54   'The Goldsbury case', Geo. Scott, letter to the editor, *Sun*, 7 October 1918, p. 4.

55   'A curious decision', *Sun*, 5 October 1918, p. 8.

56   'The Goldsbury case', 'A Briton', letter to the editor, *Sun*, 5 October 1918, p. 8.

57   'Letters to the editor', *Sun*, 7 October 1918, p. 4.

58   Numerous letters about 'The Goldsbury case' were published in the *Sun* in October 1918.

59   'Goldsbury case: Motion rescinded', *Sun*, 2 November 1918, p. 10; 'The Technical College', *Sun*, 14 January 1919, p. 5.

60   Lineham, 'Sects and war in New Zealand', p. 166; 'Military service', *Sun*, 10 July 1918, p. 3; 'A court-martial', *Sun*, 5 November 1918, p. 6; 'Reservists sentenced', *Sun*, 5 November 1918, p. 11; Robinson was sentenced to two years' imprisonment; he served 13 months before he was released from Waikeria in September 1919. Shoebridge, 'Imprisoned conscientious objectors 1916–1920', https://nzhistory.govt.nz/war/the-military-objectors-list

61   'News in Brief', *Sun*, 4 April 1918, p. 8; Cecil K. Meyers to Major Osborne Lillie, 11 July 1917; 'Religious objectors who have signed the undertaking to perform non-combatant work', 21 December 1917, AD1 733 10/407 Part 1, ANZ.

62   A. H. MacLeod, *Oxford Terrace Baptist Church: Centennial history 1863–1963*, Institute Printing and Publishing Society, Auckland, 1963; *Diamond Jubilee Souvenir 1871–1931*, Odell Print, Christchurch, 1931; Troughton, 'Christianity, peace and opposition to war', pp. 21–22.

63   'Opposed to war', *Sun*, 11 January 1917, p. 10; 'Military service', *Sun*, 16 January 1917, p. 11.

64   Thomas Nuttall to Frank Money, 25 July 1917, Frank Money's letters and diaries (photocopies), Money family collection.

65 Ibid.

66 Ibid.

67 Laurie Guy, 'Early Christian Pacifists in Christchurch: Creating division in the fight for peace', paper presented to the Anglican Pacifist Society, August 2006, p. 8. http://legacy. disarmsecure.org/Baptist%20Pacifists%20 -%20Ang%20Pac%20Conf.pdf

68 Ibid., p. 9; Wal Harris and Gerald Tisch, *The Linwood Harvest: Linwood Baptist Church 1912–1987*, The Church, Christchurch, 1987, pp. 10–11.

69 H. Bramwell Cook and Neroli Williams, *We're in the Money: The Money family history*, pp. 38–39, private collection; Margaret Lovell-Smith, 'Committed Christian Frank Money pays the price for his beliefs', 2019, http://voicesagainstwar.nz/exhibits/show/ conscription--and-those-who-ob/committed- christian-frank-mone

70 Frank Money to the Defence Department, 20 January 1917, Money family collection.

71 'F Money. My diary 1917', 11 July 1917, Money family collection.

72 Ethel Mackie to My dear Friend [Frank Money], 25 July 1917, Money family collection.

73 Frank Money to Mr and Mrs Mackie, 12 October 1918, Series 1016, Mackie Papers, CM.

74 'Paparua, 23 December 1917', Money family collection.

75 'F Money. My diary 1917', 24 June 1917, Money family collection.

76 Frank Money, 'Diary of military detention and camp life', [July 1917, p. 8.] Money family collection.

77 Troughton, 'Christianity, peace and opposition to war', p. 27.

78 Andrew Kennaway Henderson to Sir James Allen, 22 January 1918, Material relating to Kennaway Henderson, MS-0445-49, Efford Papers, ATL; Margaret Lovell-Smith, 'Kennaway Henderson: A man of principle', 2016, http://voicesagainstwar.nz/exhibits/ show/conscription--and-those-who-ob/ kennaway-henderson--a-man-of-p

79 'Court martial', *Lyttelton Times*, 8 March 1918, p. 8.

80 Winston Rhodes, *Kennaway Henderson: Artist, editor and radical*, Publications Committee of the University of Canterbury, 1988, Christchurch, p. 19; 'Conscientious objectors', *Press*, 8 March 1918, p. 4.

81 Rhodes, *Kennaway Henderson,* pp. 14, 18.

82 Ibid., p. 14; Neil Roberts, *Leonard Booth 1879–1974*, Robert McDougall Art Gallery, Christchurch, 2000, pp. 13–14.

83 Robert Owen Page's defence at his trial by court-martial, Robin Page Scrapbook, Page family collection.

84 Ibid.

85 Wayne Facer, *Prophet at the Gate: Norman Murray Bell and the quest for peace*, Blackstone Editions, Toronto, 2021, pp. 31–51, 63.

86 Ibid., p. 56.

87 Bell, Norman Murray – WW1 64795 – Army, ANZ.

88 'Conscientious objectors', B. E. Baughan, letter to the editor, *Press*, 16 March 1918, p. 7.

89 Margaret Lovell-Smith, 'Norman Bell: Scholar and peacemaker', 2016, http://voicesagainstwar. nz/exhibits/show/conscription--and-those-who- ob/norman-bell--scholar-and-peace

90 'Military service', *Sun*, 3 September 1917, p. 8.

91 Notes of interview between Hon. Sir James Allen, Minister of Defence and 8 Conscientious Objectors undergoing imprisonment at Kaingaroa, 15 November 1917, AD1 733 10/407 Part 1, ANZ.

92 C. Morgan Williams, *Memoirs*, 1963, private collection.

93 Ibid.

94 Reg Williams to [Mackie], 8 March 1919, 2017.38.3594, Mackie Papers, CM.

95 'To all whom it may concern', 27 January 1917, Lyttelton Harbour Board Letter Book, 1916–1918, ANZC; Margaret Lovell- Smith, 'Charles Edward Warden: Christian Ideals Lead to Imprisonment', 2019, http://voicesagainstwar.nz/exhibits/show/ conscription--and-those-who-ob/charles- edward-warden--christi

96 Charles Warden's 'Form of Declaration', dated 3 October 1916, Lyttelton Harbour Board Correspondence European War 1914–1918, ANZC.

97   C. Warden to the Secretary of the Lyttelton
      Harbour Board, 17 January 1917, Lyttelton
      Harbour Board Correspondence European
      War 1914–1918, ANZC.
98   Ibid.
99   For example, Theodore Gibbs, Herbert
      Church.
100 'Inconsistency', *Lyttelton Times*, 19 March
      1917, p. 8.
101 Military service', *Star*, 21 April 1917, p. 4;
      Dan Richardson, 'Silas Stedman:
      Willing to serve, not to kill', 2019,
      http://voicesagainstwar.nz/exhibits/show/
      conscription--and-those-who-ob/silas-
      stedman--willing-to-serv
102 Baker, *King and Country Call*, p. 125; 'Military
      service boards', *Press*, 10 January 1917,
      p. 5; 'The Methodist Church of New Zealand,
      Minutes of the Twelfth Annual Conference',
      February 1924, p. 16.
103 'District court martial', *Otago Daily Times*,
      19 December 1918, p. 3; RAB report, AD1
      734 10-407-15, ANZ; Bradley was released
      from Paparua prison in May 1920: *New
      Zealand Police Gazette*, June 1920, p. 358.

7 THE BEST POSSIBLE CONDITIONS? LIFE IN PRISON 1917–19

1   'Report on New Zealand prisons for the year
      1917–1918', p. 3, AJHR, 1918, H-20.
2   'Paparua Prison: In memory of those who
      suffered for conscience sake, 1916–1919',
      Miscellanea Folder, n.d., Richard Thompson
      papers, MB287-Ref51734, MBL.
3   Duncan McCormack, 'War; What for?' p. 2,
      undated transcript of radio interview, author's
      collection.
4   Religious Advisory Board report, AD1 734
      10/407/15 ANZ; Charles Mackie noted the
      frequent migrations in and out of Paparua
      prison in August 1918: Mackie to Mrs
      Ballantyne, 13 August 1918, Series 574,
      Mackie Papers, CM.
5   Robin to Freddy, 19 April 1918, Robin Page
      Scrapbook, Page family collection.
6   Meeting 14 February 1918, NPC Minute
      Book, MS 0445-F/1, Efford Papers, ATL.
7   Meeting 22 November 1917, NPC Minute
      Book, MS 0445-F/1, Efford Papers; Will to
      Annie, 15 February 1918 and Will to My
      dear Sister, 4 August 1918, Worrall family
      collection.
8   Mackie to Dr Thacker, 24 August 1917, Series
      595, Mackie Papers, CM.
9   Re Andrew Kennaway Henderson, Artist, AD1
      734 10/407 Part 3, ANZ.
10   Meetings 26 July and 22 November 1917,
      NPC Minute Book, MS 0445-F/1, Efford
      Papers.
11   Mackie to the Methodist Conference,
      23 February 1918, 2017.38.3780, Mackie
      Papers, CM. The letter was also sent to the
      Congregational Union, the Baptist Auxiliary
      and the WCTU.
12   'Recent cases of C.O.s' treatment under
      military authority in N.Z.', 31 March 1918,
      AD1 734 10/407 Part 3, ANZ.
13   Ibid.
14   Paul Baker, *King and Country Call: New
      Zealanders, conscription and the Great War*,
      Auckland University Press, Auckland, 1988,
      p. 193.
15   Robin to Auntie Nellie, 30 August [1918],
      Robin Page Scrapbook.
16   Mark Derby, *Rock College: An unofficial history
      of Mount Eden Prison*, Massey University Press,
      2020, Auckland, p. 141.
17   Will to My dear Sister, 31 March 1918, and
      Beattie to Annie, 17 April 1918, Worrall
      family collection. He was at Rotoaira by
      August 1918 and and still there when the
      RAB visited, but some time between April
      and September 1919 he was transferred to
      Waikeria.
18   This chapter draws heavily on their writings.
19   Money was detained in Hut 21 on two
      occasions, before and after his month at the
      Alexandra Barracks, and recorded an almost
      identical list of fellow religious objectors
      on both occasions: four men from the
      Richmond Mission (Church, Loomes, Dodge,
      Broughton); five from the Testimony of Jesus
      (Dixon, Blade, Hogan, Pickering, Holtham);
      one Quaker (Wright); one Church of England
      (Watson); one Brethren (King); one Free

Christian (Levett); himself as the only Baptist, and seven others – Phillips, Anderson, Read, Read, Davidson, Hopkins, Steele. 'F Money. My diary 1917'; and Frank Money, 'Diary of military detention and camp life', Money family collection.

20 Robin to Freddy, 13 April 1918, Robin Page Scrapbook.

21 Robin to Father, 16 April 1918, Robin Page Scrapbook.

22 Ruth Day to Muriel Lovell-Smith, 29 July 1918, [4 August] 1918, 11 August 1918, Day family letters, author's collection.

23 Peter Methven, *The Terrace Gaol: A short history of Wellington's prisons 1840–1927,* Steele Roberts, Wellington, 2011, pp. 67–69.

24 Shortly after arriving at the Barracks Money recorded a list of eight fellow prisoners with a summary of their beliefs. There were four COs; and other offences included smacking an officer; threatening to strike the Bombardier at Palmerston; refusing to wear uniform; an escaped agnostic; an attempted escapee; and a returned soldier who didn't want to be sent away for a second time. 'F Money. My diary 1917', 16 June and 22 June 1917, Money family collection.

25 'F Money. My diary 1917', 11 July 1917, Money family collection.

26 Robin to Freddie, 23 April 1918, Robin Page Scrapbook.

27 Robin to Mother, 19 May 1918, Robin Page Scrapbook.

28 Baker, *King and Country Call,* p. 195; Robin to Mother, 19 May 1918, Robin Page Scrapbook.

29 Frank Money 'Diary of military detention and camp life' [14 July 1917], Money family collection.

30 Robin to Freddy, 19 April 1918, Robin Page Scrapbook.

31 Frank Money, 'Diary of military detention and camp life' [July 1917].

32 Meeting 22 November 1917, NPC Minute Book, MS 0445-F/1, Efford Papers.

33 Memo from the Chief of General Staff, Colonel Gibbon, 9 August 1917, AD1 733 10/407 Part 1, ANZ.

34 Report of the work of the National Peace

Council to August 1918, 2017.38.1436, Mackie Papers, CM; Meeting 22 November 1917, NPC Minute Book, MS 0445-F/1, Efford Papers.

35 S. S. Page to My Dear Family, 28 May 1918, Robin Page Scrapbook.

36 Ibid.

37 Ibid. Page was sentenced to two years' hard labour.

38 Notes by Frank Money about his experiences since he was sentenced, dated 16 September 1917. Money family collection.

39 Methven, *The Terrace Gaol*, pp. 23, 94, 104, 110.

40 'Report on New Zealand prisons for the year 1918–1919', p. 11, AJHR, H-20.

41 Notes by Frank Money about his experiences since he was sentenced, dated 16 September 1917, Money family collection.

42 Methven, *The Terrace Gaol*, pp. 20–22. It was demolished in the 1920s to make way for the Dominion Museum.

43 Meeting 6 February 1919, NPC Minute Book No.3, MS 0445-F/3, Efford Papers, ATL; The Wellington WIL sent a letter of complaint about the two men's treatment. Sarah Beck to Hon Sir J. Allen, 9 December 1918, AD1 734 10/407 Part 3, ANZ.

44 'Report on New Zealand Prisons for the year 1917–1918', p. 10; 'Report on the New Zealand Prisons for the year 1919–1920', p. 7, AJHR, H-20.

45 'Life in Lyttelton Jail', *Maoriland Worker*, 17 January 1913, p. 8.

46 'Gaol' by H. W. Reynolds, MS 6164 0-3, Roth Biographical Notes, MS-Copy-Micro 0714-20, ATL.

47 Reg Williams, 'The truth about Lyttelton Gaol, *Repeal*, no. 2. May 1913, p. 11.

48 Winston Rhodes, *Kennaway Henderson: Artist, editor and radical*, Publications Committee of the University of Canterbury, 1988, Christchurch, p. 21.

49 'Gaol' by H. W. Reynolds, MS 6164 0-3, Roth Biographical Notes, Ms-Copy-Micro 0714-20, ATL.

50 Williams, 'The truth about Lyttelton Gaol', pp. 12–13.

51 McCormack, 'War; What for?', p. 6.

52 Douglas to his mother Ruth Day, 13 October 1918, written from HM Prison Lyttelton, Day family letters, author's collection. William Worrall experienced the complicated rules around letters and visitors at the Wellington prisons when he was at Point Halswell, where he was allowed a visit from relatives every two weeks and friends once a month, on any day but Saturday, Sunday or holidays. If he had a visitor once a fortnight, he could receive only one letter a fortnight. Beattie to Annie, 17 April 1918, Worrall family collection.

53 McCormack, 'War; What for?' pp. 7–8.

54 Alfred William Page, Ellen Saunders and Ann Saunders, *He's for the morning': Alfred William Page, his journal; also some recollections of his life by his aunts, Ellen & Ann Saunders,* Alex Wildey, Christchurch, 1939, p. 23.

55 Matthews to Mackie, 2 September 1918, Series 617; Report of the Work of the NPC, August 1918, 2017.38.1436, Mackie Papers, CM.

56 Mackie to C. E. Matthews, 22 January 1919, Series 617, Mackie Papers, CM.

57 Ibid.

58 'Report on New Zealand Prisons for the year 1917–1918', AJHR, H-20, p. 7.

59 Margaret West and Ruth Fawell, *The Story of New Zealand Quakerism 1842–1972,* Yearly Meeting of the Religious Society of Friends, Auckland, 1973, pp. 73–74. Eight Canterbury men were in Waikeria when the RAB visited: John Gray, Frank Money, Ernest Munns, Walter Robinson, Robert Stockdill, William Virtue, Reg Williams and William Young.

60 Reg Williams to Mackie, 14 September 1918, 2017.38.3590, 1 January 1919, 2017.38.3593, and 8 March 1919, 2017.38.3594; Mackie to Graham, 24 January 1921, 2017.38.4471, Mackie Papers, CM.

61 Frank Money to Mr and Mrs Mackie, 12 October 1918, Series 1016, Mackie Papers, CM.

62 'Report on New Zealand Prisons 1917–1918', pp. 6, 8, 10, AJHR, H-20. The Canterbury COs at the Invercargill Borstal at war's end were Fred Dodge, Charles Gunter, Edward Hannam, Albert Joyce, Bertie Morgan, Edward Murrane, William Ryan and Thomas Struthers.

63 Noel Hendery, 'Seven generations in New Zealand', pp. 9–10. Originally sentenced to a year and 11 months in prison, Fred was released after a year, having been found to be a 'genuine' religious objector.

64 'Report on New Zealand Prisons 1917–1918', pp. 8, 16, AJHR, H-20.

65 Notes of interview between Hon. Sir James Allen and 8 Conscientious Objectors at Kaingaroa, 15 November 1917, AD1 733 10/407 Part 1.

66 'Report on New Zealand Prisons 1917–1918', p. 7, AJHR, H-20; Will to My dear Sister, 19 January 1918, Worrall family collection; Jared Davidson, *Dead Letters: Censorship and subversion in New Zealand 1914–1920,* Otago University Press, Dunedin, 2019, p. 110.

67 The eight Canterbury men there in 1919 were: Isaac Aicken, Norman Bell, Frederick Church, Thomas Fowler, Arthur McIntyre, Robert Patton, John Stubberfield and William Worrall.

68 N. M. Bell to Charles Mackie, 22 September 1918, Series 599, Mackie Papers, CM.

69 Will to My dear Sister, 4 August 1918, Worrall family collection.

70 Robin to Father, 16 April 1918, Robin Page Scrapbook.

71 Robin to Auntie Nellie, 30 August [1918], Robin Page Scrapbook.

72 Baker, *King and Country Call,* p. 168.

73 Rhodes, *Kennaway Henderson,* p. 22.

74 'A Sketch of Gaol Life given to his mother by R. O. Page as a birthday present 1918', Robin Page Scrapbook.

75 Robin [to his family], 1 December 1918, Robin Page Scrapbook.

76 Ruth Day to Muriel Lovell-Smith, 6 October 1918, 16 October 1918, 8 December 1918, Day family letters, author's collection.

77 Ruth Day to Muriel Lovell-Smith and Margery Day, 31 December 1918, Day family letters, author's collection; E. J. Howard, 'Seditious Prisoners and Conscientious Objectors Fund', [p. 4], undated.

78 Mackie to Graham, 24 January 1921, 2017.38.4471, Mackie Papers, CM; Mary Petersen, *To the Glory of the Lord who called them to serve: The history of the Richmond Mission Christchurch, 1911–1984*, North Avon Baptist Church, Christchurch, 1995, p. 29.

79 Mackie to Graham, 24 January 1921, 2017.38.4471, Mackie Papers, CM.

80 Thomas M. Wilford to Mackie, 27 March 1918, 2017.38.1068, Mackie Papers, CM.

81 Frank Money, 'Paparua, 23 December 1917', Money family collection.

82 'F Money. My diary 1917', 2 July 1917, Money family collection.

83 'F Money. My diary 1917', 7 July 1917, Money family collection.

84 Kaiapoi District Historical Soc. Inc., known as Kaiapoi Museum. Ref. KDHS 79/85; see also Margaret Lovell-Smith, 'Horse-hair watch-guard a memento of prison life'. https://ww100.govt.nz/kaiapoi-horse-hair-watch-guard

85 Rhodes, *Kennaway Henderson*, p. 22.

86 Ibid.

87 Baker, *King and Country Call*, p. 178.

88 Robin to Auntie Nellie, 30 August [1918], Robin Page Scrapbook.

89 Ibid.

90 Meetings 11 July 1918 and 1 August 1918, NPC Minute Book No.3, 1918–1924, MS 0445-F/3, Efford Papers, ATL. While a vote on the question of consulting Findlay was lost by one vote, a statement on the rearrests, researched and written by Mackie, was sent to the *Maoriland Worker* and to parents and friends of COs.

91 Mrs G. E. Wills to James Allen, 10 June 1918, AD1 734 10/407/11, ANZ.

8 SUPPORT FOR THE CONSCIENTIOUS OBJECTORS 1917–19

1   P. S. O'Connor, 'Barmy Christchurch: A melodrama in three parts', *Comment*, June 1968, no. 35, p. 22.

2   Meetings January to December 1917, NPC Minute Book, MS 0445-F/1, Efford Papers, ATL.

3   'Labour demonstration', *Sun*, 19 March 1917, p. 8.

4   'Labour rally', *Lyttelton Times*, 19 March 1917, p. 9.

5   Ibid.

6   'The women's part,' *Lyttelton Times*, 23 April 1917, p. 7.

7   Tā Tipene O'Regan, 'He kupu whatataki', in *He Rau Mahara: To remember the journey of our Ngāi Tahu Soldiers: From the pā to the battlefield of the Great War,* Te Rūnanga o Ngāi Tahu, Christchurch, 2017, p. 13. A few South Island Māori appealed against military service on the grounds that they were Māori and therefore should not have been balloted: 'Military service board', *Star*, 16 April 1917, p. 5; 'Military service', *Star*, 28 June 1917, p. 6.

8   Monty Soutar, *Whitiki! Whiti! Whiti! E!*, David Bateman, Auckland, 2019, pp. 246–66, 257, 272–73.

9   Meetings 1, 22 August 1918, NPC Minute Book, MS Papers-0445-F/3, Efford Papers, ATL; Allen to Mackie, 19 August 1919, 2017.38.1012, Mackie Papers, CM.

10 Mackie to Maori Members of Parliament, Ngata, Pomare, Henare and Uru, 28 August 1918, 2017.38.1538, Mackie Papers, CM.

11 'Māori objection to conscription', https://nzhistory.govt.nz/war/first-world-war/conscientious-objection/maori-objection, Ministry for Culture and Heritage, updated 1-May-2020; O'Regan, 'He Kupu Whatataki', p. 12.

12 'Christchurch Branch of the Women's International League extend hearty Christmas greetings', *Maoriland Worker*, 12 December 1917, p. 11.

13 E. J. Howard, 'Seditious Prisoners and Conscientious Objectors Fund', undated.

14 'Conscientious objectors', B. E. Baughan, letter to the editor, *Lyttelton Times*, 13 January 1917, p. 10; Baughan to Allen, 17 January 1917 and 26 January 1917, AD1 734 10/407 Part 2, 1917, ANZ.

15 Nancy Harris, 'Baughan, Blanche Edith', DNZB, 1996, https://teara.govt.nz/en/biographies/3b17/baughan-blanche-edith

16 Baughan to Allen, 4 February 1918, AD1 734 10/407 Part 3, ANZ.

17 'Conscientious objectors', B. E. Baughan, letter to the editor, *Press*, 16 March 1918, p. 7.

18 Baughan to Nellie [Ellen Saunders], 16 May 1918, Robin Page Scrapbook.

19 'Conscientious objectors', *Press*, 2 April 1918, p. 3.

20 Ibid.

21 March 1918 letter signed by Jessie Mackay et al., AD1 734 10/407 Part 3, ANZ.

22 R. W. Tate to the Secretary, Recruiting Board, Wellington, 28 March 1918, AD1 734 10/407 Part 3, ANZ.

23 Territorial Force – Religious Objectors – Murray and others, AD1 734 10/407/9, ANZ.

24 'Conscientious objectors', *Sun*, 4 September 1917, p. 3; Rev H. Allen Job to Allen, 20 February and 12 June 1918, AD1 734 10/407/3 Part 2, ANZ.

25 'The deported C.O.s', *Lyttelton Times*, 8 April 1918, p. 6.

26 'Canterbury women protest', *Maoriland Worker*, 30 January 1918, p. 4.

27 'For conscience sake', *Maoriland Worker*, 27 February 1918, p. 7.

28 J. Allen, 'Conscientious objectors', 28 February 1918, AD1 734 10/407/3 Part 2, ANZ.

29 Paul Baker, *King and Country Call: New Zealanders, conscription and the Great War*, Auckland University Press, Auckland, 1988, p. 196, citing petition letter sent to every member of Cabinet regarding Archibald Baxter signed by Blanche Baughan, Jessie Mackay and Mary Johnson, 11 June 1918, AD1 10/407/3 Part 2, ANZ.

30 Petition letter from Grace Wills and 19 other women, 14 June 1918, AD1 10/407/3 Part 2, ANZ.

31 'Baxter's breakdown', *NZ Truth*, 29 June 1918, p. 6.

32 Baker, *King and Country Call*, p. 196.

33 Millicent Baxter, *The Memoirs of Millicent Baxter*, Cape Catley, Queen Charlotte Sound, 1981, p. 52.

34 Ibid.

35 'War matters', *Lyttelton Times*, 28 August 1918, p. 4.

36 Mackie to Minister of Defence, 31 August 1918, AD1 734 10/407/3 Part 1, ANZ.

37 Sarah Page, 'Wartime reminiscences', *The Working Woman*, March 1936, p. 6.

38 'Concealing deserters', *Sun*, 31 May 1918, p. 9; 'Prices sent to gaol', *Sun*, 8 August 1918, p. 8; Baker, *King and Country Call*, p. 207.

39 'Courts-martial', *Sun*, 1 July 1918, p. 9; 'Courts-Martial', *Sun*, 6 September 1918, p. 9.

40 Ibid.

41 Letter from CWI Secretary S. S. Page, 13 March 1918, AD1 734 10/407 Part 3, ANZ.

42 Baughan to Colonel R. Tate, 26 March 1918, AD1 734 10/407 Part 3, ANZ.

43 'Court-martialled', *Sun*, 22 January 1918, p. 5; 'Local and General', *Evening Post*, 24 January 1918, p. 6.

44 'News of the Day', *Colonist*, 13 May 1915, p. 4.

45 Baker, *King and Country Call*, pp. 147–49.

46 'Mobilisation scenes', *NZ Truth*, 4 May 1918, p. 4.

47 'Riots in Christchurch', *North Otago Times*, 1 May 1918, p. 7.

48 Ibid.

49 Baker, *King and Country Call*, pp. 147–49; Ministry for Culture and Heritage, 'Convictions for sedition 1915–1918', 2016, https://nzhistory.govt.nz/war/sedition-conviction-list

50 'The Second Division', *Press*, 1 May 1918, p. 6.

51 'Pay inadequate', *Dominion*, 19 April 1917, p. 4.

52 'For intellectual freedom', *Maoriland Worker*, 3 January 1917, p. 3.

53 Baker, *King and Country Call*, pp. 162–63.

54 Gwen Parsons, 'Challenging enduring Home Front myths: Jingoistic civilians and neglected soldiers', in David Monger, Sarah Murray and Katie Pickles (eds), *Endurance and the First World War: Experiences and legacies in New Zealand and Australia*, Cambridge Scholars Publishing, Newcastle upon Tyne, 2014, p. 71.

55 Elizabeth Plumridge, 'Labour in Christchurch: Community and consciousness 1914–1919', MA thesis, University of Canterbury, 1979, p. 108.

56 Mackie to Farmer, 17 September 1919, 2017.38.2894, Mackie Papers, CM.

57 C. R. N. Mackie, letter to editor, *Maoriland Worker*, 29 September 1915, p. 4.

58 'Canterbury Women's Institute', *Maoriland Worker*, 10 January 1917, p. 4.

59 'Local and General', *Evening Post*, 21 May 1918, p. 6; Minutes of meeting, 11 April 1918, 2017.38.1433, Mackie Papers, CM.

60 'Canterbury Women's Institute', *Star*, 16 August 1919, p. 9.

61 'Tears for Germany', *Star*, 16 August 1919, p. 8; While the CWI did not take part in activities set up to support the war effort, it had sent cases of clothing in response to an appeal from the British Dominions Women's Suffrage Union for warm clothing for the poor of England and Belgium. 'New Zealand's Gifts', *Rangitikei Advocate and Manawatu Argus*, 10 June 1915, p. 7; The *Star* had also published a derisory editorial directed at the NPC on 21 March 1919, titled 'Peace at any price'.

62 Sarah Page to the NPC, 24 February 1919, Series 523, Mackie Papers, CM.

63 Edmund Bohan, 'Page, Sarah', DNZB, Volume 3, 1996, https://teara.govt.nz/en/biographies/3p1/page-sarah

64 Margaret Lovell-Smith, 'The Women's International League for Peace and Freedom (WILPF): The oldest women's peace organisation in the world meets in Christchurch' 2016, http://voicesagainstwar.nz/exhibits/show/the-legacy-of-the-world-war-i-/the-women-s-international-leag

65 'The anti-militarists', *Wanganui Herald*, 31 March 1919, p. 6.

66 'Anti-militarism', *Sun*, 26 March 1919, p. 2.

67 'A stormy deputation', *Dominion*, 28 March 1919, p. 7; 'The anti-militarists', *Wanganui Herald*, 31 March 1919, p. 6.

68 Baughan to Allen, 29 June 1919, and MacKay to Allen, 4 July 1919, AD1 734 10/407 Part 3, ANZ.

69 Sarah Page to Allen, 13 May 1919 and 27 June 1919 AD1 734 10/407/3 Part 1, and 25 July 1919, AD1 734 10/407 Part 3, ANZ.

70 Baker, *King and Country Call*, p. 201.

71 Geo E. Moore to Sir James Allen, 9 December 1918; Annie C. Gadd to Sir James Allen, 10 March [1919] AD1 738 10/566/2, ANZ.

72 Mackie to Holland, 18 August 1919, and Mackie to Holland 8 October 1919, citing a letter received from Massey, Series 583, Mackie Papers, CM.

73 Religious Advisory Board Report, AD1 734 10/407/15, ANZ.

74 Kevin Ross Adams, 'The growth and development of the Society of Friends in New Zealand 1840–1920', MA thesis, University of Canterbury, 1986, p. 155, 183.

75 Meeting 6 February 1919, NPC Minute Book, MS 0445-F/3, Efford Papers.

76 Reg Williams [to Mackie], 8 March 1919, 2017.38.3594 and 5 April 1919, 2015.38.359, Mackie Papers, CM.

77 Reg Williams [to Mackie], 8 March 1919, 2017.38.3594, Mackie Papers, CM.

78 Ibid.

79 Ibid.

80 Reg Williams [to Mackie], 5 April 1919, 2017.38.3595, Mackie Papers, CM.

81 Reg Williams [to Mackie], 3 May 1919, 2017.38.3596, Mackie Papers, CM.

82 Reg Williams [to Mackie], 24 May 1919, 2017.38.3597, Mackie Papers, CM.

83 The Gaoler to the Inspector of Prisons, 13 June 1919, J40 206 1919/8/9, ANZ.

84 'Military Defaulters List', Item 990, Mackie Papers Pamphlets, CM; Minutes of meetings, 26 June 1919 and 24 July 191, NPC Minute Book, 0445-F/3, Efford Papers.

85 'Military Defaulters List', Item 990, Mackie Papers, Pamphlets.

86 Reg Williams [to Mackie], 7 June 1919, 2017.38.3598, Mackie Papers, CM.

87 'Conscientious objectors', Ann Saunders, letter to the editor, *Press*, 23 July 1919, p. 2.

88 'Peace Sunday at Christchurch', *Maoriland Worker*, 6 August 1919, p. 5.

89 Minister of Defence to Rev B Busfield, 28 August 1919, AD1 734 10/407/3 Part 1, ANZ.

90 *New Zealand Police Gazette*, 10 September 1919, pp. 549–50; and 17 September 1919, p. 556.

91 Tim Shoebridge, 'Imprisoned conscientious objectors', https://nzhistory.govt.nz/war/the-military-objectors-list

9 SOWING THAT OTHERS MAY REAP: THE LEGACY OF THE WORLD WAR I PEACE MOVEMENT

1   Ford to Mackie, 30 September 1914, 2017.38.3476, Mackie Papers, CM – a biblical allusion, probably to John 4:37.

2   Mackie to Haddy, 12 September 1919, 2017.38.3017, and 2 June 1926, 2017.38.3023, Mackie Papers, CM.

3   Memorandum for the Solicitor-General, 29 October 1919 and Memorandum for the Minister of Defence, 8 November 1919, AD10 11 19/33, ANZ.

4   Mackie believed that censorship of the NPC mail was carried out for about six years between 1915 and 1921, though the file on the 'Censorship of correspondence, National peace conference' was dated June 1915–July 1920. AD10 11 19/33, ANZ.

5   'Christchurch Technical College, Personal statement of the Director', 28 January 1919, Pacifism in New Zealand, 82-213-05, Roth Papers, ATL.

6   P. MacCallum to Allen, 2 June 1919, AD1 734 10/407 Part 3, ANZ

7   Allen to MacCallum, 2 June 1919, AD1 734 10/407 Part 3, ANZ.

8   Margaret Lovell-Smith, 'Norman Bell: Scholar and peacemaker', 2016, http://voicesagainstwar.nz/exhibits/show/conscription--and-those-who-ob/norman-bell--scholar-and-peace

9   'The coming elections', *Maoriland Worker*, 18 June 1919, p. 5.

10   'Labour personalities (no. 5) John Roberts', *The Standard*, 2 June 1938, p. 6.

11   Dan Bartlett, 'George Wears Samms: A socialist and a pacifist', 2016, http://voicesagainstwar.nz/exhibits/show/the-response-of-the-labour-mov/george-wears-samms--a-socialis

12   'Mr Frank Robinson', *Press*, 27 October 1948, p. 3.

13   Winston Rhodes, *Kennaway Henderson: Artist, editor and radical*, Publications Committee of the University of Canterbury, 1988, Christchurch, p. 24.

14   Ensom to Mackie, 4 September 1921, 2017.38.4166, Mackie Papers, CM.

15   Gordon Ogilvie, *Denis Glover: His life*, Random House, Auckland, 1999, p. 53.

16   Nuttall family information; 'Obituary Mr T. Nuttall', *Press*, 28 June 1944, p. 5.

17   Grace Adams, *Jack's Hut*, Reed, Wellington, 1968, p. 118.

18   Margaret Lovell-Smith, 'Charles Edward Warden: Christian Ideals lead to Imprisonment', 2019, http://voicesagainstwar.nz/exhibits/show/conscription--and-those-who-ob/charles-edward-warden--christi

19   The *Beacon* was a monthly publication produced in Christchurch 1920–22 to advocate for 'the coming of a better social and economic order of society at home, founded upon the principle of Mutual Aid; and to foster friendliness and co-operation with all peoples abroad', Items 7–28, Mackie Papers Pamphlets, CM.

20   Williams to Mackie, 6 September 1920, 2017.38.3599, Mackie Papers, CM.

21   David Grant, *A Question of Faith: A history of the New Zealand Christian Pacifist Society*, Philip Garside Publishing, Wellington, 2004, p. 9.

22   Munns, 'Our history', accessed 3 October 2018, https://munns.co.nz/pages/copy-of-terms-conditions

23   'Goldsbury, Noel (Ken)', Margaret West and Audrey Brodie, *Remembrance of Friends Past*, NZ Yearly Meeting of the Society of Friends, Wellington, 1999, p. 78.

24   Margaret Lovell-Smith, 'Robert Owen (Robin) Page: Canterbury College student stands up for his convictions', 2016, http://voicesagainstwar.nz/exhibits/show/conscription--and-those-who-ob/robert-owen--robin--page--cant

25   'Magistrates' Court', *Press*, 12 March 1940, p. 5.

26   James K. Worrall was secretary and Charlie Warden and William Davidson were appointed as delegates to the NPC. Bell wrote later that it had died because 'it lacked the right type of leader and sufficient individuality, as its very name shows'. Alfred William Page, Ellen Saunders and Ann Saunders, *'He's for the*

morning': Alfred William Page, his journal; also some recollections of his life by his aunts, Ellen & Ann Saunders, Alex Wildey Ltd, Christchurch, 1939, p. 56.

27 'Women's Corner', *Press*, 5 September 1921, p. 2; Mary Petersen, *To the Glory of the Lord who called them to serve: The history of the Richmond Mission Christchurch, 1911–1984*, North Avon Baptist Church, Christchurch, 1995, pp. 10–11.

28 Nancy Harris, 'Baughan, Blanche Edith', DNZB, 1996, https://teara.govt.nz/en/ biographies/3b17/baughan-blanche-edith. Mackie served as both secretary or president over many years.

29 Elizabeth Plumridge, 'Labour in Christchurch: Community and consciousness 1914–1919', MA thesis, University of Canterbury, 1979, p. 272.

30 Grant, *A Question of Faith*, pp. 9–10.

31 Page and Saunders, *'He's for the morning'*, pp. 58–59.

32 Elsie Locke, *Peace People: A history of peace activities in New Zealand*, Hazard Press, Christchurch, 1992, pp. 75–77.

33 Grant, *A Question of Faith*, p. 11.

34 Laurie Barber, 'Gibb, James', DNZB, 1993, https://teara.govt.nz/en/biographies/2g5/ gibb-james. Gibb, a Presbyterian minister, had become anti-war partly through the influence of Charles Murray of Christchurch.

35 Margaret Lovell-Smith, 'Taylor, Elizabeth Best', DNZB, 1996, https://teara.govt.nz/en/ biographies/3t9/taylor-elizabeth-best

36 Grant, *A Question of Faith*, p. 11.

37 Page and Saunders, *'He's for the morning'*, p. 56.

38 Ibid., pp. 24–25.

39 Ibid., p. 25.

40 Ibid., pp. 26–35.

41 Margaret Lovell-Smith, 'Fred Page and the No More War Movement', 2016, http:// voicesagainstwar.nz/exhibits/show/the-legacy- of-the-world-war-i-/fred-page-and-the-no- more-war-

42 'Canterbury socialists', *Maoriland Worker*, 8 August 1917, p. 3.

43 'Picnic at Pleasant Point', *Maoriland Worker*, 9 January 1918, p. 4; 'Socialist Party', *Star,* 23 February 1918, p. 13.

44 'Socialist Sunday Schools', Ann Saunders, letter to editor*, Press*, 16 November 1922, p. 8; 'Golden Sayings' MS 0445-47 Efford Papers, ATL.

45 Locke, *Peace People*, p. 72.

46 Elwyn Clements, 'The life of a woman: Muriel Morrison', 1994, http://legacy.disarmsecure. org/Muriel%20Morrison%20Part%201.pdf

47 Grant, 'A question of faith', p. 12.

48 'Muriel Morrison's tribute to Lincoln Efford', MS 7202-315 Locke Papers, ATL.

49 Ibid.

50 The other editors were B. Anan, D. Thorne, Lily Samms, Lincoln Efford, R. Macfarlane and C. Bloomfield. *The International Sunbeam*, Items 63–78, Mackie Papers Pamphlets, CM; see also 'The Christchurch Socialist Sunday School starts its own press', *Maoriland Worker*, 20 June 1923, p. 7.

51 'The Socialist Party', *Press*, 30 May 1932, p. 3; David Grant, 'Standing up for peace', *NZ Listener*, 19 July 1986, p. 12.

52 Fred Page to Mr Atkinson, 3 February 1928, MS 82-213-07, Roth Papers, ATL; Mackie to Cole, 7 September 1929, Series 1010, Mackie Papers, CM.

53 Page and Saunders, *'He's for the morning'*, p. 57.

54 Ibid., p. 60.

55 Ian Dougherty, *The People's University: A centennial history of the Canterbury Workers' Educational Association 1915–2015*, Canterbury University Press, Christchurch, 2015, p. 85; 'Charitable bequests', *Press*, 15 June 1929, p. 19.

56 See Series 1059 and 1281, Mackie Papers, CM, for correspondence about the Ensom Trust Fund.

57 Ada Wells to Mackie, 9 March 1933, Series 515, Mackie Papers, CM.

58 Sarah Page to the National Peace Council, 2 March 1932 and Programme for Round Table Conference, 28 September 1932, Series 1010, Mackie Papers, CM.

59 Circular letter from C. R. N. Mackie and H. A. Atkinson, 24 May 1934, Series 1343, Mackie Papers, CM.

60 The Constitution of the National Peace Council of New Zealand, undated, 2017.38.1216, Mackie Papers, CM.

61 Tim McKenzie, 'J. R. Hervey, 1889–1958', *Kōtare*, vol. 7, no. 3, 2008, pp. 105–14, https://www.academia.edu/55742007/J_R_Hervey_1889_1958; 'Vicar retires', *Press*, 26 July 1934, p. 10.

62 'New pacifist society', *Press*, 30 September 1935, p. 17.

63 'Peace Pledge Union', *Press*, 11 June 1938, p. 15. The first acting secretary, Russell Thurlow Thompson (d. 1985), was the father of Richard H. Thurlow Thompson (1924–2006), who became a dedicated peace worker in his turn.

64 'Department and Minister for Peace', *North Canterbury Gazette*, 10 August 1939, p. 7.

65 'Same wretched bugles', *North Canterbury Gazette*, 24 August 1939, p. 4: Taylor had recently returned from England where he had visited the PPU and seen it at work.

66 Ibid.

67 'The pacifists', C. R. N. Mackie, letter to the editor, *Press*, 31 May 1938, p. 7.

68 'The pacifists', L. A. Efford, letter to the editor, *Press*, 31 May 1938, p. 7.

69 'The pacifists', J. R. Hervey ,letter to the editor, *Press*, 31 May 1938, p. 7.

70 'Open-air meetings'. C. R. N. Mackie, letter to editor, *Press*, 5 October 1939, p. 3.

71 'Neutrality for New Zealand', *Press*, 2 September 1939, p. 3; 'Pacifist views stated', *Press*, 17 November 1939, p. 6.

72 Jim McAloon, 'Radical Christchurch', in John Cookson and Graeme Dunstall (eds), *Southern Capital Christchurch: Towards a city biography 1850–2000*, Canterbury University Press, Christchurch, 2000, p. 181; Geoffrey W. Rice, *Christchurch Changing: An illustrated history*, Canterbury University Press, Christchurch, 1999, pp. 85–86, 92, 97.

73 'Armed Forces Board', *Press*, 12 July 1941, p. 4.

74 Jim McAloon. 'Armstrong, Hubert Thomas', DNZB, 1996, https://teara.govt.nz/en/biographies/3a20/armstrong-hubert-thomas

75 *Press*, 19 January 1940, p. 10.

76 'Resignation accepted with regret', *Bay of Plenty Times*, 26 August 1949, p. 2.

77 J. E. Cookson, 'Mackie, Charles Robert Norris', DNZB, 1996, https://teara.govt.nz/en/biographies/3m20/mackie-charles-robert-norris

78 Ibid.

79 Meeting 8 March 1943, NPC Minute Book 1934–1946, MS Papers-0445-H/08, Efford Papers, ATL.

80 Melanie Nolan, *Kin: A collective biography of a New Zealand working-class family*, Canterbury University Press, Christchurch, 2005, p. 49.

81 Brent Efford, 'Lincoln Efford', presentation to the Canterbury WEA, September 2018.

82 Grant, *A Question of Faith*, p. 14.

83 Efford, 'Lincoln Efford'.

84 Nicola Barnett, 'Efford, Lincoln Arthur Winstone', DNZB, 2000, https://teara.govt.nz/en/biographies/5e1/efford-lincoln-arthur-winstone

85 Lincoln Efford to Blanche Baughan, 21 April 1946, MS-Papers-0445-02 Efford Papers, ATL.

86 Locke, *Peace People*, p. 166.

87 Maire Leadbetter, *Peace Power and Politics: How New Zealand became nuclear free*, Otago University Press, Dunedin, 2013.

88 Locke, *Peace People*, p. 316.

BIBLIOGRAPHY

BOOKS, CHAPTERS AND ARTICLES

Adams, Grace, *Jack's Hut*, Reed, Wellington, 1968.

Armstrong, John, 'Review: *Gallipoli: The scale of our war*, Museum of New Zealand Te Papa Tongarewa, April 2015–April 2019', *New Zealand Journal of Public History*, vol. 5, no. 1, 2017, pp. 59–63.

Baker, Paul, *King and Country Call: New Zealanders, conscription and the Great War*, Auckland University Press, Auckland, 1988.

Baxter, Archibald, *We Will Not Cease,* Cape Catley, Auckland, 2003.

Baxter, Millicent, *The Memoirs of Millicent Baxter*, Cape Catley, Queen Charlotte Sound, 1981.

Bracher, S. V., *Ripa Island: A lesson for conscriptionists*, Peace Committee of the Society of Friends, London, 1913.

Brodie, Audrey and J. W. Brodie, *Seeking a New Land: Quakers in New Zealand: A volume of biographical sketches*, New Zealand Yearly Meeting of the Society of Friends, Wellington, 1993.

Brosnahan, Seán, '"Shaming the Shoneens": The *Green Ray* and the Maoriland Irish Society in Dunedin, 1916–1922', in Lyndon Fraser (ed.), *A Distant Shore: Irish migration and New Zealand settlement*, Otago University Press, Dunedin, 2000, pp. 117–34.

Cunnington, Eveline Willett, *The Lectures and Letters of E.W. Cunnington*, printed by Lyttelton Times, Christchurch, 1918.

Davidson, Jared, *Dead Letters: Censorship and subversion in New Zealand 1914–1920*, Otago University Press, Dunedin, 2019.

Derby, Mark, *Rock College: An unofficial history of Mount Eden Prison*, Massey University Press, Auckland, 2020.

Devaliant, Judith, *Kate Sheppard: The fight for women's votes in New Zealand: The life of the woman who led the struggle*, Penguin Books, Auckland, 1992.

Devere, Heather, Kelli Te Maihāroa, Maui Solomon and Maata Wharehoka, 'Regeneration of indigenous peace traditions in Aotearoa New Zealand', in Heather Devere, Kelli Te Maihāroa and John Synott (eds), *Peacebuilding and the rights of Indigenous peoples*, vol. 9, Springer, Cham, 2017, pp. 53–63.

Dougherty, Ian, *The People's University: A centennial history of the Canterbury Workers' Educational Association 1915–2015*, Canterbury University Press, Christchurch, 2015.

Dunick, Mark, 'Who were the Clarion Settlers?', *Labour History Project Bulletin,* vol. 65, 2015, pp. 18–25.

Eldred-Grigg, Stevan, *The Great Wrong War: New Zealand society in WWI*, Random House, Auckland, 2010.

Facer, Wayne, *Prophet at the Gate: Norman Murray Bell and the quest for peace*, Blackstone Editions, Toronto, 2021.

Fletcher, John Percy and John Francis Hills, *Conscription under Camouflage*, John Francis Hills Publisher, Adelaide, 1919.

Ford, Charles Reginald, *The Defence Act: A criticism*, National Peace Council of New Zealand, Christchurch, 1911.

——, *The Case Against Compulsory Military Training*, National Peace Council of New Zealand, Christchurch, 1912.

——, *The Cost of War and Militarism*, National Peace Council of New Zealand, Christchurch, 1912.

Franks, Peter and Jim McAloon, *Labour: The New Zealand Labour Party 1916–2016*, Victoria University Press, Wellington, 2016.

Gardner, W. J. (Jim), *Colonial Cap and Gown*, University of Canterbury, Christchurch, 1979.

——, 'Tradition and conscience: Canterbury College and R. O. Page, Conscientious Objector, 1918–1919', *History Now*, vol. 9, no. 2, 2003, pp. 6–9.

Gee, David, *The Devil's Own Brigade: A history of the Lyttelton Gaol 1862–1920*, Millwood Press, Wellington, 1975.

——, *My Dear Girl*, TreeHouse, Christchurch, 1993.

Gosset, Robyn, *The History of Mrs Pope Ltd*, Mrs Pope Ltd, Christchurch, 1981.

Grant, David, *A Question of Faith: A history of the New Zealand Christian Pacifist Society*, Philip Garside Publishing, Wellington, 2004.

——, *Field Punishment No. 1*, Steele Roberts, Wellington, 2008.

——, *Out in the Cold*, Reed Methuen, Auckland, 1986.

——, 'Standing up for peace', *NZ Listener*, 19 July 1986, p. 12.

——, 'Where were the peacemongers? Pacifists in New Zealand during World War One', in Steven Loveridge (ed.), *New Zealand Society at War 1914–1918*, Victoria University Press, Wellington, 2016, pp. 220–34.

Guy, Laurie, 'Three countries, two conversions, one man – J. J. Doke: Baptists, humanity and justice', in David Bebbington and Martin Sutherland (eds), *Interfaces: Baptists and others*, Paternoster, Milton Keynes, 2013, pp. 265–76.

Harris, Wal and Gerald Tisch, *The Linwood Harvest: Linwood Baptist Church 1912–1987*, The Church, Christchurch, 1987.

Holland, H. E., *Armageddon or Calvary: The conscientious objectors of New Zealand and 'the process of their conversion'*, H. E. Holland, Wellington, 1919.

Holt, Betty, *Women in Council: A history of the National Council of Women of New Zealand 1896–1979*, National Council of Women of New Zealand, Wellington, 1980.

Howard, E. J., *Seditious Prisoners and Conscientious Objectors Fund*, undated.

Hucker, Graham, '"The Great Wave of Enthusiasm": New Zealand reactions to the First World War in August 1914 – a reassessment', *New Zealand Journal of History*, vol. 43, no. 1, 2009, pp. 59–75.

Hutching, Megan, '"Mothers of the World": Women, peace and arbitration in early twentieth-century New Zealand, *New Zealand Journal of History*, vol. 27, no. 2, 1993, pp. 173–85.

——, 'The Moloch of War: New Zealand women who opposed the war', in John Crawford and Ian McGibbon (eds), *New Zealand's Great War: New Zealand, the Allies and the First World War*, Exisle Publishing, Auckland, 2007, pp. 85–95.

King, Michael, *The Penguin History of New Zealand*, Penguin Books, Auckland, 2003.

Laing, Robert M., *Shall War and Militarism Prevail?*, L. M. Isitt, Christchurch, 1911.

Lange, Doreen, *Cricklewood*, Doreen Lange, Invercargill, 1982.

Leadbetter, Maire, *Peace, Power and Politics: How New Zealand became nuclear free,* Otago University Press, Dunedin, 2013.

Lineham, Peter, 'First World War religion', in John Crawford and Ian McGibbon (eds), *New Zealand's Great War: New Zealand, the Allies and the First World War*, Exisle Publishing Ltd, Auckland, 2007, pp. 467–92.

——, 'The rising price of rendering to Caesar: The churches in World War One', in Steven Loveridge (ed.), *New Zealand Society at War 1914–1918*, Victoria University Press, Wellington, 2016, pp. 190–205.

——, 'Sects and war in New Zealand', in Geoffrey Troughton (ed.), *Saints and Stirrers*, Victoria University Press, Wellington, 2017, pp. 163–82.

Littlewood, David, *Military Service Tribunals and Boards in the Great War: Determining the fate of Britain's and New Zealand's conscripts*, Routledge, Oxford, 2018.

Locke, Elsie, 'Wilhelmina Sherriff Bain', in Charlotte MacDonald (ed.), *The Book of New Zealand Women: Ko Kui Ma Te Kaupapa*, Bridget Williams Books, Wellington, 1991.

——, *Peace People: A history of peace activities in New Zealand*, Hazard Press, Christchurch, 1992.

Lovell-Smith, Margaret, *Easily the Best: The life of Helen Connon 1857–1903*, Canterbury University Press, Christchurch, 2004.

Loveridge, Steven, *Calls to Arms*, Victoria University Press, Wellington, 2014.

Loveridge, Steven and James Watson, *The Home Front: New Zealand society and the war effort, 1914–1919*, Massey University Press, Auckland, 2019.

Low, Peter, 'New Zealand's identity was not created by war: "The Glorious Anzac Myth"', *Friends Newsletter*, vol. 96, no. 4, September 2014.

MacLeod, Angus H., *The First Hundred Years: A centennial history of Oxford Terrace Baptist Church, Christchurch, 1863–1963*, Institute Printing and Publishing Society, Auckland, 1963.

MacLeod, Nellie G. H., *The Fighting Man: A study of the life and times of T. E. Taylor*, Dunbar and Summers, Christchurch, 1964.

Marshall, Chris, 'Remembering Jesus on Anzac Day: Just war or just another war?', in Geoffrey Troughton and Philip Fountain (eds), *Pursuing Peace in Godzone: Christianity and the peace tradition in New Zealand*, Victoria University Press, Wellington, 2018, pp. 213–27.

McAloon, Jim, 'Radical Christchurch', in John Cookson and Graeme Dunstall (eds), *Southern Capital Christchurch: Towards a city biography 1850–2000*, Canterbury University Press, Christchurch, 2000, pp. 162–92.

Methven, Peter, *The Terrace Gaol: A short history of Wellington's prisons 1840–1927*, Steele Roberts, Wellington, 2011.

Murray, Sarah, *A Cartoon War: The cartoons of the* New Zealand Freelance *and* New Zealand Observer *as historical sources, August 1914–November 1918*, New Zealand Cartoon Archives Monograph Series, no. 1, Wellington, 2012.

Nolan, Melanie, *Kin: A collective biography of a New Zealand working-class family*, Canterbury University Press, Christchurch, 2005.

——, (ed.), *War and Class: The diary of Jack McCullough*, Dunmore Publishing, Wellington, 2009.

O'Connor, P. S., 'Barmy Christchurch: A melodrama in three parts', *Comment*, no. 35, June 1968, pp. 21–28.

——, 'The awkward ones: Dealing with conscience, 1916–1918', *New Zealand Journal of History*, vol. 8, no. 2, 1974, pp. 118–36.

Ogilvie, Gordon, *Denis Glover: His life*, Random House, Auckland, 1999.

O'Regan, Tā Tipene, 'He Kupu Whatataki', in *He Rau Mahara: To remember the journey of our Ngāi Tahu soldiers: From the pā to the battlefield of the Great War*, Te Rūnanga o Ngāi Tahu, Christchurch, 2017.

Oxford Terrace Baptist Church, *Diamond Jubilee Souvenir 1871–1931*, Odell Print, Christchurch, 1931.

Page, Alfed William, Ellen Saunders and Ann Saunders, '*He's for the morning': Alfred William Page, his journal; also some recollections of his life by his aunts, Ellen & Ann Saunders*, Alex Wildey Ltd, Christchurch, 1939.

Page, Dorothy, *The National Council of Women: A centennial history*, Auckland University Press with Bridget Williams Books, Auckland, 1996.

Page, Sarah, 'Wartime reminiscences', *The Working Woman*, March 1936, pp. 6–7.

——, 'Paths to permanent peace', *The Working Woman*, October 1936, pp. 8–9.

Parsons, Gwen, 'Challenging enduring Home Front myths: Jingoistic civilians and neglected soldiers', in David Monger, Sarah Murray and Katie Pickles (eds), *Endurance and the First World War: Experiences and legacies in New Zealand and Australia*, Cambridge Scholars Publishing, Newcastle upon Tyne, 2014, pp. 66–85.

——, 'Debating the war: The discourse of war in the Christchurch community', in John Crawford and Ian McGibbon (eds), *New Zealand's Great War: New Zealand, the Allies and the First World War*, Exisle Publishing, Auckland, 2007, pp. 550–68.

Pearce, Cyril, *Comrades in Conscience: The story of an English community's opposition to the Great War*, Francis Boutle Publishers, London, revised edition, 2014.

Petersen, Mary, *To the Glory of the Lord Who Called Them to Serve: The history of the Richmond Mission Christchurch, 1911–1984*, North Avon Baptist Church, Christchurch, 1995.

Phillips, Jock, 'War and national identity', in David Novitz and Bill Willmott (eds), *Culture and Identity in New Zealand*, GP Books, Wellington, 1990, pp. 91–110.

Plumridge, Libby, 'The necessary but not sufficient condition: Christchurch Labour and working-class culture', *New Zealand Journal of History*, vol. 19, no. 2, 1985, pp. 130–50.

Rhodes, Winston, *Kennaway Henderson: Artist, editor and radical*, Publications Committee of the University of Canterbury, Christchurch, 1988.

Rice, Geoffrey W., *Christchurch Changing: An illustrated history*, Canterbury University Press, Christchurch, 1999.

Richardson, Len and Shelley Richardson, *Anthony Wilding: A sporting life*, Canterbury University Press, Christchurch, 2005.

Roberts, Neil, *Leonard Booth 1879–1974*, Robert McDougall Art Gallery, Christchurch, 2000.

Roth, Herbert, 'In memoriam: Harry Albert Atkinson', *Here and Now*, June 1956, pp. 18–20.

——, 'The Labour churches and New Zealand', *International Review of Social History*, vol. 4, no. 3, 1959, pp. 361–66.

——, 'Hell, no, we won't go', *Monthly Review*, October 1970, pp. 20–22.

Scotter, W. H., *A History of Canterbury, Volume III 1876–1950*, Whitcombe & Tombs, Christchurch, 1965.

Soutar, Monty, *Whitiki! Whiti! Whiti! E! Māori in the First World War*, David Bateman, Auckland, 2019.

Thorn, James, *The Formation and Development of Trades Unionism in Canterbury*, Standard Press, Wellington, 1950.

Tolerton, Jane, *Ettie: A life of Ettie Rout*, Penguin Books, Auckland, 1992.

Troughton, Geoffrey, 'Christianity, peace and opposition to war', in Geoffrey Troughton (ed.), *Saints and Stirrers*, Victoria University Press, Wellington, 2017.

Troughton, Geoffrey and Philip Fountain (eds), *Pursuing Peace in Godzone: Christianity and the peace tradition in New Zealand*, Victoria University Press, Wellington, 2018, pp. 17–29.

Weitzel, R. L., 'Pacifists and anti-militarists in New Zealand, 1909–1914', *New Zealand Journal of History*, vol. 7, no. 2, 1973, pp. 128–47.

West, Margaret and Audrey Brodie, *Remembrance of Friends Past*, NZ Yearly Meeting of the Society of Friends, Wellington, 1999.

West, Margaret and Ruth Fawell, *The Story of New Zealand Quakerism 1842–1972*, Yearly Meeting of the Religious Society of Friends, Auckland, 1973.

Williams, Morgan, *The Great White Elephant*, Repeal Printery, Christchurch, 1914.

THESES

Adams, Kevin Ross, 'The growth and development of the Society of Friends in New Zealand 1840–1920', MA thesis, University of Canterbury, 1986.

Anderson, Ross, 'New Zealand Methodism and World War I: Crisis in a liberal church', MA thesis, University of Canterbury, 1983.

Bodman, Ryan, '"Don't be a conscript, be a man!": A history of the Passive Resisters' Union, 1912–1914', Postgraduate Diploma in Arts in History dissertation, University of Auckland, 2010.

Clark, Kath, 'A history of the Canterbury Trades and Labour Council 1889–1937', MA thesis, University of Canterbury, 1966.

Dunick, Mark, 'Making rebels: The New Zealand Socialist Party, 1901–1913', MA thesis, Victoria University of Wellington, 2016.

Hutching, Megan, '"Turn back this tide of barbarism": New Zealand women who were opposed to war 1869–1919', MA thesis, University of Auckland, 1990.

McAloon, Jim, 'Working class politics in Christchurch 1905–1914', MA thesis, University of Canterbury, 1986.

Plumridge, Elizabeth, 'Labour in Christchurch: Community and consciousness 1914–1919', MA thesis, University of Canterbury, 1979.

Taylor, James E., '"To me, socialism is not a set of dogmas but a living principle": Harry Atkinson and the Christchurch Socialist Church, 1890–1905', MA thesis, Victoria University of Wellington, 2010.

DICTIONARY OF NEW ZEALAND BIOGRAPHY (DNZB)

The following articles were originally published in the Dictionary of New Zealand Biography; they can be found at https://teara.govt.nz/en/biographies

Atkinson, Neill, 'Mack, Matthew Joseph', 1996.

Barber, Laurie, 'Gibb, James', 1993.

Barnett, Nicola, 'Efford, Lincoln Arthur Winstone', 2000.

Bohan, Edmund, 'Page, Sarah', 1996.

Brodie, James W., 'Howell, John Henry', 1996.

Chapple, Geoff, 'Chapple, James Henry George', 1996.

Clark, Kath, 'John William Roberts', 1998.

Cookson, J. E., 'Mackie, Charles Robert Norris', 1996.

Harris, Nancy, 'Baughan, Blanche Edith', 1996.

Hutching, Megan, 'Bain, Wilhelmina Sherriff', 1996.

Keenan, Danny, 'Te Whiti-o-Rongomai III, Erueti', 1993.

Lovell-Smith, Margaret, 'Taylor, Elizabeth Best', 1996.

Lowe, Peter, 'Ford, Charles Reginald', 1998.

McAloon, Jim, 'Armstrong, Hubert Thomas', 1996.

——, 'Cooke, Frederick Riley', 1996.

——, 'Howard, Edwin John', 1996.

——, 'Hunter, Hiram', 1996.

——, 'Thorn, James', 1998.

Nicholls, Roberta, 'Cunnington, Eveline Willett', 1996.

Nolan, Melanie, 'McCullough, John Alexander', 1996.

Roth, Herbert, 'Atkinson, Harry Albert', 1993.

Somerville, Ross, 'Te Maiharoa, Hipa', 1990.

VOICES AGAINST WAR

The following articles were published on the Voices Against War website; they can be found at http://voicesagainstwar.nz/

Bartlett, Dan, 'Bob Semple: Miner, unionist and Labour politician', 2016.

——, 'Fred and Harry Cooke: The father and son who stood up for socialism', 2016.

——, 'George Wears Samms: A socialist and a pacifist', 2016.

——, 'Ted Howard: A champion of the working class', 2016.

——, 'Tim Armstrong: "A very seditious character"', 2016.

Crick, Martin, 'John Percy Fletcher, the Society of Friends and the campaign against compulsory military training in New Zealand, 1909–1914', 2020.

Lovell-Smith, Margaret, 'Ada Wells: First woman councillor outspoken in the peace cause', 2016.

——, 'The case of Noel Goldsbury: A Quaker whose "leave of absence" caused a furore', 2016.

——, 'Charles Edward Warden: Christian ideals lead to imprisonment', 2019.

——, 'Charles Mackie and the National Peace Council', 2016 updated 2019.

——, 'Charles Morgan Williams: The anti-war Kaiapoi farmer who became a Labour MP', 2018.

——, 'Committed Christian Frank Money pays the price for his beliefs', 2019.

——, 'David Gray: Transported to Europe in error', 2016.

——, 'Douglas Henry Day: Christian conscientious objector who identified with Christ's suffering', 2016.

——, 'Ellen and John Howell: Active members of the National Peace Council', 2016.

——, 'Fred Page and the No More War Movement', 2016.

——, 'Help from abroad: T.C. Gregory and the Advice to Emigrants Campaign', 2020.

——, 'Henry William Reynolds: Bootmaker pays the penalty for promoting peace', 2017.

——, 'James Chapple: The socialist preacher who was jailed for sedition', 2016.

——, 'Kennaway Henderson: A man of principle', 2016.

——, 'Norman Bell: Scholar and peacemaker', 2016.

——, 'Peter Scott Ramsay: Long-standing member of the peace and Labour movements defies conscription', 2016.

——, 'Reg Williams: A passionate opponent of militarism', 2016 updated 2017.

——, 'Robert Owen (Robin) Page: Canterbury College student stands up for his convictions', 2016.

——, 'Rose Atkinson: A long-standing commitment to peace', 2016.

——, 'Sarah Saunders Page: A courageous advocate for peace', 2016.

——, 'The Women's International League for Peace and Freedom (WILPF): The oldest women's peace organisation in the world meets in Christchurch', 2016.

——, 'Thomas Nuttall: A Baptist Sunday School teacher who resisted compulsory military training', 2016.

——, 'Worrall family showed united front against militarism', 2017.

Richardson, Dan, 'John and James Roberts: Socialist brothers against conscription', 2019.

——, 'Silas Stedman: Willing to serve not to kill', 2019.

OTHER ONLINE RESOURCES

Binney, Judith, 'Māori prophetic movements – ngā poropiti – Te Whiti and Tohu – Parihaka', Te Ara – the Encyclopedia of New Zealand, 2011, http://www.TeAra.govt.nz/en/maori-prophetic-movements-nga-poropiti/page-4

Bloomberg, Simon, 'Waitaki: Water of tears, river of power', *New Zealand Geographic*, issue 51, May–June 2001, https://www.nzgeo.com/stories/waitaki-water-of-tears-river-of-power/

Clements, Elwyn, 'The life of a woman: Muriel Morrison', 1994, http://legacy.disarmsecure.org/Muriel%20Morrison%20Part%201.pdf

Davidson, Jared, 'Dissent during the First World War: By the numbers', 2016, https://blog.tepapa.govt.nz/2016/06/28/dissent-during-the-first-world-war-by-the-numbers/

Grant, David, 'Social conflict and control, protest and repression (New Zealand)', 1914–1918-online, International Encyclopedia of the First World War, https://encyclopedia.1914-1918-online.net/article/social_conflict_and_control_protest_and_repression_new_zealand

Guy, Laurie, 'Early Christian pacifists in Christchurch: Creating division in the fight for peace', paper presented to the Anglican Pacifist Society, 2006, http://legacy.disarmsecure.org/Baptist%20Pacifists%20-%20Ang%20Pac%20Conf.pdf

Heritage New Zealand Pouhere Taonga, 'Fort Jervois', undated, https://www.heritage.org.nz/the-list/details/5306

Hill, Marguerite, 'The taonga of HMS New Zealand', 2016, https://ww100.govt.nz/the-taonga-of-hms-new-zealand

Hutching, Megan, 'Women's International League for Peace and Freedom 1916– ', first published in Anne Else (ed.), *Women Together: A history of women's organisations in New Zealand / Ngā rōpū wāhine o te motu*, Daphne Brassell Associates and Historical Branch, Department of Internal Affairs, Wellington, 1993, updated in 2018, https://nzhistory.govt.nz/women-together/womens-international-league-peace-and-freedom

Lovell-Smith, Margaret, 'Canterbury Women's Institute 1892 – c.1920', first published in Anne Else (ed.) *Women Together: A history of women's organisations in New Zealand / Ngā rōpū wāhine o te motu*, Daphne Brassell Associates and Historical Branch, Department of Internal Affairs, Wellington, 1993, https://nzhistory.govt.nz/women-together/canterbury-women%E2%80%99s-institute

——, 'Horse-hair watch-guard a memento of prison life', 2018, https://ww100.govt.nz/kaiapoi-horse-hair-watch-guard

McKenzie, Tim, 'J. R. Hervey, 1889–1958', *Kōtare* 7, no. 3, 2008, pp. 105–114, https://www.academia.edu/55742007/J_R_Hervey_1889_1958

Ministry for Culture and Heritage, 'Conscientious objection and dissent in the First World War', updated 2020, https://nzhistory.govt.nz/war/first-world-war/conscientious-objection

——, 'Convictions for sedition 1915–1918', updated 2016, https://nzhistory.govt.nz/war/sedition-conviction-list

——, 'Imprisoned conscientious objectors, 1916–1920', updated 2016, https://nzhistory.govt.nz/war/the-military-objectors-list

——, 'Invasion of pacifist settlement at Parihaka', updated 2021, https://nzhistory.govt.nz/occupation-pacifist-settlement-at-parihaka

——, 'Māori objection to conscription', updated 2020, https://nzhistory.govt.nz/war/first-world-war/conscientious-objection/maori-objection,

——, 'Military defaulters list, 1919', updated 2017, https://nzhistory.govt.nz/war/military-defaulters-list

——, 'Preparing for war', updated 2017, https://nzhistory.govt.nz/war/first-world-war-overview/nzs-contribution

——, 'Turning boys into soldiers', updated 2014, nzhistory.govt.nz/war/children-and-first-world-war/cadet-training

Munns Menswear, 'Munns: Our history', accessed 3 October 2018, https://munns.co.nz/pages/copy-of-terms-conditions

Museum of New Zealand Te Papa Tongarewa, 'HMS New Zealand: "A grim and formidable fighting machine"', undated, https://collections.tepapa.govt.nz/topic/1049

New Zealand Baptist, https://www.baptistresearch.org.nz/digital-baptist?_open=1

Wilmers, Annika, 'Feminist pacifism', 1914–1918-online, International Encyclopedia of the First World War, 2015, https://encyclopedia.1914-1918-online.net/article/feminist_pacifism

NEWSPAPERS AND OFFICIAL PUBLICATIONS

Appendices to the Journals of the House of Representatives
Ashburton Guardian
Canterbury Times
Evening Post
Lyttelton Times
Maoriland Worker
New Zealand Police Gazette
Otago Daily Times
Otago Witness
Press
Southland Times
Star
Sun
White Ribbon

UNPUBLISHED SOURCES

Alexander Turnbull Library

Ormond Burton Papers
Lincoln Efford Papers
Elsie Locke Papers
Herbert Roth Papers

Archives New Zealand Te Rua Mahara o te Kāwanatanga, Christchurch

Lyttelton Harbour Board Letter Book, 1916–1918: XBAA CH518 Box 1090, XBAH-A003-24, R25018918
Lyttelton Harbour Board Correspondence European War 1914–1918: XBAA CH518 Box 793, XBAH-A002-1008, R25017755

Archives New Zealand Te Rua Mahara o te Kāwanatanga, Wellington

Army Department (AD1, AD10)
Justice Department (J40)
New Zealand Expeditionary Force NZEF 1917 and 1918

Canterbury Museum

Charles Mackie Papers and Pamphlets
Harry A. Atkinson Papers
Minute book of general meetings, October 1905 to May 1908, Canterbury Women's Institute
Wilhelmina Sherriff Elliot, née Bain, Papers
Women's Christian Temperance Union Minute Books of Canterbury Branches, 1886–1988

Macmillan Brown Library

Richard Thompson Papers
Society of Friends Christchurch Minutes 1913–1938

Other

Duncan McCormack interviewed by Alwyn Owen, 'A matter of principle', Spectrum 305, 1979, https://ngataonga.org.nz/collections/catalogue/catalogue-item?record_id=177242
McCormack, Duncan, 'War; What for?', undated transcript of radio interview, provenance unknown
WILPF Series III, Folders 11–13, 1915–25, Archives and Special Collections, University of Colorado, Boulder

Private collections

C. Morgan Williams, 'Memoirs', 1963, Williams family collection
Cook, H. Bramwell and Neroli Williams, 'We're in the Money: The Money family history', undated, private collection
Day family letters, author's collection
Efford, Brent, 'Lincoln Efford', presentation to the Canterbury WEA, September 2018
Frank Money's letters and diaries (photocopies), Money family collection
Harding, Bruce, 'To serve them all his days': Rewi Alley's schooling for war, and the birth of a people's warrior', unpublished paper, 2018
Hendery, Noel, 'Seven generations in New Zealand: The history of the Hendery family', private collection, 2018
Jack, Hilary, 'Early days in Oxford', private collection
Robin Page scrapbook, Page family collection
William Worrall letters, Worrall family collection

IMAGE CREDITS

1/2-150372-F. Alexander Turnbull Library, Wellington

p. 85 CCL-PhotoCD04, IMG 0050, Christchurch City Libraries

p. 86 Box 30, Folder 136, Charles Mackie collection, Canterbury Museum

p. 88 James McCombs, 1873–1933. Original prints from ATL Photograph Section loose print sequence. Ref: PAColl-3861-29-14. Alexander Turnbull Library, Wellington

p. 91 Palliser family collection, Canterbury Museum, 1991.345.3

p. 92 Charles Mackie collection, Canterbury Museum, Item 186

p. 93 Heathcote Mann, *Maoriland Worker*, 11 July 1913, p. 1. Papers Past

p. 94 Ron Nuttall

p. 95 Worrall family

p. 101 Charles Mackie collection, Canterbury Museum, Item 175

p. 102 Auckland Libraries Heritage Collections, AWNS-19140423-40-1

p. 103 Charles Mackie collection, Canterbury Museum, Item 206

p. 115 Edward Brodie Mack, *New Zealand Free Lance*, 19 November 1915, p. 1. Papers Past

p. 116 William Blomfield, *New Zealand Observer*, 2 October 1915, p. 1. Papers Past

p. 117 *NZ Truth*, 9 October 1915, p. 5. Papers Past

p. 118 Ken M. Ballantyne (unsigned), *New Zealand Free Lance*, 2 June 1915, p. 1. Papers Past

p. 120 Canterbury Workers' Educational Association

p. 123 Wheeler & Son, Presbyterian Research Centre (Archives)

p. 124 Canterbury Workers' Educational Association

p. 125 Hamurana Spring, group portrait, 27 April 1914, Blencowe photograph, Canterbury Museum, 2018.129.4

p. 130 The Worker Print, Charles Mackie collection, Canterbury Museum, Item 721

p. 131 *New Zealand Truth*, 29 January 1916, p. 7. Papers Past

p. 133 Edward Brodie Mack, *New Zealand Free Lance*, 1 June 1916, p. 1. Papers Past

p. 136 PH-NEG-C5769, Auckland War Memorial Museum Tāmaki Paenga Hira

p. 139 Credited to Colborne in the *Edinburgh Socialist*; *Maoriland Worker*, 16 June 1915, p. 1. Papers Past

p. 140 William Blomfield, *New Zealand Observer*, 11 December 1915, p. 13. Papers Past

p. 145 Frederick Riley Cooke. Holland, Roy, 1894–1975: Portraits of Labour politicians, and lantern slides compiled by Harry Holland; also WW2 veterans on parade, including Sir Stephen Weir. Ref: 1/2-068608-F. Alexander Turnbull Library, Wellington

p. 146 Charles Mackie collection, Canterbury Museum, Item 805

p. 148 Andrew, Earle William, 1909–1986: Hubert Thomas Armstrong. Original photographic prints and postcards from file print collection, Box 10. Ref: PAColl-6208-44. Alexander Turnbull Library, Wellington

p. 149 Charles Mackie collection, Canterbury Museum, Item 491

p. 150 H. H. Clifford collection, Canterbury Museum, 1980.175.69030

p. 154 Worrall family

p. 155 Crown Studios (Christchurch), Worrall family

p. 157 Green and Hahn, MB 14 ref. 49, Canterbury Trades and Labour Council records, Macmillan Brown Library, University of Canterbury

p. 159 Efford family

p. 161 Patricia Smith

p. 164 Portrait of James Henry George Chapple, 1865–1947. Gee, Maurice Gough, 1931–: Photographs. Ref: 35mm-14541-4-F. Alexander Turnbull Library, Wellington

p. 165 William Blomfield, *New Zealand Observer*, 18 December 1915, p. 1. Papers Past

p. 175 AAYS 8638 10/407/3 R22429763, Archives New Zealand Te Rua Mahara o te Kāwanatanga

p. 177 Tolputt & Clarke (Rangiora), Vallance family

p. 181 H. H. Clifford collection, Canterbury Museum, 1980.175.57704

p. 182 Author's collection

p. 183 Author's collection

p. 184 H. H. Clifford collection, Canterbury Museum, 1980.175.22715

p. 186 William Blomfield, *New Zealand Observer*, 1 July 1916, p. 16, Papers Past

p. 187 Crown Studios (Christchurch), Ron Nuttall

p. 191 Canterbury Society of Arts art class. Canterbury Society of Arts art class and hanging committee. Ref: PAColl-5374-2. Alexander Turnbull Library, Wellington

p. 192 Robin Page scrapbook, Page family

p. 193 H. H. Clifford collection, Canterbury Museum, 1980.175.7415

p. 194 H. H. Clifford photo, Williams family

p. 195 Charlie Warden collection, Canterbury Museum, 1989.28.1

p. 196 Stedman family

p. 201 MB 287 ref. 51734, Richard Thompson Papers, Macmillan Brown Library, University of Canterbury

p. 205 Mount Cook Prison and buildings on Buckle Street, Wellington. Smith, Sydney Charles, 1888–1972: Photographs of New Zealand. Ref: 1/1-020192-G. Alexander Turnbull Library, Wellington

p. 206 Fred Page photo from Robin Page Scrapbook, Page family

p. 207 Extended Money family

p. 212 Terrace Gaol and gardens, Wellington. Fry, Pat: Photographs, chiefly of the Ohakune district. Ref: 1/2-058369-F. Alexander Turnbull Library, Wellington

p. 214 Ref: 14985.30. Online collection 1136038. Te Ūaka The Lyttelton Museum

p. 216 ABGU 6875 Posref 10 R16952153, Archives New Zealand Te Rua Mahara o te Kāwanatanga

p. 217 *The Working Woman*, March 1936, Ref: S-L-1584-11, Alexander Turnbull Library, Wellington

p. 218 ABGU W3777 149 R18388398, Archives New Zealand Te Rua Mahara o te Kāwanatanga

p. 221 ACGS 16225 1918/8/6 R3195153, Archives New Zealand Te Rua Mahara o te Kāwanatanga

p. 223 ABGU 6875 Posref 9 R16952152, Archives New Zealand Te Rua Mahara o te Kāwanatanga

p. 224 Robin Page Scrapbook, Page family

p. 225 Robin Page Scrapbook, Page family

p. 226 Ref: KDHS 79 85, Kaiapoi Historical Society, known as Kaiapoi Museum

p. 230 Steffano Webb photo, Charles Mackie Collection, Canterbury Museum, 19xx.2.262, 13709

p. 231 Edwin John Howard. Hocken Library: Portraits of E. J. and Mabel Howard. Ref: PAColl-0146-01. Alexander Turnbull Library, Wellington

p. 234 H. H. Clifford photo, 1980.175.5575, Canterbury Museum

p. 236 H. H. Clifford photo, J. K. Stone collection, Canterbury Museum, 1972.121.1

p. 238 Edward Brodie Mack, *New Zealand Free Lance*, 4 July 1918, p. 3. Papers Past

p. 239 James Allen. General Assembly Library: Parliamentary portraits. Ref: 35mm-00089-e-F. Alexander Turnbull Library, Wellington

p. 242 William Blomfield, *New Zealand Observer*, 18 May 1918, p. 1. Papers Past

p. 244 Acc032, Box 100, Ara Institute of Canterbury

p. 253 Harry Holland, leader of the Labour Party. S. P. Andrew Ltd: Portrait negatives. Ref: 1/1-018348-F. Alexander Turnbull Library, Wellington

p. 259 Extended Nuttall family

p. 260 *Ellesmere Guardian*, 26 March 1935, p. 3. Papers Past, Stuff Limited

p. 261 Page family

p. 265 Page family

p. 266 Efford family

p. 267 Canterbury Workers' Educational Association

p. 269 Efford family

p. 270 Page family

p. 271 Efford family

p. 277 Patricia Smith

INDEX

Page numbers in **bold** indicate photographs and other images. Page numbers in the form 302n67 indicate information in notes, in this case note 67 on page 302.